Research Methods for Pedagogy

BLOOMSBURY RESEARCH METHODS FOR EDUCATION SERIES

Edited by
Melanie Nind, University of Southampton, UK

The *Bloomsbury Research Methods for Education* series provides overviews of the range of sometimes interconnected and diverse methodological possibilities for researching aspects of education such as education contexts, sectors, problems or phenomena. Each volume discusses prevailing, less obvious and more innovative methods and approaches for the particular area of educational research.

More targeted than general methods textbooks, these authoritative yet accessible books are invaluable resources for students and researchers planning their research design and wanting to explore methodological possibilities to make well-informed decisions regarding their choice of methods.

Forthcoming:

Place-Based Methods for Researching Schools,
    Pat Thomson and Christine Hall
Research Methods for Education in the Digital Age,
    Maggi Savin-Baden and Gemma Tombs
Research Methods for Understanding Practitioner Learning,
    Vivienne Baumfield, Elaine Hall, Rachel Lofthouse and Kate Wall

BLOOMSBURY RESEARCH METHODS FOR EDUCATION

Research Methods for Pedagogy

MELANIE NIND, ALICIA CURTIN AND KATHY HALL

Bloomsbury Academic
An imprint of Bloomsbury Publishing Plc

B L O O M S B U R Y
LONDON · OXFORD · NEW YORK · NEW DELHI · SYDNEY

Bloomsbury Academic

An imprint of Bloomsbury Publishing Plc

50 Bedford Square
London
WC1B 3DP
UK

1385 Broadway
New York
NY 10018
USA

www.bloomsbury.com

**BLOOMSBURY and the Diana logo are trademarks
of Bloomsbury Publishing Plc**

First published 2016

British Library Cataloguing-in-Publication Data
A catalogue record for this book is available from the British Library.

ISBN: HB: 978-1-4742-4282-0
PB: 978-1-4742-4281-3
ePDF: 978-1-4742-4284-4
ePub: 978-1-4742-4283-7

Library of Congress Cataloging-in-Publication Data
Names: Nind, Melanie, author. | Hall, Kathy, 1952- author. | Curtin, Alicia,
author.
Title: Research methods for pedagogy / Melanie Nind, Kathy Hall and Alicia
Curtin.
Description: London, UK ; New York, NY : Bloomsbury Academic, an imprint of
Bloomsbury Publishing, Plc, [2016] | Series: Bloomsbury research methods
for education series | Includes bibliographical references and index.
Identifiers: LCCN 2016005913 (print) | LCCN 2016019087 (ebook) | ISBN
9781474242820 (hb : alk. paper) | ISBN 9781474242813 (pb : alk. paper) |
ISBN 9781474242844 (ePDF) | ISBN 9781474242837 (ePub) | ISBN 9781474242837
(epub) | ISBN 9781474242844 (epdf)
Subjects: LCSH: Education–Research–Methodology. |
Teaching–Research–Methodology.
Classification: LCC LB1028 .N55 2016 (print) | LCC LB1028 (ebook) | DDC
370.72–dc23
LC record available at https://lccn.loc.gov/2016005913

Series: Bloomsbury Research Methods for Education

Cover design by Clare Turner

Typeset by Deanta Global Publishing Services, Chennai, India
Printed and bound in India

CONTENTS

LIST OF TABLES

ABOUT THE AUTHORS

Melanie Nind PhD, professor of education, University of Southampton, UK, has a long history of teaching and researching focused on the interactive, the inclusive and the pedagogical. She is currently researching the pedagogies applied in short courses in advanced social science research methods. This is part of a programme of pedagogical research for the National Centre for Research Methods, where Melanie is a co-director. She co-edits *International Journal of Research & Method in Education* and is the director of the Centre for Research in Inclusion at Southampton Education School.

Alicia Curtin PhD, lecturer at University College Cork, Ireland, conducts research employing sociocultural theory to explore issues highly relevant to education and learning. These include adolescent literacies in and out of school; language and identity; and neuroscientific perspectives on literacy and learning. Her most recent research project (with Kathy Hall) investigates the professional workplace learning of experienced teachers.

Kathy Hall PhD, professor of education and head of school, University College Cork, Ireland, is an experienced teacher, researcher, lecturer and author with a long-held interest in pedagogy in the broadest sense. Her recent publications include *Networks of Mind: Learning, Culture, Neuroscience* (2013), with Curtin and Rutherford.

ACKNOWLEDGEMENT

We are grateful to Cristina Azaola for providing feedback as a critical friend during the drafting of this book.

SERIES EDITOR'S PREFACE

The idea of the *Bloomsbury Research Methods for Education* series is to provide books that are useful to researchers wanting to think about research methods in the context of their research area, research problem or research aims. While researchers may use any methods textbook for ideas and inspiration, the onus falls on them to apply something from social science research methods to education in particular, or from education to a particular dimension of education (pedagogy, schools, the digital dimension, practitioner learning to name some examples). This application of ideas is not beyond us and has led to some great research and also to methodological development. In this series though, the books are more targeted, making them a good place to start for the student, researcher or person wanting to craft a research proposal. Each book brings together in one place the range of sometimes interconnected and often diverse methodological possibilities for researching one aspect or sector of education, one research problem or phenomenon. Thus, readers will quickly find a discussion of the methods they associate with that bit of education research they are interested in, but in addition they will find less obvious and more innovative methods and approaches. A quick look at the opening glossary will give you an idea of the methods you will find included within each book. You can expect a discussion of those methods that is critical, authoritative *and* situated. In each text the authors use powerful examples of the methods in use in the arena with which you are concerned.

There are other features that make this series distinctive. In each of the books, the authors draw on their own research and on the research of others making alternative methodological choices. In this way they address the affordances of the methods in terms of real studies; they illustrate the potential with real data. The authors also discuss the rationale behind the choice of methods and behind how researchers put them together in research designs. As readers you will get behind the scenes of published research and into the kind of methodological decision-making that you are grappling with. In each of the books, you will find yourself moving between methods, theory and data; you will find theoretical concepts to think with and with which you might be able to enhance your methods. You will find that the authors develop arguments about methods rather than just describing them.

In *Research Methods for Pedagogy* I was delighted to team up with Alicia Curtin and Kathy Hall, not the least because I knew that the process of writing this book would involve lots of wonderful conversation about things that matter to us, plus we would all learn from each other along the way. This has been the case, and as series editor, I'm pleased that, with my co-authors, I am contributing to the series. The widespread focus on teaching and learning is not the same as a critical look at pedagogy, and is rarely matched with detailed attention to how we research pedagogy in ways that do not reduce it to something less complex than it necessarily is. In this book you will find ideas about how we can think about pedagogy interwoven with ideas about how we can research it. Equally importantly, you will find arguments about how the two, do and must, form a coherent pairing.

This book (nor any in the series) cannot be the only book you need to read to formulate, justify and implement your research methods. Other books will cover a greater range of methods and others still, more operational detail. The aim of this series, though, is to provide books that take you to the heart of the methods thinking you will want and need to do. They are books by authors who are equally passionate about their substantive topic and about research methods and they are books that will be invaluable for inspiring deep and informed methods thinking.

Melanie Nind
Series editor

A GLOSSARY OF RESEARCH METHODS AND APPROACHES

This glossary comprises only those methods and approaches covered in the book; those marked with a * are more fully discussed and exemplified. We have indicated when methods appear in particular chapters rather than recurring across the book.

*Action research** A systematic approach for practitioners to understand and improve their own practice through a focus on their own practical actions and their own reflections on data about the effects of those actions. This often involves cycles of planning, implementing, recording and analysing a change in process.

At-home ethnography Ethnographic research conducted in familiar settings by researchers who are already active participants in them. See also ethnography.

Autoethnography An approach that combines life history, ethnography and self-narrative in either an ethnographic study of oneself in the social and cultural context or an autobiographical account that includes ethnographic data. See also ethnography.

Best evidence synthesis See systematic review.

*Case study** In-depth, intensive analysis of the single (or multiple) case within its naturalistic context, valuing its particularity, complexity and relationships with the context. This approach uses multiple methods and perspectives to look at the case holistically.

Child-centred or child-friendly methods Research methods designed or developed to be accessible, attractive and engaging for children. These methods often involve activities for young children or draw on youth culture for young people. See Chapter 4.

Communicative daily life stories One of the methods within critical communicative methodology in which the researcher and participant co-construct reflective accounts of everyday experiences. See Chapter 2.

Communicative focus groups One of the methods within critical communicative methodology in which the focus group, including the researcher, works towards a consensus or collective interpretation. See Chapter 2.

Communicative observations One of the methods within critical communicative methodology whereby observations of practice involve the researcher and observed participants in constant communication towards reaching a joint interpretation and account. See Chapter 2.

Conversation analysis* An approach for studying in detail audio-/video-recorded social interaction and conversation, paying particular attention to how the conversation works in terms of turn taking, sequences, functions for the social context. See Chapter 5.

Correlational analysis The use of statistical correlation to evaluate the strength of the relationship between variables.

Critical communicative methodology/CCM A combination of methods to bring together the contributions of different educational agents (teachers, pupils, parents, administrators, policy makers) so that analysis of the social situation reflects their reality and produces knowledge that is usable to them. See Chapter 2.

Critical incident analysis A method to focus the researcher on a critical incident or turning point, exploring people's behaviour and experience before, during and after the incident to analyse its meaning for those involved. Incidents are usually explored via interview and are significant or revelatory in relation to what interrupts or enables everyday practices. See Chapter 3.

Discourse Analysis/Critical Discourse Analysis/CDA* A term given to various approaches to the analysis of texts (which can be verbal or written but which communicate something of what is taken for granted in the social situation). Discourse analysts, for example, examine texts for what they say about what is doable, sayable and thinkable in a classroom situation. See Chapter 5.

Documentary analysis More often used by social science researchers as a supplementary rather than a main method, this involves analysis of documents (pre-existing artefacts or written texts) for what they can tell us about the phenomenon under study.

Drawing A visual method used particularly with children to offer an alternative or supplement to verbal or written accounts. Participants may be asked to draw a picture to depict the phenomenon, for example classroom, lesson, learning support teacher. Drawings can be analysed alone or alongside recorded conversations to offer another perspective on what is under study.

Ecological momentary assessment A method of experience sampling used for capturing the emotional states and behaviours of participants as they happen at a series of moments in time. See Chapter 7.

Emancipatory research An approach to research in which the subjects of social inquiry take control of the research process to ensure that the process and product of the research works for social transformation for their benefit.

Ethnographic case study* A type of case study using an ethnographic approach. This usually involves a shorter, less intensive degree of immersion in the context by the researcher than in an ethnography. The focus is on the case – the individual, event or phenomenon – rather than on the culture of the group. See case study. See ethnography.

Ethnography* A research approach aimed at understanding an insider perspective on a particular community, practice or setting by focusing on the meaning of social action from the point of view of the participants. Methods of progressively focused observation and interview are used by the researcher who is immersed in the situation, generating complex, detailed data to enable deep descriptions and theorization of the cultural context.

Factor analysis The use of statistical methods to reduce correlational data to a smaller number of dimensions regarded as the basic variables accounting for the interrelations observed in the data.

Focus group A group interview method in which participants are invited to explore a given topic in group discussion. Participants respond to each other, to activities or stimuli rather than just to the researcher's questions. The researcher aims to facilitate discussion as much as direct it.

Group data surgery A method in which a number of researchers and/or participants come together to jointly share, discuss and analyse data.

Hierarchical multiple regression analysis Standard multiple regression is a statistical method used to evaluate the relationship between a set of independent variables and a dependent variable. Hierarchical regression evaluates this same relationship but controls for the impact of a different set of independent variables on the dependent variable.

*Identity research** Research that employs identity construction as a method for analysing and theorizing social actions and behaviour. See Chapter 6.

*Inclusive research** An umbrella term for research approaches that respond to the call for democratization of the research process. This includes for example, participatory, emancipatory and partnership research. The emphasis is on ensuring the relevance of the research to the people concerned, so that it is important and beneficial to them, so that they are involved in the process and decision-making, and so their views and experiences are treated with respect. See Chapter 2.

*Interview** The method of asking participants to respond to questions, usually by reflecting on their experiences or views. Interviews may be structured, semi-structured or unstructured and conducted with individuals or groups.

*Lesson study** An education research method within practice-based inquiry. The plan for a lesson is shared with other practitioners/researchers who observe the live lesson and collaboratively analyse it. There follows a process of reflection with the purpose of using the data to improve professional practice. See Chapter 7.

Longitudinal research Research conducted over an extended period of time in which time is a unit of analysis. Examples include cohort studies in which individuals experiencing the same event are observed at repeated intervals to examine changes, panel studies involving a cross section of a population surveyed at multiple points in time, and qualitative longitudinal research often involving returning to interviewees on multiple occasions over time.

Mapping A visual method in which participants individually or in groups map out (write or draw) their experiences, often including a space/time dimension. The researcher may record and explore production of these maps alongside the maps produced.

Meta analysis See systematic review.

Mosaic approach* A combination of participatory and visual methods designed to bring together data generated by young children and adults making sense of their everyday experiences. The resulting Mosaic is co-constructed by them and the researcher. See Chapter 4.

Multilevel statistics/modelling Advanced statistical method for handling clustered or grouped data.

Multimodal analysis* An approach that takes into account multiple modes of communication (gesture, gaze, movement, speech, drawing, etc.) without taking for granted any as most important. The researcher reads different texts and embodied actions for what they say about the phenomenon under study. See Chapters 4 and 8.

Multimodal transcription* An early stage of analysing or representing multimodal data that retains some of the complexity of the ways in which modes of communication interact. See multimodal analysis. See transcription. See Chapter 8.

Observation* A method for recording what can be seen in the research site. Observation can be naturalistic, conducted by participant or non-participant observers. It can be systematic and structured using time or event sampling and pre-prepared schedules.

*Participatory action research** Action research that goes beyond technical action for instrumental improvement. PAR involves participants in the planning, change and reflection processes, often considering underlying issues of power and social justice as part of a transformatory process. See action research.

*Participatory/partnership research** A research process that involves those being researched or implicated in the research in the decision-making and conduct of the research.

*Pedagogical documentation** A combination of observation, record-keeping, analysis and reflection on the pedagogical process (often carried out in collaboration) to inform understanding and action for teachers and researchers. See Chapter 4.

*Phenomenology** A research approach that asks questions about the subjective experience of research participants and how meaning is made in the moments of practice as individuals experience the world. Participants identify what is meaningful to them about particular practices and the researcher explores this with them. See Chapter 6.

Photo ethnography The use of digital or mobile technology to visually record ethnographic data and experiences. See ethnography.

Photo questionnaire The use of photos related to the research question as stimuli for focused or open-ended response from participants.

Practice-based inquiry A research strategy for practitioners (individually or collectively) to systematically and rigorously study their own practice. Related to action research, this is a way to support the development of knowledge contextualized within specific contexts of practice, emphasizing the role of collaboration and reflection in the inquiry and learning process.

Quasi-experimental design Research that takes an experimental style approach without the core ingredient of random assignment of subjects to groups. Quasi-experimental designs are more commonly used in education than experimental designs as they raise fewer ethical concerns and fit better with real life contexts. See Chapter 7.

Questionnaire Administration of a pre-prepared set of (usually written) questions for obtaining data usually for statistical analysis.

Randomized control trial An experimental design in which study participants are randomly allocated to different treatments (e.g. treatment and non-treatment control group) to gain robust evaluation of efficacy.

Reflection A method used by researchers or participants to probe experiences or feelings about experiences in detail. Reflections may be shared between participants, between researchers or between participants and researchers to encourage further discussion and reflection.

*Sensory ethnography** An ethnographic approach encompassing sensory embodied experiences. See ethnography. See Chapter 8.

*Sensory methods** Methods used to focus on the sensory bodily experience, recording data gained through multiple senses. See Chapter 8.

*Spatial research methods** Methods employing physical, social, temporal, experiential and/or virtual aspects of space to understand the experiences of participants in a research site. See Chapter 9.

Survey An approach used to discover broad, general or comparative information on a selected topic by surveying (often a large) number of participants. This may involve no personal contact between researcher and participant.

Systematic review A method for synthesizing findings from many studies on one theme using an explicit, transparent, replicable and accountable protocol. A systematic search strategy and application of inclusion/exclusion criteria and quality thresholds allow for claims to be made about the best evidence and strength of evidence.

*Think-aloud methods** A range of methods designed to enable researchers (and participants) to access participants' introspective mental processes. See Chapter 7.

Time series design One form of quasi-experiment design involving capturing data at multiple data points (not just before and after an intervention) that allows comparison with baseline levels and trends. See Chapter 7.

Transcription* A method of deciding what is described and how it is represented so that audio or video data are transformed for the purpose of analysis.

Video methods* Methods that allow researchers to produce and analyse audiovisual data including naturally occurring video data, video diaries, researcher-produced or elicited video films, etc. Analysis may treat the video as a record or as an impression of events.

Video-stimulated recall/reflection/dialogue* Video of participants in action is used to stimulate their recall of, or reflection and dialogue about, the recorded event or interaction. It is used to probe what participants were thinking or feeling at the time. Control of the selection of units of analysis can be shared or handed over to participants. See Chapter 7.

Videography* An ethnographic approach to video making that regards video as an aesthetic object and a reflexive mirror for researchers and participants to use in reorienting the power of researcher gaze. See Chapter 8.

Virtual ethnography* An approach adapting ethnographic research methods for online research contexts. Netnography is one example. See ethnography. See Chapter 9.

Introduction

In recent decades pedagogy has attracted considerable attention from policy makers, politicians, researchers and, of course, educators. Enabling learners to acquire understanding, attitudes and skills in different domains, sectors and settings is of immense importance to societies and cultures. The strides that have been made in our understanding and conceptions of learning, children, teaching and culture account for some of the growing interest in pedagogy internationally.

Historically, pedagogy has frequently been positioned in contrast to knowledge and the specified curriculum, so the complexities and subtleties of supporting and organizing the learning of learners could, in this view, be consigned to irrelevancy and invisibility. In being underrated in the past, pedagogy was therefore under-explored and certainly under-theorized. Pedagogy has surfaced in more recent times as a vital area of professional learning, practice and research. It is increasingly recognized as complex and important, and teachers are seen as requiring considerable professional expertise. In some countries, pedagogy is taken very seriously indeed in the training and education of teachers, and is viewed as a field of study in its own right. In many countries in continental Europe, for example, teacher education policy requires that all those entering the teaching profession be highly qualified pedagogically, represented by the requirement for a Master's degree in education, in which pedagogy is central.

The major reason for the elevation in the status of pedagogy stems from the greater awareness of the work of several scholars on learning itself, for instance, the work of Lev Vygotsky, Jerome Bruner and, more recently, cognitive anthropologists such as Barbara Rogoff, Jean Lave and Etienne Wenger. The realization offered by such scholars of the person as sense-maker, interpreting and intentional, at once shaped by and shaping the world, brought new thinking to the process of how we support the learning of others. Understanding the constraints and affordances of different contexts, relations, values, knowledges and ways of knowing contributed to a significant appreciation of pedagogy, no longer as something effortless and inconsequential, but as something that merits serious attention, research and scrutiny. It thus becomes necessary to pay attention to the interpreting, meaning-making responsive mind and to reconsider the complexities of situations and contexts, and their mediating role in learning and human accomplishment. From this perspective, researching pedagogy comes to be recognized as tremendously challenging, because all of the following assume importance: relations, prior experience and histories, knowledge, opportunity to learn, meanings, actions, identities, agency, communities, participation and time and space. And all these features are dynamic and indeterminate – they manifest and emerge differently in settings.

In the light of this relatively new perspective on the complexity of pedagogy and its significance for researchers, the scale and scope of studies of pedagogy have expanded considerably. Dedicated journals, books, theses and even research programmes have been devoted to the study of pedagogy in recent years. Just two examples of research journals are *Pedagogy, Culture and Society,* and *Pedagogies: An International Journal.* This growth is not surprising since, as this book hopefully demonstrates, the field is such a rich landscape for research.

Also not surprising is that the research methods considered appropriate for the exploration of such a complex view of pedagogy are rich in scale and scope. In this perspective on pedagogy the tacit, the often hidden from view, the silences, the absences and the usually invisible become relevant, alongside traditionally more explicit dimensions such as the specified curriculum, the learning outcomes sought, the assessment approaches and so on. Research methods need to be fit for purpose and, in the case of pedagogy, need to be consistent with the fundamentals of the substantive area itself. Methods of researching pedagogy have to align with what we assume pedagogy is. This is the challenge we set for ourselves in writing this book.

We set out to produce a book that would help the pedagogy researcher become well informed about the possible research approaches that could be considered suitable for exploring pedagogy as a complex activity while, *inter alia*, highlighting some of the pedagogic foci of contemporary pedagogy researchers. It is important to point out that this is not a book about methods per se, but about methods in context – methods for specific purposes related to understanding pedagogy. Our motivation for writing this book arose from our interest in researching pedagogy and our experience of supporting and supervising pedagogy research studies. Our work with research students who are interested in documenting and analysing the sociocultural work of teachers and students made us aware of the need for a resource that conceptualized pedagogy and its associated research methods in a way that would offer choices, possibilities and new ways of thinking to the pedagogy researcher. Thus, we wished to provide readers with tools for researching and debating pedagogy, thereby enabling them to expand their pedagogic repertoire, innovate and reform pedagogy in their own and others' contexts.

Within a broadly sociocultural frame, the book examines various aspects of pedagogy, and the implications of these aspects and dimensions for how it is researched. A key feature we sought to make clear throughout and a key 'take home message' is the importance of fit across theoretical stance, pedagogical context and research approach. In elaborating on this with reference to a wide range of contexts and sectors of education, we illustrate our conceptualizations and analyses by referring to case examples of studies from our own and others' work.

We pay particular attention to the everyday and the hard-to-know in the study of pedagogy. The subtleties and nuances of pedagogy require research methods and approaches to capture such implicit workings. This is tremendously challenging for the researcher; therefore, we devote considerable space to describing and discussing the principles and procedures that might be useful in embarking on pedagogic research and making wise decisions about research foci, assumptions, methods, evidence, analyses and ethics, alongside issues of scale and scope.

For us, pedagogy encompasses teaching and learning, plus matters of curriculum, assessment, relationships and values; it encompasses what people perceive to be meaningful, important and relevant as they interact, engage and participate in activity. By providing the reader with sociocultural insights into pedagogy as articulated, pedagogy as enacted and pedagogy as experienced, along with other conceptual tools, we shed light on the arena of methodological decision-making for researchers of pedagogy. We examine what pedagogy researchers look at, where they look, how they look and what is visible and invisible from different angles and points of view. Pedagogy is inevitably about perspective-taking, and the perspective adopted has implications for the research tools one chooses. We consider an extensive range of research methods but, throughout, we have tried to make explicit the assumptions and principles underlying methods and approaches, and of course the pedagogic stance of the researcher.

Overall, the predominant methodological focus of the book happens to be more qualitatively than quantitatively oriented. This would seem to reflect the field of pedagogic research, though we would point out that statistical methods are certainly not absent from the literature. However, given the stance on pedagogy we have outlined in the first three chapters, it is likely that research designs and methods chosen for pedagogic understanding will need to be appropriately flexible to align with the underlying notion of pedagogy assumed by the researcher. Certainly, on the basis of our experience of working on funded projects and with doctoral students, there is a tendency to embrace what might be termed an ecological model [of pedagogy] that 'explores the complex embeddings and mediations of teaching and learning within cultures and discourses, systems and everyday practice' (Luke 2006: 3).

We outline the focus of the different chapters in our descriptions of the book's three parts. A glossary appears at the beginning of the book, rather than more conventionally at the end. This is designed for the convenience of the reader in gaining a sense of the key methods and approaches that feature in the various chapters.

We hope that the book invites the reader to be thoughtful about methods, and perhaps to ask and seek to answer research questions that reflect and build on a sociocultural understanding of pedagogy.

PART ONE

Conceptions of pedagogy and implications for research

Introduction to part one: Conceptions of pedagogy and implications for research

These three chapters explore, problematize and interweave conceptions of pedagogy and pedagogy research in ways that only become visible from a researcher perspective. Together they define and explore pedagogy, pedagogical research and our understanding of the integrated and complex relationships between theoretical stance, pedagogical context and research approach in ways that support our distinctive and applied focus on these elements in Parts Two and Three as inseparable and combined.

Chapter 1 offers an introduction to pedagogy and how to investigate it. Integrating central theoretical perspectives on pedagogy, we share our definition of pedagogy for the pedagogical research explored throughout this text. Understanding the dynamic relationship between theory and method, we explore the implications of our conceptualization of pedagogy as the specified, enacted and experienced dimensions of practice for the methodological approaches presented in later chapters. Investigating what pedagogy does alongside what pedagogy is, this chapter reveals how pedagogy is negotiated in policy and practice through pedagogical scripts and histories of participation. **Case study** examples in this chapter from the United Kingdom and the United States focus on primary and inclusive education.

Chapter 2 delves further into the complexities inherent in defining and researching pedagogy by looking at a number of different pedagogies and pedagogical concepts, and their particular implications for research methods. Understanding pedagogy as not just a generic concept, this chapter exemplifies the roles of context (social, cultural, historical and political) and values in pedagogical research. Critical pedagogy, radical pedagogy, engaged pedagogy, social pedagogy and inclusive pedagogy are taken in turn and explored, highlighting a core message of coherence between theories, methods, values and subject matter. Examples from our own research are also discussed in detail, alongside case study examples from Australia, Scotland and Europe focusing on school and disadvantaged settings.

Chapter 3 turns to historical and metaphorical conceptions of pedagogy and its various positionings as either art, craft or science. This chapter examines these positions and implicated research approaches, and in so doing offers researchers new ways of looking at and thinking about pedagogical research in different contexts, such as those discussed in Chapter 2. Problematizing ways of knowing, the knower and the known in pedagogical research, this chapter examines the relationships between our understanding of the world and our simultaneous construction of it through our interactions, experiences and practices in pedagogical research. Employing case studies from the United States, Europe and the United Kingdom of early years, secondary and third level settings, this chapter builds on the framework for pedagogical research developed in the previous two chapters while indicating some challenges for pedagogical research.

CHAPTER ONE

Pedagogy – theoretical perspectives and methodological implications

Introduction

This chapter is an introduction to pedagogy and how to investigate it. We present our understanding of pedagogy, and within this we consider and integrate central theoretical perspectives on it. We explore the methodological implications of our definition of pedagogy for pedagogical research. We begin by identifying and exemplifying three key interrelated dimensions of pedagogy as we understand them (what pedagogy does), before offering in the second half of this chapter a definition of pedagogy (what pedagogy is).

Three dimensions of pedagogy

Simply put, pedagogy is about teaching and learning. It incorporates the following elements: teaching, learning, curriculum and assessment. It also concerns relationships and values. Pedagogy is fundamentally concerned with what people perceive to be meaningful, important and relevant as they engage in teaching-related activity and develop competence and expertise in a practice. Since we cannot assume what is salient to people as they engage in tasks, whether in school or work, we have to reflect on and study the way experience is organized and authorized, produced, reproduced and transformed in settings. According to Bruner (1996: 63), 'A choice of pedagogy inevitably communicates a conception of the learning process and the learner. Pedagogy is never innocent. It is a medium that carries its own message.'

As a medium that is never neutral, we understand pedagogy as having three key, interrelated dimensions. We outline these three dimensions here, but we return to them throughout the book as they offer an important sociocultural framework that we think will prove helpful in researching pedagogy in various settings. We take the view, shared by many who come from a sociocultural theoretical perspective, that opportunities and contexts for learning are all around us – they are not just bound to places explicitly designed to promote learning, such as schools and colleges. Opportunities and contexts for learning are 'everywhere' and 'everyday'. As such, learning transcends time, place, age and setting. Pedagogy, therefore, as something involving the support and promotion of learning, is inseparable from how learning opportunities are afforded and denied to people, how learning is resisted by people and how knowledge is produced. Learning concerns how people change the way they participate in practices and activities; and pedagogy concerns how people are enabled, supported or constrained in how they participate in practices and activities, and how their histories mediate and are brought to bear by the teacher and by the setting. This is the case regardless of whether one is talking about becoming a secondary school student, a reader, a hairdresser, a doctor or a teacher – all involve changes in participation and all involve ways of affording (and constraining) that participation.

The first dimension of pedagogy we present is the dimension of what is assumed to be an appropriate way to teach and learn. We can think here in the context of schooling, for example, about the official curriculum – the specified curriculum is part of pedagogy for it conveys messages about what society deems valuable and valued. Similarly, there may be a notion of a specified pedagogy, or accepted ways of teaching and learning, in a given curriculum domain (e.g. early reading) or for a particular phase of schooling that is perhaps generally endorsed by a society through national policy. For convenience, we can label this 'pedagogy as specified'.

A second dimension of pedagogy is about enactment. It is one thing to have a notion of what constitutes an appropriate pedagogy, but it is quite another to enact it. Enacted pedagogy, which incorporates an enacted curriculum, inevitably depends on the enactor and how that person breathes life into the policy or the specified or official version of pedagogy through their actions in the classroom or other learning environments. It is important who the enactor is; it matters how that person interprets the specified pedagogy; this, in turn, depends upon the person's own history of experience and competence, as well as their power to make decisions and exercise judgement. It also depends on their relationships with and conceptions of other actors around them, for instance students, other teachers, parents, the head teacher and so on. For convenience, we can label this dimension, 'pedagogy as enacted'.

The third dimension is about experience. How is the pedagogy experienced by the actors involved, particularly by the teachers/mentors/guides and the learners, all of whom are constantly decoding and interpreting what is happening, and how it is happening? How are the actors affected, positioned and transformed by the enactment, and the experience of the pedagogy? The subjective experience of all involved is important. We can refer to this dimension as 'pedagogy as experienced'.

These sociocultural features of pedagogy provide important analytic tools for its exploration as a dynamic phenomenon. The assumption of this model of pedagogy is that how to support learning cannot be separated from social identities, power relations, interests, purposes, agendas of participants, availability of resources, and existing organizational and institutional practices. It is an approach to pedagogy that takes account of the lived realities, experiences, conventions and perspectives of teachers, mentors and learners, which are treated as significant and relevant. As we develop this chapter and the book, we unpack this version of pedagogy further and bring out its many implications and possibilities for the pedagogy researcher. In particular, we explore the three dimensions of pedagogy collectively and individually.

The next section considers an approach to pedagogy that became dominant, especially in the United States and United Kingdom, in the past decade. We explore this pedagogical approach through the lens of the three dimensions just described to exemplify further what this sociocultural understanding of what pedagogy means for our understanding of what pedagogy is and how we engage in pedagogy research.

Pedagogy as a treatment: 'What works'?

The idea that teaching should become 'an evidence-based profession' came to prominence when various researchers and policy makers called for a closer connection between research, policy and practice (see e.g. Slavin 2002, 2004; Sebba 2004). The notion of 'evidence-informed practice' stems from this initiative. The idea is that pedagogy should be based on 'what works', so for the pedagogy researcher the issue becomes how to define and establish 'what works'.

The research method assumed to be most appropriate for answering 'what works' research questions is the **randomized control trial** (RCT, often termed the 'gold standard'), involving randomized allocation of, for example, people to particular teaching approaches or treatments. The assumption is that this research methodology can demonstrate the effectiveness of interventions or treatments 'beyond reasonable doubt' (Slavin 2002: 16). Once the variable of participants is removed (because participants are randomly allocated to groups), then pedagogy becomes akin to a treatment. The reasoning offered for such an approach frequently likens education to medicine and so the claim is made that pedagogy enacted is akin to a medical intervention, like a new drug or diet.

Unlike the framework we briefly outlined in the introduction, the assumption of this approach is that the researcher can separate the phenomenon of how to support learning from social identities, power relations, people's interests and purposes, participants' meaning-making, availability of resources, and existing organizational and institutional practices. The focus is on the relationship between teacher behaviour (process) and learner outcomes (product) though, as Muijs and Reynolds (2005) observe, eradicating other variables is difficult. The approach renders invisible the lived realities, experiences and perspectives of teachers and learners – these are seen as irrelevant and so can be entirely glossed over. Alternatively, these realities may be seen as too politically sensitive in bringing to light individual teacher effectiveness (Muijs and

Reynolds 2005). This approach to pedagogy is often described as rational, technical or neutral. It has become ever more sophisticated, with advanced statistical techniques, yet it is reductionist in that pedagogy is largely reduced to prescriptions about what actions to take, that is, what methods to use to ensure learning. This is similarly one of the criticisms of a **systematic review** approach, where decontextualization can be a problem (Hammersley 2001). In this way pedagogy becomes isolated parts of the enactment. As Lave (1996: 158) observes, 'It takes the teacher out of the teaching. It reduces teaching to curriculum, to strategies or recipes for organizing kids to know some target knowledge. It also takes learners' learning out of the picture.'

A controversial example of a study that adopted this technical approach to pedagogy sought to assess the relative effectiveness of two approaches to the teaching of early reading based on two different ways of developing phonic knowledge (Johnston and Watson 2005). The two different approaches were applied in classrooms in Scotland and their effectiveness was judged on the basis of differences in reading test scores of pupils undergoing the different 'treatments'. With an interest in research methods for pedagogy, we need to ask what assumptions the researchers are making in this approach.

The first assumption is of a direct link between teaching and learning, an assumption deeply challenged by a sociocultural pedagogy (see Lave 1996). This view of pedagogy also assumes that the intentions and beliefs of the different teachers about the different teaching approach and phonic programme assigned to them would not influence the way they applied the methods or phonic programme. Claims were subsequently made about the relative merits of one approach over the other, and since then these claims have been influencing the direction of national policy on the teaching and learning of early reading in England (though, interestingly, not in Scotland where the study was done!).

From a sociocultural perspective, such studies can of course provide important illumination, but they cannot ever deliver a person-proof pedagogy. The idea of 'what works' is seductive, given policy concerns with measurable outcomes as indicators of the success of educational systems. However, it matters what is judged as research; and in terms of education, particularly pedagogy, an evidenced-based approach as defined in this example, is, we think, simplistic. This is because of the view of learning it brings with it – it assumes neutrality on the part of the people involved in the 'treatment', where all the participants are assumed to stand outside the phenomena under investigation. The assumption of impartiality on the part of enactors of pedagogy in the 'what works' way of thinking about effectiveness has been heavily criticized, not just in education but in other aspects of social life (e.g. Slee, Weiner and Tomlinson 1998; Biesta 2007; Hollway 2001; Hedges 2012).

Specifications of pedagogy as in the 'what works' approach include a number of important assumptions that the pedagogy researcher needs to notice. One is the assumption that meaning can be 'given'. From a sociocultural viewpoint, meaning has to be perceived; it cannot simply be handed over. Another is the assumption that, because meaning can be given, then practice can be homogenized. The latter gives us the notion of the lesson that seeks to bypass the teacher. Neither of these assumptions makes sense. Accounts or abstractions from practice can, and do, signal what is deemed important for attention, but on their own they cannot determine practice. This assumption leads in turn to the privileging of the programme or method over the agents, a move that makes them invisible and undermines their participation. It is people who implement policy directives about pedagogy and associated curriculum programmes. The implementers, as agents, have views, perspectives and beliefs about the world and what works in their context, and with their learners. Furthermore, assuming that one programme can be equally effective with all learners ignores the different histories of teachers and how those histories inevitably mediate practice. Case example 1.1 illustrates this point.

Case example 1.1: Teachers' interaction with policy (Woodgate-Jones 2014)

Context: A study of teachers engaging with the Primary Modern Foreign Language Initiative (PMFL) in England.

Goal: To explore teachers' responses to the government's introduction in 2002 of their intention to introduce modern foreign languages into all primary schools for children aged 7–11 by 2010.

Case example 2.1

The policy advocated primary teachers teaching the subject thereby facing change as they adopted the reform. The study aimed to see how head teachers, subject coordinators and class teachers felt about the initiative and responded in practice.

Outcomes: 'The unmanageable number of initiatives combined with the rise of accountability led to schools and teachers implementing the PMFL initiative hurriedly and with little time dedicated to its introduction. The low status of PMFLs compared with the core subjects of English and Maths meant that the importance placed on teachers' subject knowledge was downplayed. This resulted in some teachers trying to teach French with insufficient subject knowledge, and with mixed feelings about their own language learning. A lack of appropriate professional development sometimes 'led to teachers not making progress with their subject knowledge either in terms of competence or confidence', yet 'the high level of compliance amongst teachers was striking'. Some, therefore, taught PMFL to provide enjoyable curriculum experiences rather than facilitate linguistic progress. This may be seen as a 'lethal mutation' (McLaughlin 2008: 183) of policy, diverting from the government reformers' intent.

Methods: A case study approach was designed to gain in-depth understanding of the policy implementation in two schools. It included periods of extended engagement with the schools, building rapport, having informal conversations, experiencing the culture, interviewing head teachers, class teachers and subject coordinators and undertaking participant **observation** of lessons. A grounded theory approach was used to analyse data and thereby to generate theory from the dataset.

From a sociocultural perspective, participants (learners, teachers/ mentors) act and negotiate their meanings in the course of engaging with particular tasks within particular sets of relations, roles, interests and expectations, and broader institutional practices and imperatives. This makes a universal notion of pedagogy untenable and challenges the assumed direct connection between specified, prescribed or so-called effective teaching methods and learning.

Our sociocultural frame seeks to recognize the dynamic interplay between the social order – or pedagogy as specified – and the experienced world, where practice emerges through the actions and interactions of actual people – pedagogy as experienced. However, in the move towards a view of practice as synonymous with 'what works', the individual is taken out of the analysis and pedagogy becomes generalizable across people and across contexts. This is highly problematic in a sociocultural view of pedagogy. At a very minimum, the pedagogy researcher needs to consider the assumptions underlying a given pedagogical approach and be able to consider the research implications critically.

The role of pedagogical scripts in doing pedagogy (research)

Official directives and guidelines frequently refer to pedagogy and urge teachers to teach in a particular way. Consider OfSTED reports of schools in the United Kingdom as an example. Official policies make assumptions about what constitutes good pedagogy, in general or in particular reference to a curriculum area. For instance in many, especially English-speaking, countries in recent years, governments have encouraged and occasionally mandated schools to use specified pedagogic practices to develop literacy and numeracy. Some of this push stems from international assessments such as the Programme for International Student Assessment (PISA). Thus, there is an increasing attempt to determine the *what* and the *how* of the pedagogy. Such directives function to shape the thinking and the practices of those who support learning in institutions. They act as scripts, tools or guides to action. At times, such scripts may be taken for granted and assumed to be 'the' way to teach.

Such policy directives also work to shape public consciousness about what constitutes a 'good', 'outstanding', 'adequate', 'effective' way to support learning. In addition, the popular press may pick up and reinterpret such descriptions, **drawing** on intuitive theories about 'the way things should be'. Making explicit the implicit theory underlying representations of pedagogy invites a critical understanding of how beliefs are constructed and reconstructed. Being able to examine the explicit and implicit theory underlying representations or scripts of pedagogy is important for the pedagogy researcher. The scripts available to us structure our activity and guide our actions. In the case of pedagogy then, identifying what those scripts are requires consideration if we are to research how, for example, classroom interaction and behaviour are shaped, and how practitioners and learners are positioned.

The media headlines listed below position and reposition practitioners and pedagogy in particular ways.

1 'Bad teaching kills reading skills' (Jennifer Buckingham, *The Australian*, 30 September 2013)

2 'Poor teachers set students back years' (Andrew Stevenson, *The Sydney Morning Herald*, 27 August 2011)

3 'Our schools need tough guys teaching teenage boys, not feminised men changing infants' nappies' (Kathy Gyngell, *Daily Mail*, 17 July 2012)

4 'Discipline fears as female teachers outnumber male peers by 12 to 1' (*Evening Standard*, September 2006).

Relevant sociocultural questions for the pedagogy researcher might be:

1 What story lines or ways of thinking do these headlines legitimate?

2 What assumptions are being made that may mediate practice? and

3 How are practitioners being positioned, given these assumptions?

To focus more specifically on the thrust of the last two, the script being communicated in these headlines is that men are needed to ensure discipline in schools. One piece goes on to state that 'to our cost, teaching has become a female-dominated profession in both secondary and primary schools', and that, 'with the elimination of so many single-sex schools, boys today can go through their entire schooling without ever being taught by a man'. The author asserts, 'This is quite, quite wrong. I would go so far as to say it is a disaster.' The last piece threatens a classroom discipline crisis as boys miss out on authority role models, positioning men as the only authority figures. The headline implies that an attribute of effective pedagogy for boys is one in which they are controlled, and the headline positions boys as incapable of identifying with authority figures that are not male.

One might imagine how, in response to such claims about pedagogy, institutions of the state might adopt a policy of encouraging more men to pursue teaching as a career based on the script of men as better authority and role figures for boys, better able to discipline students, especially boys, than women. Such claims, at the same time, create a belief that there is a crisis of discipline in *all* schools. At the level of schools, one could imagine how the script could be taken up to influence recruitment, school practices to ensure compliant pupil behaviour, and who is taught together, by whom and in which ways. So, at the level of practice, this script may emerge as the way the world ought to be. In this way a particular script is affirmed and reproduced, but it is important to note that this is not an inevitable process. In a sociocultural view, the person is always agentive and what happens in practice depends on the lived experience of all the actors, and their previous histories and values, such that scripts can be resisted and can emerge in ongoing practice in various diverse ways. This captures something of the complexity of pedagogy and broader social human action. As researchers, we need to be reflexive about the scripts we are adopting and reinforcing.

Returning to the three dimensions of pedagogy noted in the framework introduced at the beginning of the chapter, we can imagine the kind of interconnection across the three permeable dimensions shown in Table 1.1.

The kind of script about gender and pedagogy evident in the last two headlines may restrict participation in some activities – female

Table 1.1 An exemplar of the three dimensions at work

Pedagogy as specified ↓	Authority, discipline, order and being male	Recruit more males
Pedagogy as enacted ↓↑	Discipline, single-sex groupings	Segregation by sex group
Pedagogy as experienced ↑	Competitive, controlling approach	

teachers employed as authority figures – and enhance participation in others – male teachers as authority figures. Scripts are useful for understanding how practice is structured and how people may be variously positioned to participate in a practice and so experience themselves as developing competence in it. Different scripts afford and constrain particular ways of participating. The way ideas that are taken up in settings or communities will influence people's opportunities to participate and belong to those communities. The key message for the pedagogy researcher here is that the three dimensions are intimately interconnected. As enactment and experience occur, the pedagogy as specified is confirmed, revitalized (or resisted) or reproduced. Through enactment the policy is affirmed, albeit with the nuances and idiosyncrasies of the local, the latter dependent on the actors in the setting. Case example 1.2 shows how resistance to pedagogy as specified was fostered by one group of teachers and researchers.

Case example 1.2: Resisting dominant narratives (Broderick et al. 2012)

Context: A study of the 'everyday, lived experiences' of inclusive educators in Columbia, USA, who are dually certified to teach Grades 1–6 and disabled students, and who are facing narratives of disability in education that they wish to challenge. Their teacher education is imbued with a critical theoretical disability studies perspective, 'which holds that constructs of both ability and disability are socially, culturally and politically constructed facets of identity and experience, rather than innate, static or objective attributes of an individual's physical or psychological makeup' (Broderick et al. 2012: 825). This is a rejection of 'individualistic discourses that position dis/ability as individual attributes' (ibid.), and there is a commitment to upholding this in practice when 'working actively, deliberately and collaboratively' (p. 826) with pre-service and in-service teachers in pedagogical work.

Goal: To make explicit the dominant narratives (or pedagogical scripts) about disability in education, and share and illustrate ways of resisting and transgressing them with a view to supporting inclusive education teachers through their preparation and practice.

Case example 1.2

Outcomes: Confirmation of the painful, draining and difficult nature of resistance, which was lonely and burdensome. Clarification of the dominant narratives, discourses and myths, and affirmation of their own agency to transgress these.

Methods: A collaborative inquiry circle involving an inclusive teacher educator and seven classroom teachers, working to enable dialogue 'with colleagues who share a similar lens, reminding ourselves of our common commitments as well as the challenge of working with colleagues that we trusted to continue to critically challenge each other and ourselves' (p. 827). A response to acknowledgement that 'teachers who espouse a DSE [disability studies in education] perspective do engage in myriad acts of resistance on a daily basis, as they live and interact within the institutional, bureaucratic and discursive structures of special education, structures that are grounded in medicalized, objectivist, often deficit-driven conceptualisations of disability, knowledge and experience' (p. 828). Inquiry to develop counter-narratives including reading theoretical and methodological texts together, positioning counter-storytelling as a pedagogical and methodological tool, each member identifying a particular challenge to pursue individually and collectively. Generating as data over one year their own reflective journals documenting their own experiences, student work, other artefacts, commentary on these, dialogues around articulated issues and essays. Analysis conducted first by the teacher educator with other inquiry circle participants commenting, making suggestions, revisions, and clarifications or confirmations.

Taking a sociocultural view means recognizing the distributed nature of human action. With reference to pedagogy, this means it is insufficient to look exclusively at one of the dimensions without regard for the other two. If, as pedagogy researchers, we attend only to the dimension of policy (pedagogy as specified), we may get a sense of what society values and while that is a guide to action, it is not action itself, so it only offers a partial, impoverished account of pedagogy in a given setting. If we look exclusively at enactment, such as the teacher's practice in the classroom without reference to the specified pedagogy (be that at national or local level), it too will be a limited account as it bypasses the 'guides to action' and the reifications that direct and structure practice. Similarly, enactment without reference to the experience of the central actors (e.g. students) is also limited, since enactment is shaped by the perspectives, expectations and experiences of the students and the teachers. Pedagogy, in the sense that we are developing our position in it here, is fundamentally concerned with what people perceive to be meaningful and relevant as they engage in activity. Since we cannot assume what is relevant to people as they engage in tasks, we have to seek ways of establishing it to understand practice. The task of the pedagogy researcher is therefore a complex but fascinating one.

Official scripts of enactment as negotiations of pedagogy

In England and Wales, OfSTED reports are based on inspectors' observations of practice. The observations are made against published frameworks of criteria for effective practice, and therefore, they draw implicitly on theories of pedagogy. The reports and frameworks are part of the ongoing political, social and economic structuring of meanings. Versions of pedagogy are manifest in these texts, and these manifestations are variously negotiated, reproduced and recreated as agents interpret and apply them in the present to their different settings and activities.

One can think of OfSTED reports as projections of meanings about what effective pedagogy is through portrayals of practice. As such, they seek to capture experiences and practices to pin them down in a fixed form, which is used to guide and change practices (Wenger 1998). Schemes of work to deliver subject-specific national curriculum standards are designed to influence practice in a way society legitimates. In each case they draw on idealized notions of effective and 'best' practice, and implicit theories of pedagogy. For example, OfSTED reports of individual schools, OfSTED Annual Reports, Qualifications and Curriculum Authority (QCA) guidelines and the schemes of work available through the Standards Site all provide portrayals that allow the pedagogy researcher to consider assumptions about learning, teaching and knowledge. However, as projections, inevitably they are incapable of capturing the richness of lived experience. They must still submit to negotiation at the level of communities of actors, because the negotiation of meaning cannot be predetermined.

An example of a domain-specific, official pedagogic directive for early reading in primary schools is found in the UK Department for Education and Skills framework for the early years, focused on pace. We unpack the assumptions underlying this portrayal of pedagogy. Schools are urged to use a particular approach in the teaching of phonics. They are expected to adhere to the programme 'with fidelity', and the programme is expected to be applied consistently and used regularly, avoiding drawing in too many elements from different programmes. The guidance states:

- be systematic, with a clearly defined and structured progression for learning all the major grapheme–phoneme correspondences: digraphs, trigraphs, adjacent consonants and alternative graphemes for the same sound

- be delivered in discrete daily sessions at a brisk pace that is well matched to children's developing abilities

- be underpinned by a synthetic approach to blending phonemes in order all through a word to read it, and segmenting words into their constituent phonemes to spell them

- make clear that blending and segmenting are reversible processes

Source: http://www.standards.dfes.gov.uk/primaryframeworks/ foundation/early/pace/

While being able to decode print is assumed to be important in the early years of school, the extract could also be assuming that children find learning to read difficult and that teachers find teaching reading difficult. In recognition of these assumptions, the directive urges teachers and schools to draw on a single prescribed pedagogic approach and adhere faithfully to sequenced content (a specified curriculum and pedagogy) to be successful in their endeavours. This pedagogic approach is characterized as systematic, isolated from other aspects of learning, fast-paced and matched to learners' abilities. In this way, the assumed difficult tasks of teaching reading and learning to read are simplified, the potential confusion for learners is minimized and a single best way is assumed to be available. This approach aligns well with many official texts on the teaching of early reading and with media reports (such as the one noted above). The extract portrays a view of pedagogy as transmission and it prioritizes the rote learning of carefully organized sequential steps. The child as imitative learner seems to underpin this approach. An assumption underlying this pedagogic approach is that learners are more or less the same in relation to their previous experiences and their previous opportunities to learn to read, and also in terms of what they will find relevant and engaging. Indeed, the assumption is that that they are pre-competent as readers. They are competent only in terms of reading as defined by the test and by the opportunities made available to read by the test and test conditions.

A sociocultural view of pedagogy would not isolate school learning from everyday learning and would treat children as knowledgeable (e.g. Bruner 1996). Purpose, interest and reading for oneself from street signs, television and other environmental print sources would be judged as reading. Moreover, a socioculturalist pedagogy would keep things simple, not by isolating bits to be learned, but by embedding them in the context in which they will be used, that is, in this case to situate learning phonics in the context of the overall social practice of reading. Brown and Duguid (1996) develop this sociocultural pedagogic strategy very well in their aptly titled chapter, 'Stolen Knowledge'. They make the point that it is important not to break down or fragment tasks simply to be able to monitor and assess their mastery by individuals. They suggest that any breaking down of the task should be done by attending not to the task itself or to the learner in isolation, but by attending to the learner's need to locate the decomposed task in the broader context of the social practice of which the task is a part. Brown and Duguid argue that it is the presence of the full social context that enables the learner to 'steal' what is needed and what she or he finds most appropriate. These authors go on to say that classrooms tend to be 'secured against theft', by which they mean that the actual practice in question in the extract – real reading – may not be available for learning: only the replica, phonics, is. The difficulty with the notion of pedagogy in this extract is that the learner is isolated from the meaningfulness, the purpose of the act of reading. Denied is the idea that young people are not simply learning to read, but that they are becoming socialized into a range of literacy practices with meaning, motivation, power and attraction.

Researching the enactment of pedagogical scripts

In 2000, Robin Alexander published *Culture and Pedagogy*, an in-depth comparative study of pedagogy in primary classrooms in five countries: India, Russia, the United States, England and France. The study illustrates how different priorities, purposes and values, at country level, influenced pedagogy. He showed how teaching was variously organized and how learning was variously demonstrated, according to the values enacted by the teachers in each country. His study involved in-depth observations in the five countries over a considerable period of classroom life. The study is of particular interest to the pedagogy researcher for a number of reasons. It represents the first large-scale cross-cultural examination of pedagogy in any country of which we are aware, and it acknowledges teachers as enactors who draw on theories about pedagogy that are shaped by policies and cultural beliefs and values.

Comparisons of pedagogy across countries are useful in drawing the attention of 'insiders' of that community or country to hitherto taken-for-granted assumptions and practices (Rogoff 1995). Our purpose in highlighting Alexander's (2000) study is to expose the different ways in which researchers, policy makers and professionals define and understand pedagogy. His conceptualization of pedagogy is not a static one (unlike the 'what works' notion of pedagogy just discussed). His notion of pedagogy is dynamic, insofar as he does not assume that the specified pedagogy is simply that which is enacted. Alexander (2000) argues that the fact that there was no national curriculum in England until 1988 contributed to curriculum issues rather than pedagogic issues being the subject of decision-making, debate and contestation, in contrast to several other European countries that have had a national curriculum for much longer. Insofar as the notion of a specified curriculum exists in France and

Russia, he argues it is simply taken as a given. Alexander describes how pedagogy failed to become a matter for debate and research in England when, in relation to pedagogy, educational theory and practice diverged. He relates this continuing phenomenon to right-wing policies and individual actors who supported anti-intellectual approaches and denigrated the role of theory in the practice of school teaching.

Overall, Alexander's (2000) study provides insight into what is valued at the level of specified and enacted pedagogy and curriculum in each country he studied. He demonstrates how the cultural beliefs mediating the enactment or practice of teachers are not all the same in each country. He describes the situation in England and the United States, where he argues that pedagogy is subsidiary to curriculum, and contrasts this with the continental European tradition where pedagogy, as an overarching concept and as a broad intellectual field of study, enjoys high status in the education of teachers, and is strongly articulated in teachers' explanations for their classroom decisions. He describes the culturally specific traditions or theories of pedagogy and refers to a central European tradition where the focus is on what to teach and how to teach it, rather than on the child. He views the concern with the tension between the child and the subject as characteristic of Anglo–American practice. For instance, he demonstrates that US teachers, and some in England, seem to place more emphasis on practices that enable negotiation with learners ('negotiated pedagogy') than their counterparts in France, Russia or India.

Alexander, therefore, argues that how curriculum is understood is significant in understanding approaches to pedagogy. In the Anglo–American tradition, curriculum has both a broad sense, similar to the continental use of pedagogy, and a narrow one related to teaching method. However, when content becomes contested and narrowed to subject outcomes, as it is in most countries, curriculum is what is prescribed and is detached from pedagogy, which similarly narrows. For these reasons, Alexander argues the case for a focus on pedagogy as enacted, that is, to do with every aspect of what goes on in schools and classrooms. Curriculum for Alexander (2000: 325) is the '"framing" component of the act of teaching before it is transformed into task, activity, interaction, discourse and outcome'.

Teachers, Alexander (2000) argues, draw on different cultural legacies that reflect the values and beliefs of previous generations and that are approved by their societies in the shape of different specified curricula. However, as he is at pains to point out, institutions and schools take up scripts of pedagogy in different ways depending on context. Thus, he describes a pedagogy characteristic of French and Russian classrooms where the teacher is the giver of information and acquisition of objective knowledge is prioritized. Pedagogy in this view would not give value to collaboration to enable shared meaning-making, as this would not be an issue if meanings are given, not constructed and having to be perceived. Hence, practice based on this approach would not work with students' ideas and experiences. In both countries, however, Alexander observed that some teachers did pay attention to the personal authenticity of tasks to enable learners to make links with their prior experience. Further, he observed how some teachers used practices that enabled learners to draw on their expertise and local knowledge.

In India, where transmission and didactic delivery were the primary form of pedagogy observed, Alexander noted instances in certain subjects where approaches to pedagogy congruent with a sociocultural view of learning could be discerned. This was in an apprenticeship approach that enabled novice dancers and musicians to move more deeply into practice and achieve a trajectory of expertise. In US and UK classrooms, in contrast, he saw no examples of apprenticeship approaches to pedagogy. He observed practice where the negotiation of meaning to enable mutual engagement was apparently evident, but questioned the extent to which this was successful.

Pedagogy, for Alexander (2000: 540), involves more than teaching: it 'incorporates theories, beliefs, policies and controversies that inform and shape it'. The main point about Alexander's study is that he moves thinking from specification to enactment, thus addressing the cultural shaping of pedagogy. His study offers in-depth observations of what teachers do, what teaching is like. He did not intend to provide insights into the teachers' beliefs, intentions or explanations for their practices, or how learners, and what they bring to settings also shape practice.

This absence of insight is important. While Alexander's version of pedagogy recognizes the importance of culture and beliefs, his comparative study did not extend to probing the participants' experiences and thinking in this particular study. On the basis of our sociocultural framework, the teachers and the learners are enmeshed. The nature of the enacted pedagogy is mediated by both the teacher and the learners – it emerges in practice, in the moment-by-moment interactions based on what people deem to be meaningful and salient in a situation (see Benjamin, Nind, Collins, Hall and Sheehy 2003 for an example of research showing this). To understand pedagogy, researchers need to attend to the enacted and the experienced curriculum, and their shaping by the institutional framework and social structures – policy, theories and cultural beliefs in wider society. It is arguable that, though innovative and pioneering, at the level of the experienced pedagogy Alexander's (2000) conception of pedagogy is limited because it does not address the full dynamic nature of pedagogy.

Teaching and Learning Research Project (TLRP): Towards a definition of pedagogy

Before concluding this chapter, we consider the largest programme of educational research on pedagogy ever mounted in the United Kingdom. Introduced in 2002 and spanning a decade, this initiative involved 700 researchers and almost a hundred projects. Funded by the Economic and Social Research Council (ESRC), it sought to improve outcomes for learners and to understand the teaching and learning processes. It is important to this chapter because its researchers sought to define pedagogy and to offer a perspective on 'effective' pedagogy, and did so largely from a sociocultural perspective. In attempting to pull together the key findings from the many projects, the directors chose to present them in the form of evidence-informed principles of effective pedagogy. They were keen to avoid specifying detailed instructional prescriptions that tell teachers what to do, recognizing the highly situated, indeterminate and contingent nature of classroom life. It seems to us that the approach to pedagogy assumed by the TLRP leaders was deeply sociocultural in orientation. This is how they describe how the research in the different projects precluded prescribing pedagogy:

> The expectation that the research would be carried out in authentic settings made it impossible to control all the variables operating at any one time. But it enabled researchers, working with

practitioners, to grapple with the issues of implementation that so often confound best efforts to 'scale up' promising innovations. Furthermore, it enabled practitioners to use their knowledge, of the features of particular settings and characteristics of learners, to develop and refine generalisations from the original research. (James and Pollard 2011: 283)

The first of the TLRP's ten principles bears on educational values and goals:

> Learning should aim to help people to develop the intellectual, personal and social resources that will enable them to participate as active citizens and workers and to flourish as individuals in a diverse and changing society. This implies a broad view of learning outcomes and that equity and social justice are taken seriously. (James and Pollard 2011: 283)

The remaining nine principles cluster under three headings and are taken from the article by James and Pollard (2011):

1   curriculum, pedagogy and assessment ('Effective pedagogy engages with valued forms of knowledge'; it 'recognises the importance of prior experience and learning'; it 'requires learning to be scaffolded'; and it 'needs assessment to be congruent with learning');

2   personal and social processes ('Effective pedagogy promotes the active engagement of the learner'; it 'fosters both individual and social processes and outcomes'; it 'recognises the significance of informal learning');

3   teachers and policies ('Effective pedagogy depends on the learning of all those who support the learning of others'; 'Effective pedagogy demands consistent policy frameworks with support for learning as their primary focus.')

Although not without their critics (e.g. Dochy et al. 2011; Hogan 2011), these principles of pedagogy appear to recognize its dynamic nature; it depends on context, lived experiences, agendas as well and broader policy and political contexts. A key question arising from the TLRP research concerns how research is transformed through use, through practitioners' awareness and understanding of it. Collectively, the principles and the authors' analysis of them speak to a view of the learner and the teacher as agentive, while not taking it for granted that extending agency for learners is straightforward or inevitable. They acknowledge the complexities, in particular, around aligning assessment and learning. This includes how, for instance, aspects such as classroom dialogue and formative assessment, while well recognized for their importance by practitioners, are frequently undermined in the rush to 'cover' content. They prioritize a narrow version of learning outcomes associated with testing, or alternatively, are routinized and ritualized, losing their intended impact of negotiating and personalizing learning. What the directors of TLRP emphasize is that the process of learning is an interactive one of negotiating meaning. The need for negotiation of meaning through taking part with others in recognizing and resolving dilemmas is central to a sociocultural pedagogy (Lave 1996) and also to the pedagogic approach described by Alexander (2000). Value is given to learners being given 'hands-on' experience and having their prior knowledge recognized, rather than just learning abstract knowledge.

Overall, the TLRP's stance on pedagogy and effectiveness is a sophisticated one that acknowledges that expectations, roles, conventions, power relations and rules influence what is done and what can be done in a setting. Teacher beliefs, along with the mediational means, whether whiteboards, language or resources, human and material, all have a shaping influence on action. The pedagogy researcher in this view has to attend to a wide range of issues in understanding practice, a task that is enormously demanding methodologically. On the one hand, there are conversations, dialogue, joint action among teacher and learners, texts that can provide valuable evidence for the pedagogy researcher. These aspects are easily evident. Less obvious aspects include personal histories of previous interactions as well as the historical expectations and conventions of particular contexts and settings, which assume particular ways of acting in the world (Edwards 2007; Rogoff 2008). All these are also relevant, as they give insight into the constraints and affordances of action. A key question becomes: What is possible to do in certain situations within certain sets of relationships, bearing in mind the decoding mind of the actors? In later chapters we examine the kind of field studies that would begin to capture pedagogy, in this view.

Conclusion

This chapter presents an introduction to our conceptualization of pedagogy and the implications of this for methodological approaches in pedagogy research that we develop and expand throughout the book. We encourage you to reflect on your own conceptualization and any different methodological implications it may have. For us, pedagogy is complex, incorporating specified, enacted and experienced dimensions in practice. Researching pedagogy requires researchers to be aware of and to attend to many different concerns, but in particular:

- The enmeshed/constitutive nature of the above elements

- How people construct positions for themselves and each other within classrooms and other settings that reflect their histories of participation

- How practice is mediated by learners' subjectivities and how they position themselves and are positioned in the moment-by-moment unfolding of a setting

- How interactional practices are pivotal to understanding how learners and teachers are positioned and position themselves and others (shaped and shaping)

- Learners' understanding of how they learn, and the means that support this.

CHAPTER TWO

Different pedagogies – different research methods: Values into practice

Introduction

Pedagogy is not just a generic concept. There is a range of particular pedagogies or pedagogical concepts, each with its own theorization and implications for research methods and approach. First in this chapter, we discuss a family of pedagogies encompassed within a broad label of critical pedagogies, including radical, progressive and engaged pedagogy. There are subtle differences between them, but our main purpose in this chapter is to explore their associated research approaches and to illustrate the explicitly value-laden nature of the research of pedagogy. Critical pedagogy is well known in the pedagogical literature, yet the research methods for studying it are under-developed or implicit. Second in the chapter, we discuss inclusive pedagogy, where there is a smaller, newer literature but perhaps more explicit implications for methods.

Pausing early on in the book to look at different pedagogies is important because, as Williams (2009) argues, we need to understand pedagogy within its social, cultural, historical and political context. Some pedagogical movements have grown up in response to particular values contexts and, 'once we view pedagogic practice through the profoundly important lens of values we find ... that the relationship between structure, culture and (pedagogic) agency is more complex still' (Alexander 2009: 18). Values, according to Alexander (ibid.), 'spill out untidily at every point in the analysis of pedagogy', yet too often they are neglected. Looking at pedagogy where the values are particularly transparent may help with exposing what this means for making methodological decisions. If we understand pedagogy, as Alexander does, as 'the act of teaching together with its attendant discourse' (p. 11), then this attendant discourse takes on particular importance in our examples of critical pedagogy or inclusive pedagogy.

This chapter considers the methodological implications of a critical pedagogy stance and those of researching inclusive pedagogy. They are together here, because they each make a particular position explicit for pedagogy researchers. The former is more overtly about the political, cultural, economic and social landscape. Critical pedagogies challenge the what, why and how of curriculum and pedagogy in asking 'whose interests are being served?' Inclusive pedagogy is about who is included, how and in whose interests, but without necessarily taking such a critical approach to the curriculum itself. We begin with a brief account of the philosophy of critical pedagogy; case example 2.1 exemplifies the critical pedagogy principles and illustrates an associated methodological approach. We go on to explain more of the conceptualization before attending in depth to inclusive pedagogy; subsequent case examples elaborate on pertinent issues to researching inclusive pedagogy, highlighting the complexities and interconnections of theory and method.

Critical pedagogy and where it leads methodologically

Simply put, critical pedagogy is 'preoccupied with social injustice and examines and promotes practices that have the potential to transform oppressive institutions or social relations, largely through educational practices' (Keesing-Styles 2003: 2). Paulo Freire is often regarded as 'the inaugural philosopher of critical pedagogy' (McLaren 2000: 1) (although he rarely used the term himself), because of his concern with issues of relational power in the learning–teaching relationship. For Freire, education – and pedagogy – *is* politics. This is best reflected in his concept of praxis, which is about the critical reflection and action that need to be implemented within educational practices 'with the goal of creating not only a better learning environment, but also a better world' (McLaren 2000: 3). Comber (2001: 301) refers similarly to critical literacies, which involve 'asking complicated questions about language and power, about people and lifestyle, about morality and ethics, about who is advantaged by the way things are and who is disadvantaged'.

As we have already made clear, our stance in this book is that theories, practices, research approaches and methods messily and inevitably intertwine. Critical pedagogy, critical literacy and so on are rooted in critical theory. Critical pedagogy 'focuses on issues related to opportunity, voice and dominant discourses of education and seeks more equitable and liberating educational experiences' (Keesing-Styles 2003: 3). Here, pedagogy cannot be reduced to technique or method (Sellar 2009). The curriculum is never neutral (Shor 1992): it is always political text (Keesing-Styles 2003). The coming together of the teacher and learner and the production of knowledge is a political process with inherent implications for teaching practice. For example, Luke and Gore (1992: 1) make explicit: 'As feminist educators, we all attempt on a daily basis to create pedagogical situations which "empower" students, demystify canonical knowledges, and clarify how relations of domination subordinate'; their stance both encompasses and confronts 'male-authored critical pedagogy'.

In terms of implications for research, one of the goals of critical pedagogical research might be to describe and better understand empowering pedagogical processes. Keesing-Styles (2003), for example, argues that this is what Shor (1996) does in *When Students Have Power,* looking at what happens when liberating practices are implemented in classrooms. Luke and Gore (1992) discuss the importance of exposing classroom and curricular gender (and other) inequalities that affect policy and practice, and attempts at changing one's own practice. Critical pedagogical stances (and these are many and varied) do not divorce taking a critical look from taking critical action. Therefore, research approaches can be neither apolitical nor inert. There is no suggestion of 'single-strategy pedagogies of empowerment, emancipation and liberation' (Luke and Gore 1992: 7), nor of single-strategy research approaches. There is, however, a strong steer to research approaches that involve taking action, such as **participatory action research**.

Research methods for critical pedagogy can be hard to tease from the texts, which are largely embroiled in the philosophical and political argument. Yet there is a strong sense that such methods are highly unlikely to involve researching what is going on in pedagogical encounters without engaging with what could or should be going on. Researchers are implicitly involved in the transformational process of liberation. They are likely to be teachers, or working with teachers, in the process of promoting practices that address oppression in and through education. This is the point of praxis. Keesing-Styles (2003: 2) argues: 'If knowledge is to be produced, the pedagogue must systematically reflect on the role of the teacher in relation to the learners and must also examine such critical aspects as the social milieu that influences and is subsequently influenced by the learning experience.' Similarly, there must be systematic reflection on the role of the researcher in respect of that social milieu; the researcher is part of it, s/he will change it, and within critical pedagogy, should do so with clear transformational intent.

We turn now to our first case example, which encapsulates research designs and methods for critical pedagogy. Mindful of the distinction we drew in Chapter 1 across specified, enacted and experienced pedagogy, this study interrogates all three dimensions. For instance, it challenges the specified or official by introducing an 'unofficial curriculum' of popular culture and out-of-school learning interests.

Case example 2.1: Collaborative methodology in the Redesigning Pedagogies in the North (RPiN) project (Sellar 2009)

Context: A collaboration of university researchers and a cohort of around thirty teachers from one primary and ten secondary schools 'on the geographic and socioeconomic fringe' (Sellar 2009: 348) of Adelaide in South Australia.

Goal: To work together 'to theorize and redesign more life connected and thus engaging pedagogies for students in disadvantaged schools' ... 'to make a difference for students not traditionally well-served by institutional schooling' (ibid.). 'To identify and describe

Case example 2.1

pedagogical practices that have potential to improve students' engagement with schooling by making connections to knowledge that is valued in their out-of-school lives' (p. 349). Wanting to engage students in learning through strong and meaningful connections between the school curriculum and the local community, the pedagogical and research approach involved the negotiation of curriculum projects with learners so they became researchers of their own lives, on which they were regarded as experts.

Outcomes: Various pedagogies 'focused on different areas such as community knowledge, popular culture, critical literacy, or mathematics and science education' (ibid.). An understanding that teachers struggle to articulate their practice, which they see as 'all about relationships', practice which is 'inherently relational, emergent and non-linear' (p. 350), and hard to know other than in the conduct of pedagogical practice.

Research methods: Creating time and space for **reflection** by the community involved to engage in 'a series of whole-group round table meetings and numerous smaller meetings between subsets of teachers and university researchers … to reflect on their work in ways not often possible amidst the triage of daily life in disadvantaged schools' (p. 349). Use of anecdotal and more formal discussions of working practice 'to sustain rich ongoing conversations about pedagogy' and to provide 'space for teachers to engage in collaborative practice-referenced theory building' (ibid.). Use of prompts for discussion, such as the suggestion that 'pedagogical decisions are primarily ethical rather than technical or methodological' (p. 353).

In this case example, praxis was at the heart of the research as Sellar, the doctoral researcher stimulating much of the discussion, reflects in the first of our excerpts in which researchers reflect on their choice and use of methods:

I modified my thinking and research in response to our discussions, and teachers borrowed aspects of my theoretical vocabulary when it proved useful. While similar in format to semi-structured **focus groups**, the sessions were framed as opportunities for collaboration. Although I gave my research concerns some emphasis, the teachers were encouraged to take ownership of our discussions by critiquing or developing concepts I posed, or deviating from these if other issues seemed of greater significance. (Sellar 2009: 349)

In one of several publications based on this project, the team talks about their 'framing approach' or 'methodo-logic' for it. Hattam et al. (2009: 304) explain that by this they 'do not mean research methods or even methodology, but rather the logic of an approach for chasing socially just change through research, including guiding principles that underpin decisions and activities in all points and dimensions of the project'. In practice, this meant that the research team sought to build a language among its participants 'for shifting from deficit to asset perspectives' (p. 306). It also meant that all those participating had to become well versed with the nuances of the political context, such as media attention that tended to demonize students and schools from less advantaged catchments.

To describe analysis of the discussion, Sellar (2009) uses Massumi's (2002) expanded empiricism, that is, the idea of a commentary on collaborative theory building. Rather than respond to attempts to translate the teachers' anecdotes into theoretical knowledge, they talked about 'situated negotiation through which the teacher–learner relationship unfolds against its contextual backdrop' (p. 356). Sellar highlights this phenomenon in the conclusion that 'the relationality of pedagogy prevents it from being readily translated into an object of knowledge prospectively or retrospectively' (p. 358). For our current discussion of research methods for critical pedagogy, what is most pertinent is the collaborative approach employed in this project, which positioned teachers as co-researchers and actively involved them in attempting a simultaneous process of changing pedagogy and translating this into something they could articulate. As Sellar is aware, this approach is as important for liberating teachers as it is for pupils as, 'if teachers cannot give theoretical voice to their pedagogy then they risk exclusion from emerging scholarship and policy debate in which "good" pedagogy is being described, and has the potential to become increasingly prescribed' (p. 348).

Moving on from this case example, but keeping with the idea of articulating critical pedagogy, Arnot and Reay (2007: 312) discuss how '"the pedagogic encounter" offers a conceptual language and understanding of the relations of power and control and the ways in which they shape the educational system'. They advocate 'a sociology of pedagogic voice which engages with the power relations which create voices' (ibid.), and argue that this stance has serious implications for how we engage theoretically in these voices. Importantly, such a critical theoretical stance would lead researchers away from a naive concept of research methods that capture the voices of pupils or teachers as if they are in a political vacuum. Instead, they remind us of Bernstein's (1990) argument that the 'voice of pedagogy' 'is constituted by the pedagogic device' (p. 316). This points researchers towards addressing how voice is 'produced within classroom settings' and 'created by particular *pedagogic contexts*' (p. 317, original italics). Arnot and Reay (2007: 321), therefore, remind the researcher that

consulting pupils, eliciting and hearing their voices assumes the value of such pupil talk in challenging the hierarchical relations between teacher and taught and in reshaping pedagogic practices in line with students' expressed needs. However, the process of student consultation is not substantially different from other pedagogic encounters. It too requires recognition and realisation rules. Being a learner involves considerable skill and familiarity with the expectations of such a communicative setting.

Research methods for critical pedagogy need to recognize power relations at every turn.

Bell hooks' (1994) 'engaged pedagogy' is, as Keesing-Styles (2003) notes, directly attributed to inspiration provided by Freire, hooks' mentor. Engaged pedagogy brings together 'anticolonial, critical, and feminist pedagogies ... for interrogating biases in curricula that reinscribe systems of domination ... while simultaneously providing new ways to teach diverse groups of students' (hooks 1994: 10). It describes a teaching process that is respectful and caring of students; central to this, for hooks, is that the teacher reveals her or his vulnerability by sharing lived personal experiences, facilitating the student in doing likewise and, in turn, facilitating an authentic connection to the curriculum for teacher and student. In terms of research methods, the implication is that the researcher, too, is required to make her or himself known and vulnerable, so that engaging with lived experience is reciprocal.

Berry (2010) provides a useful discussion of the way in which critical pedagogy and engaged pedagogy deal with dialogue, including the right to speak and the asymmetry in the power of the teacher and student. There are criticisms that hooks' engaged pedagogy fails to address these asymmetrical positions, which again raise questions about whether researchers, in selecting their methods for researching pedagogy, should aspire to address their asymmetry and whether this is achievable. For hooks, 'teacher/professor vulnerability via revealment has the potential to shift the power relationship' (Berry 2010: 23). We discuss other routes to disrupting the power relationship in both pedagogy and research in our later examination of inclusive pedagogy.

Also related to critical pedagogy is the concept of social pedagogy. A bit like pedagogy itself, social pedagogy is a most comfortably used as a concept within mainland Europe. Chavaudra et al. (2014: 55) argue that the concept takes us into the broadest realm of education and into informal learning processes. Kyriacou et al. (2009) describe it as referring to the theory and practice underpinning the work of professionals involved in supporting the personal development, social education and overall welfare and care of the whole child. Critical pedagogy generally does not exclude concerns with holistic well-being, but the holism in social pedagogy is more central, perhaps, than the concern with rights and empowerment. In common with many of these pedagogies, social pedagogy is less about prescribing techniques than about an ethical stance pervading practice. Similarly, the practice of action is always connected to theory. The implications of social pedagogy in terms of research methods are in the expansiveness of what those methods need to capture and the interpretations they need to facilitate.

We would not want to end our deliberation of critical pedagogy and its relatives without touching briefly upon post-critical pedagogies. Lather (1992: 120) is helpful here in citing the argument of Ulmer (1985: 52), that 'pedagogy must itself be a text'. Lather reminds us of the role of deconstruction as a 'way of thinking' that is necessary to 'keep things in process, to disrupt'. Thus, she points us to a definition of pedagogy from Lusted (1986: 3) that concerns 'the transformation of the consciousness that takes place in the intersection of three agencies': the teacher; the learner; and 'the knowledge they produce out of the interactions'. Lather argues that this challenges ideas of the teacher as 'neutral', the student as 'passive' or knowledge as 'immutable material to impart' (p. 121). Critical pedagogy, she maintains, is 'that which attends to practices of teaching/learning intended to interrupt particular historical, situated systems of oppression' (ibid.). She goes on to argue, however, that 'too often, such pedagogies have failed to probe the degree to which "empowerment" becomes something done "by" liberated pedagogies "to" or "for" the as-yet-unliberated, the "Other", the object upon which is directed the "emancipatory" actions' (p. 122). This too, is a good warning to the researcher who may be looking to find research approaches or methods that might empower or liberate, which in itself requires problematization (Comber 2001; Gallacher and Gallagher 2008; Nind 2014a).

Inclusive pedagogy and where it leads methodologically

Turning now to inclusive pedagogy, this is a dimension of inclusive education, and is inherently political. Just as inclusive education is a contested and slippery concept, so too is inclusive pedagogy. Understandings of inclusive pedagogy are contextual rather than universal (Corbett 1999; Makoelle 2014). Not unrelated to critical pedagogy, however, inclusive pedagogy focuses on the educational culture and promotes change. For Corbett (2001), this is a culture of accommodating all learners through the use of diverse teaching strategies. She links it to her concept of connective pedagogy in which she advocates first connecting learners with their own learning, and then connecting their learning to the curriculum. For Florian (2009), inclusive pedagogy is about the totality of teaching methods, approaches, forms and principles that enhance learner participation. For Corbett and Norwich (2005), it may mean any combination of pedagogies common to all, pedagogies specific to some, and individual, unique pedagogies. For Hart, Dixon, Drummond and McIntyre (2004), in contrast, it is always about pedagogies for everyone.

Much more is written on inclusive education in terms of its values, philosophy and policies than its pedagogy. Even less is written on how to research inclusive pedagogy. Florian and Black-Hawkins (2011) build their definition of inclusive pedagogy on Alexander's (2004: 11) definition of pedagogy as 'the act of teaching and its attendant discourse'. This informs their study of teachers' craft knowledge, exploring those teachers' inclusive pedagogy 'in terms of what they do, why and how' including what they 'know and believe about inclusive classroom practice' (p. 814). Their focus on what people do reflects their understanding that this gives meaning to the concept of inclusion. Somewhat unusually then, they are explicit about their research methods for exploring inclusive pedagogy, as shown in our next case example 2.2.

Case example 2.2: Applying the *Framework of Participation* in examining inclusive pedagogy (Florian and Black-Hawkins 2011)

Context: A Scottish study of teachers' craft knowledge for inclusive pedagogy.

Goal: 'To encourage teachers to articulate how they make meaning of the concept of inclusion in their practice. Thus, a primary purpose of the research was not only to observe the teachers' inclusive pedagogy, but also to encourage them through **interview** to articulate their thinking about that practice' (Florian and Black-Hawkins 2011: 815).

Outcomes: Understanding that 'inclusive pedagogy is defined not in the *choice* of strategy but in its *use*' (p. 820).

Research methods: An iterative process of classroom observations and subsequent interviews within an adapted and extended application of the 'framework of participation' (Black-Hawkins, Florian and Rouse 2007), whereby 'the *Framework* structured the observation but the informal conversations focused it' (p. 816). Examination of the intertwining of what teachers do, know and believe in inclusive pedagogy, using the argument that any two

Case example 2.2

of these will enhance the third. Use of informal conversations: 'to clarify any immediate questions about the observations; to encourage the practitioners to begin to think about their inclusive pedagogy; and to help to build rapport in preparation for the extended interviews' (p. 816). Application of their 'own developing theoretical understandings of inclusive pedagogy' to help identify 'tangible examples of their inclusive pedagogy in action' (p. 816) with the process of analysis: (i) beginning with using emergent theory to identify events from the observational data for discussion; (ii) asking of the data 'What teaching strategies help to increase the participation and achievement of *all* children, including those identified as having special educational needs or requiring additional support for learning?' in a deductive approach; and (iii) reflecting on practice 'through the lens of our developing theoretical ideas' combined with 'a more inductive approach, allowing further ideas and concerns relating to the teachers' inclusive pedagogy to emerge from the interviews, which in turn helped to shape our analytical themes' (p. 818).

This is an interesting example of research methods designed for working with the idea from Hart et al. that inclusive pedagogy is about pedagogy for everybody and extending those authors' work in *Learning without Limits* with teachers who reject the notion of ability as fixed.

Another interesting example comes from the European INCLUDE-ED project where the interest in pedagogy is just part of an overall concern with research and its translation 'into actions and reforms that contribute towards overcoming educational inequality' (Puigvert, Christou and Holford 2012: 513). The 2006–11 European Commission project's focus was on 'Strategies for Inclusion and Social Cohesion in Europe from Education'. Puigvert, Christou and Holford (2012, p. 513) explain that their starting position was 'that educational research needs to employ methodologies that invite the contributions of all educational agents (i.e. teachers, students, parents, administrators, and policy makers) in order to generate meaningful analyses of social reality and produce usable knowledge'. In pursuit of their transformative agenda, their methodological approach of **critical communicative methodology (CCM)** (Gómez, Puigvert and Flecha 2011) is crucial as depicted in case example 2.3.

Case example 2.3: Critical communicative methodology (CCM) (Puigvert, Christou and Holford 2012)

Context: The (2006–2011) European Union-funded INCLUDED project, addressing 'Strategies for Inclusion and Social Cohesion in Europe from Education' and involving fifteen partners from fourteen countries in seven projects.

Goal: To research 'the question of social exclusion and education from different perspectives including the role of social structures, policies, and social agents' (Puigvert, Christou and Holford 2012: 517), including to analyse 'the relationship between school failure or success in four areas of society: employment opportunities, housing, health, and social and political participation'.

Outcomes: The outcomes are too complex to communicate here, but they included findings about the critical communicative methodology (CCM) approach, such as that it requires considerable reflection by participants and that 'egalitarian dialogue is not immediately possible just because researchers are seeking it' (p. 523).

Research methods: CCM aims to analyse social reality to help transform it. 'Within this approach the object of study is based on the reflections and interpretations of the actors who are experiencing the social reality that needs to be transformed. Researchers incorporate both theories and research-based knowledge into dialogue, and contrast them with the participants' knowledge. Using this methodology, researchers identify both the elements that reproduce inequalities and the elements that transform them by differentiating between the dimensions that are

Case example 2.3

exclusionary and those that are *transformative'* (original italics, p. 514). Specific methods include:

Communicative daily life stories, used 'to obtain a reflective narration on the everyday experiences … a dialogic reflection during which interviewer and interviewee work together to create an understanding of the world and to provide explanations for the problem of social exclusion' (p. 518).

Communicative focus groups: similarly based on these principles, but involving a group or community of participants with, unlike usual focus groups, the aim of trying to reach a consensus, that is, 'to construct a collective interpretation of what can transform social reality' (p. 519) with the researcher as an active participant in the process.

Communicative observations: conducted in schools and aimed at observing how participation in the learning process unfolds; in this, 'the researchers constantly interact with participants to understand the meaning of what they do and talk about' and together they 'must reach a consensus based on a process of ongoing joint interpretation' (p. 520).

The stance that the CCM researchers take on research methods is embedded in their concern with egalitarian dialogue. This connects back to radical pedagogy in that the theoretical basis of the methodological approach is guided by Freire's dialogism as well as the concept of communicative action from Habermas (1987) and ethnomethodology from Garfinkel (1967). Again, we see that choice of research methods is theoretical and imbued with values of the researcher in relation to the object of the research. For Puigvert, Christou and Holford (2012), it was important to reject a hierarchical position in which the researchers' knowledge and arguments counted for more than those of the teachers, learners and so on. Instead, influenced by Freire (1970), they sought to raise the critical consciousness of everyone involved through dialogue that 'takes into account the inherent power struggles not only in the subject of study – educational and social inequality – but also in the relationship between researchers and the research participants' (p. 517).

The value of this work, from our perspective in this book, is that Puigvert, Christou and Holford (2012) articulate three specific research methods that work very well for the study of pedagogy if one's standpoint is influenced by radical or inclusive pedagogy. Their dialogic ethic is applied also to methods of analysis, in which the most important dimension of validity relates to 'the ability of the knowledge to become transformative' (Lincoln, Lynham and Guba 2011: 114, cited by Puigvert, Christou and Holford 2012: 522).

The core message of the coherence between methods, values and subject matter has been echoed in our own work. Melanie (Nind 2014a) advocates that inclusive education (and inherent in this, inclusive pedagogy) is researched using **inclusive research**, that is, 'approaches reflecting a turn towards democratisation of the research process' (p. 527). In inclusive research approaches, the research needs to be relevant to the people concerned, of importance and benefit to them, and respectfully connecting with their views and experiences (Walmsley and Johnson 2003). What this means for research methods in practice varies greatly, with some researchers developing particular so-called **child-centred or child-friendly methods**, others offering participants choice of methods, other consulting over the process, even sharing control over it or having the control taken from them (see Nind 2014b). There is common ground between inclusive pedagogy and inclusive research that makes the latter a good fit when considering methodological options for studying the former.

Examples of this common ground being translated into real research projects are not as common as one might expect (Nind 2014b). Nonetheless, there are: (i) 'studies that involve teachers and connect with the drives for their involvement as change agents in **participatory action research** style projects'; (ii) 'studies that attempt to empower teachers as producers of knowledge; studies connected with the movement for pupil/student voice' and (iii) 'studies conceptualised as explicitly aligned with the goal of **emancipatory research** in not just giving voice but enabling students and teachers to take new and rightful positions in research' (Nind 2014a: 530). Ainscow, Booth and Dyson (2004) describe their action research network, 'Understanding and Developing Inclusive Practices in

Schools', as involving extensive practitioner–academic partnerships working 'to define and evaluate practices that can help to improve outcomes for marginalised learners' (p. 126), using mutual dialogue to learn 'how to learn from differences' (p. 131). Melanie (Nind 2014a: 531) also identified the example of Jones, Whitehurst and Hawley (2012), whose 'accessible research cycle' was a codification of their desire for teachers 'to generate and complete research about their own practice; thereby becoming the initiators and owners of the research'. In contrast, the collaborative inquiry circle developed in New York and discussed by Broderick et al. (2012) is a method reflecting a more emancipatory and transgressive agenda (see case example 1.2). Inclusive research approaches seek to include missing perspectives in a transformative project, thus for inclusive pedagogy this offers potential to develop a body of knowledge about inclusive education generated through inclusive research. This, Nind (2014a: 536) argues, 'could do much to secure the trust of the educational community, who after all would be invested in, party to and co-producers of that knowledge'.

In a study that Melanie Nind and Kathy Hall worked on with colleagues to explore inclusive cultures, practices and pedagogies in two English urban, multi-ethnic classes of ten- and eleven-year-olds, it was mostly through an **ethnographic case study** approach that we could see inclusion and exclusion 'renegotiated moment-by-moment by pupils and teachers' (Benjamin et al. 2003: 547). Moreover, it was our theoretical lens that enabled us to understand that these negotiations were 'played out in classroom contexts framed by overlapping sets of micro-cultures' and 'the struggle for power and prestige within those worlds' (ibid). Thus, we argue that

[the] children in our study were produced, by their schools, as differently able, gendered, classed, racialised and embodied subjects. All the children played an active role in their subjectivity: they could take up, resist and manoeuvre around the subject positions on offer to them. That activity, however, always took place in relation to the identity resources available, and the discursive practices in play. (Benjamin et al. 2003: 548)

Getting to these findings relied upon the research team addressing a series of methodological challenges (Nind et al. 2004) that reflect some of the connectedness between inclusive education and inclusive research. It was in making creative use of these challenges that dialogue was, once again, at the forefront of our methodology – or at least of our methodological decisions. One of our aims in this book is to make transparent some of the methods thinking that pedagogical researchers have engaged in. In this study, we actually made such decision-making public as shown in the reflective excerpts we rehearse again here:

> We spent a good deal of time discussing ... two main dilemmas: did we want to examine 'good' practice or 'everyday' practice, and did we primarily want to enhance inclusive practice or enrich our own understandings about the processes of inclusion. We were conscious too, that these were, largely, false dichotomies. As a group of academics with very varied theoretical and practitioner backgrounds we had varied amounts of experience in **ethnography**, action research and experimental methods, and we had a variety of recent and not-so-recent experiences of teaching in primary, secondary, further education and special school settings. Without extensive dialogue on the tensions arising from our distinct backgrounds and perspectives we could not proceed. Dyson et al.'s (2002) systematic review identified a relative lack of observational evidence in the existing literature as well as an inadequacy of the research base regarding students' experiences of inclusion. Our intention was to foreground student voices and experiences and to offer portrayals of inclusive schools that are grounded in extensive observational evidence. What held us together was our interest in what goes on in classrooms (and playgrounds, assemblies, etc.) in interactions between teachers and pupils, and pupils and pupils, and teachers and teachers. ... Our decision to adopt a case study approach drawing on ethnographic methods was relatively straightforward in that we shared a general agreement about the fitness of this for our purpose. Less straightforward was our next challenge of communicating our intentions to others. This meant establishing a common language amongst ourselves, and a way of describing our project and key concepts that was meaningful for the schools, parents and children. We grappled somewhat with others' desire to know precisely our definitions and concepts when we were comfortable with these still being very fluid. (Nind et al. 2004: 260)

In reflecting on the methodological process, we continue:

> The methodological challenges that followed ranged from the pragmatic to the ethical and more often than not combined the two. For example, 'how might we interview the children?' incorporated how can it feasibly be done and how can it be done responsibly, as equitably as is possible, and without causing harm. Similarly, 'when will the teachers find time to talk to us?' meant both finding the actual time and judging whether it was acceptable to take time away from teachers' contact with pupils. (p. 261)

The research methods ultimately took the form of fieldwork in two schools with each of the researchers immersing themselves in the school and one classroom within it for a week, followed by a series of single days spent similarly. The dataset comprised field notes, interview transcripts (head teacher, class teacher and groups of children) and audio and video recordings of lessons. Data generation and analysis reflected a mix of openness to emergent themes and pursuit of pre-specified questions. The dilemmas included how to identify schools with inclusive practices to study and what to do once we had negotiated entry to them:

> One option was to study practice in schools whose inclusiveness was already in the public domain, but there was something uncomfortable about over-researching these schools at the expense of others doing equally good but under-explored inclusion work. To somehow build up 'hero schools' seemed to undermine the concept that processes of inclusion (and exclusion) go on in everyday schools every day of the week. Alternatively, we could devise our own criteria for deciding that a school is inclusive and therefore worthy of our study. This, however, felt a little like answering our own research question without even entering a school! ... Ultimately we decided on a mixture of recommendation by others – senior advisory staff in LEAs [Local Education Authorities], combined with self-identification – schools with an interest in further understanding their own inclusive practices. (p. 262)

We faced the challenge of seeing through the layers of what we found in schools: the official culture, the school culture, classroom culture, playground culture, subcultures related to class, ethnicity, gender, sexuality and so on. Moreover, we needed to see through the pressures upon the schools that shape their culture, such as the pressure of financial survival in the market economy. While needing to be aware of the bigger picture, we sought to examine the microcosm of school interactions.

In aspiring to keep children and their experience at the centre of research on inclusion, as stressed by Corbett (2001), we sought to talk to the children, incidentally and in interview, so that we might build connections with them that could give us insights into their perspectives. We could see practices, such as [one of the school's] 'bottom six' (p. 264) going to literacy/numeracy with the deputy head/Special Educational Needs coordinator, which we could judge as excluding, but we wanted to know if these were actually experienced as such by the children.

Ultimately, while we reflected at the time on these methodological contemplations in relation to studying inclusive school cultures, the contemplations apply equally well to studying inclusive pedagogy. Questions like 'who is at risk of marginalization and exclusion in this classroom/school?' (p. 264) help to sharpen the methods as part of any inclusive pedagogic research showing a continual desire not to pathologize or objectify children. The transformative agenda informs the methods thinking, too:

> We could not research processes of inclusion/exclusion without being a part of their construction. We would be a part of the understandings we developed not separate from them. Our very involvement as researchers in the schools meant that we changed them (Goodey 1999); we could accept this passively or we could seek to make a difference. ... We had to decide not once, however, but over and over again, whether to answer the 'call for action' we felt from seeing exclusionary practice. Moreover, we had to think about how we might make taking action empowering rather than threatening for the teachers. (Nind et al. 2004: 264)

Conclusion

In this chapter we have shown a little of how pedagogic and research values translate into practice. This might be the decision-making surrounding the broad methodological approach or, more specifically, with the methods themselves. You might find it useful to put your values onto paper to examine them and their implications. At the heart of all the different pedagogies and the different research approaches and methods is the valuing of the different social actors involved in (the practice and discourse of) pedagogy and the valuing of their different ways of knowing, their different knowledge. Thus, the chapter has also shown that research methods for pedagogy, when driven by such values, are research methods that put dialogue at the centre of the research process.

Further reading

Hattam, R., M. Brennan, L. Zipin and B. Comber (2009), 'Researching for Social Justice: Contextual, Conceptual and Methodological Challenges', *Discourse: Studies in the Cultural Politics of Education*, 30(3): 303–16. This paper is useful in its discussion of methodology from a critical pedagogy perspective.

Nind, M. (2014), *What is Inclusive Research?* London: Bloomsbury. This short book provides detailed exploration of the approaches, methods and debates at the heart of participatory, emancipatory and collaborative research. Inclusive research and its fit with other research approaches are important for any research focusing on critical or inclusive pedagogies.

Puigvert, L., M. Christou and J. Holford (2012), 'Critical Communicative Methodology: Including Vulnerable Voices in Research through Dialogue', *Cambridge Journal of Education*, 42: 513–26. This paper elaborates some of the methods discussed in case example 2.3.

CHAPTER THREE

Teasing out pedagogy: The art, craft and science

Introduction

In education theory and research, pedagogy is variously positioned as an art (Eisner 1979), a craft (Brown and McIntyre 1993) or science (Kornbeck and Jensen 2009). Understanding pedagogy within and across these positions has particular implications for our understanding of what counts as research, the methods we use and what we need to consider in our designs. This chapter sheds light on the debates, dilemmas and concerns for the researcher inherent in each of these positions, aligning each with a particular way of knowing and doing research. The purpose of this chapter is not to provide the reader with ready-made research toolkits, or to consider methods out of context of the research site, but to offer ways of looking at and thinking about pedagogy research in different contexts around the following four questions: What do we, as researchers, look at? Where do we look? How do we look? What is visible and invisible from different points of view?

Ways of knowing, the knower and the known

Where two people have different ways of knowing, they will come to know different things, and acknowledging these different knowers and knowns is central to a study of pedagogy (Fenstermacher 1994). The relationship between our understanding of the world and our simultaneous construction of it through our interactions, experiences and practices is foregrounded in a study of pedagogy through the guiding metaphors of art, craft and science. This chapter unearths and explores these metaphors, showing that what is 'hard to know' is influenced by how and where we look and, for the purpose of this chapter, dependent on which metaphor for pedagogy we prioritize in our research design.

Considering and employing these three metaphors of art, craft and science in pedagogy research is helpful for researchers exploring their own or others' practice, as metaphor 'is a vehicle uniquely well designed to negotiate and make sense of the creative space between what is personal and what becomes public' (Hunt 2006: 317). Here, Hunt highlights one of the central dilemmas in researching pedagogy across all three metaphors: that the researcher and what is researched are often inextricably linked, so that the spaces chosen for pedagogical research are also the spaces in which teachers (and researchers) shape their personal and professional identities in complex ways. Researching pedagogy in spaces that are simultaneously personal and public challenges teachers as researchers to make visible and verbalize the hidden and the hard-to-know of their practice in many different ways. Locating our thinking within these metaphors for pedagogy allows us as researchers to simplify the complex and abstract aspects of our worlds (Farrell 2006) and provides a solid basis to understand the unfamiliar of our practice in familiar terms (Saban 2010).

To do some more metaphorical thinking, we can consider an artist, a carpenter and a scientist who we ask to design a structure for habitation – a dwelling. The considerations of each will differ based on their previous experience and understanding of the form and function of the structure. In his planning the artist may prioritize form and focus on shape, symmetry, colour and the relationship of these to each other in the creation of an aesthetically pleasing design. The carpenter might consider her materials and how each piece of wood can bend, flex and fit together at her will to realize her vision. Finally, the scientist may consider what functions the dwelling will provide in terms of light and warmth and look to the organization and design of other similar structures to inform ideas and decisions of what is required to achieve functionality. Which structure will be better or worse and according to whose judgements and definitions is not the point of this metaphorical exercise. Rather, it is about considering what is seen and unseen, heard and unheard, and prioritized and sidelined from a particular point of view.

This example, though generalized and over-simplified, illustrates quite clearly the different ways individuals can approach a given task and the different ways of thinking they apply to everyday practice. In introducing pedagogy as an art, craft or science, similar polarizations can be drawn. Pedagogy as art focuses our attention on care and relationships in intuitive and responsive practices. Involving imagination, creativity and emotion, the artful elements of pedagogy can be obscured from sight by the very practices and relationships that sustain them. Pedagogy as craft is centred on the notion of practice itself – doing, making, being and becoming – in communities of practice, and suggests a professional action-oriented knowledge base in teaching around the day-to-day experiences of teachers. The science of pedagogy links to research-informed decision-making and involves systematic observation or experiment in practice. This is often seeking proof around that which is assumed to be good or effective teaching practices.

We suggest thinking about the affordances and constraints inherent in each of these metaphors for pedagogy research in terms of methodological issues. This prompts us to reflect on what questions are being asked, by whom, how the study is designed and documented, what counts as evidence, measurement, validity and so on. This, in turn, allows us to focus on the hard-to-know in pedagogy research and creates new opportunities for the collection, analysis, presentation and discussion of data and the meaning of evidence in each unique research site and study. In pedagogy research, there are serious epistemological challenges to researching what is hard to know, and identifying as knowledge what teachers believe, imagine, sense and reflect upon (Fenstermacher 1994). In this chapter in particular, but also in the sociocultural approach to pedagogy research we take throughout this text, we address this issue. We understand knowledge not as something separate to the practices of teaching and learning but as something intrinsic to it, a part of the very hidden and hard-to-know that permeates and constitutes relations of being and becoming in educational life.

The aim of this chapter is to move both through and beyond these polarizations of pedagogy as an art, craft or science. This first involves asking what is different about our approach to pedagogy research, if we understand pedagogy as art, craft or science. Ultimately, it is about understanding pedagogy as what people see as meaningful as they engage in practice. We offer a methodological blend of these central pedagogical metaphors, exploring how they interact, intersect and inform research positions and become themselves legitimate tools for thinking about research methods and design. Conceptualizing pedagogy as a multilayered set of interactions grounded in our understandings of pedagogy as art, craft and science facilitates research design that gets to the heart of what teachers know as a result of their experiences as teachers. It offers many layers and ways of looking at practice, and in particular, the elusive and out-of-focus ways of knowing, doing and being that remain unnamable and make up the hard-to-know of our pedagogical experiences.

A scientific approach to pedagogy research: Effective decision-making in the hard high ground

Working through the three metaphors in reverse order, starting with a look at the more visible aspects, we begin with the metaphor of pedagogy as science. We explore how this understanding of the form and functions of pedagogy leads to a scientific approach in research methodology and design, questioning what this means for our research in terms of the four questions highlighted at the beginning of this chapter. Understanding pedagogy as science frames the research process as an attempt to understand the world around us, bringing the outside in through structured and scientific methods. Educational science has made some practical contributions to education, for example, work with success criteria and testing, learning outcomes, feedback practice, monitoring, motivating, expectancy and wait time. Most recently, neuroscience has been positioned within current debates on education practice, and its allure is fast claiming ground in this area (Hall, Curtin and Rutherford 2014). From this scientific perspective, the researcher begins as an increasingly sophisticated consumer of other people's knowledge and in due course plays a participatory role in the creation and use of further knowledge in the field (Cochran-Smith and Lytle 1993). Table 3.1 summarizes a scientific approach to pedagogy research influenced by the idea that pedagogy itself is a science.

Table 3.1 Pedagogy as science: Implications for research design

Nature of questions asked	<ul><li>what is good or effective pedagogy?</li><li>what models, frameworks or toolkits can be developed?</li><li>what can be known about quality and causality by implementing interventions and quantifying change?</li></ul>
Role of the researcher	<ul><li>an objective investigator, testing hypotheses informed by previous research positions</li><li>a producer of findings that can be replicated elsewhere</li></ul>
Goal of the research	<ul><li>knowing that …</li><li>addressing a problem or gap</li><li>widespread and general improvement of pedagogy through the development of generic and transferable models or principles of effective pedagogy</li><li>explaining pedagogy as measurable</li><li>isolating the 'here and now' under research from the history and context of the practice</li></ul>
Methods	<ul><li>conventional quantitative, qualitative or mixed</li><li>highly dependent on selection of sample</li></ul>
Data collection	<ul><li>systematic and structured</li><li>linear</li><li>closed</li><li>possibly multisite</li></ul>

Data presentation	• charts and graphs showing patterns and cause and effect • reporting of data captured
Data analysis	• deductive • informed by previous research and driven by research questions/hypotheses
Meaning of evidence	• understood as captured through the research design and knowledge constructed is understood to be proven through the findings
Measurement	• highly visible practice saturated with models and frameworks from research • theoretically informed • triangulated and generalized • value added (through national and international comparability)
Ethics	• primarily concerned with confidentiality, anonymity, design and use of instruments in an ethical way

From the pedagogy as a science perspective, researchers start from the premise that it is possible to use research to elucidate effective or best teaching practice and principles. The intention is to apply accepted theory and practice as an intervention that improves practice in a way that is measurable and recordable, or to distil from practice markers of effective teaching for further study. Gage (1985: 8) defines scientific knowledge as law like in that 'it holds for the more or less general case under specified conditions with all, or all but a few, other variables held constant'. There is a danger that the researcher can become insulated from the world we are researching through an over-reliance on previous theories, research or policy, without questioning the constructed nature of this knowledge (Hall and Curtin 2015). Despite this, a scientific approach to researching pedagogy can be favoured in large-scale national and international pedagogy research, as exemplified in case example 3.1.

56

RESEARCH METHODS FOR PEDAGOGY

Case example 3.1: Pedagogy as science: Measuring the effectiveness of secondary maths teachers (Clark et al. 2013)

Context: A comparison of efficacy in mathematics pedagogy in the United States according to the training model.

Goal: To explore the effectiveness of secondary maths teachers from the Teach for America (TFA) and Teaching Fellows (TF) programmes, compared to other teachers, teaching the same maths courses in the same schools.

Outcomes: Finding that TFA teachers were more effective than comparison teachers and that TF teachers did not differ in effectiveness from comparison teachers overall, but some differences were evident in the subgroups. Additional finding that teacher effectiveness increased with teacher experience and declined with increasing amounts of teacher coursework during the school year.

Research methods: The study was designed to ensure that the measured mathematical achievement of students could be attributed to teacher effectiveness rather than differences in the characteristics of students or the schools, thus it involved the following methods: the identification of classroom matches in each participating school and random assignment of students to each comparison class; a sample of 8689 students, 229 classroom matches, 89 schools and 289 maths teachers; a survey of teachers to identify their characteristics and a test of their mathematical competency; measurement of effectiveness through standard deviations from the mean.

Treating pedagogy as science and applying scientific methods for research, this case study prioritizes certain ways of knowing, knowns and features of research design that align with the researchers' own scientific view of the world and beliefs about teaching and learning. Employing quasi-experimental research designs call for consideration of validity, reliability and generalizability, as Clark et al. (2013) show. An advantage of this approach to research design is that it assumes that the essence of pedagogy research – the outcome of pedagogy – is easily visible and can be known and shared with others to improve practice. There is an extensive research literature of this kind in the United States, but very little in the United Kingdom. This observation by Muijs and Reynolds (2005) is explained by them as, in part, due to

> the historical belief that teaching was more like a creative subject than a scientific 'technology of practice' that could be learned, in which case there was little point in studying it because teaching reflected the influence of things 'deep down' in the psyches and constitutions of teachers that determined whether they were effective or not, just as the quality of the work that the artist produces reflects his or her deep structure. (p. 4)

From the scientific perspective, though, researchers need to concern themselves with the impact of observable teacher behaviour, and with test results and outcomes in particular, and do so in a way that does little to problematize these outcomes or the judgements through which they have been made. Evidence drawn from this perspective is visible precisely because of the perception that the values and beliefs on which the research and pedagogy are based do not require questioning. Using final-year test scores to evaluate teacher effectiveness in case example 3.1 does not allow for any consideration of variables other than those that have been controlled for in the design. The influence of other more nebulous processes becomes irrelevant to the research.

Schön has been influential in suggesting that thinking of pedagogy as a science alone is unwise, since such thinking rests on a fundamental misconception of what professionals do. For Schön (1983: 42), teacher knowledge is not the knowledge of science that occupies the 'high, hard ground populated with research-based theory, but rather is the knowledge of practice, found in the swampy lowland where situations are confusing messes, incapable of technical solutions'. If we understand the field (pedagogy) in this light, then we must also consider our approach to researching pedagogical practice to achieve a best fit for our particular research questions and purposes.

In our next section we leave this high, hard ground of pedagogy as science as we introduce the implications for research practice of understanding pedagogy as craft.

A craft approach to pedagogy research: Everyday experiences and angles of repose

Brown and McIntyre (1993: 12) explain that 'it is impossible to have direct access to teachers' thinking while teaching [therefore] it is important that theoretical accounts of teachers' classroom thinking should be grounded in teachers' own way of making sense of the particular things they do'. Pedagogy as craft centres on action-oriented knowledge used by teachers in their day-to-day classroom teaching, which is not generally made explicit and which teachers themselves might find difficult to articulate, or be unaware of using (Ruthven and Goodchild 2008) (see Chapter 7). Pratte and Rury (1991) explore how this knowledge is embodied and experientially learned rather than acquired in a systematic and highly formal manner. The craft of pedagogy is difficult to verbalize as, according to Gamble (2009), understanding pedagogy as craft implies tacit principles implicit in the actions of teachers that form a basis for professional judgement.

In a series of empirical studies with craftspeople, Gamble (2001, 2002, 2004) found that cabinetmakers neither talk nor act with explicit awareness of the knowledge principles they apply in their practice. Gamble suggests that these craftspeople recognize their embodied knowledge through being able to visualize the relationship between parts and the whole, but that they cannot explain what they do in scientific or principled terms. Thus, understanding pedagogy as craft complements and extends possibilities for research, as it allows researchers to bring into focus pedagogy as process alongside the consideration of its products favoured in the scientific approach.

The craft idea is also reflected in Lave's (1996) study of the teaching and learning of tailors in Liberia. In this, master tailors showed great difficulty communicating their craft, and even invented pedagogical monologues to apprentices (advising, for example, that the fly should always be sewn on the front of the trousers). Lave comes to see these apprentice tailors as mappers in cloth of complex Liberian social relations; the tailors came to see themselves not as sewers of trousers but master tailors, as their skill as artisans was only a small part of their social identities and engagement with practice. These studies of craft have many implications for the design of research into the craft of pedagogy, some of which we outline in Table 3.2.

Table 3.2 Pedagogy as craft: Implications for research design

Nature of questions asked	• what teachers know as a result of their experiences? • how can personal practice be better understood? • what is the nature of daily classroom practice? • how do the teacher, the practice and the values and beliefs interact? • how does practical and applied knowledge develop?
Role of the researcher	• an explorer at the heart of naturalistic enquiry recording, interpreting and forming new understandings • an interpreter of each unique study context
Goal of the research	• knowing how ... • interpreting individual experience in a social world • depicting evolving practice • understanding pedagogy in context
Methods	• bound to context • suited to emergent and flexible design (ethnography, reflective journals, case studies ...)
Data collection	• non-linear – evolving and emergent, dependent on experience
Data presentation	• stories and narratives of experience • offering questions as well as answers • richly engaging with (rather than explaining) experience • intermingled with (not separate from) analysis
Data analysis	• inductive • emergent – driven by experiences

Meaning of evidence	<ul><li>understood as situated and local and not necessarily replicated at another site</li><li>helping to show the how and why of pedagogy, rather than what is effective and ineffective</li><li>the power of the evidence lies in the experiences of teachers and learners</li></ul>
Measurement	<ul><li>largely visible practice bound by time, place and situation</li><li>teachers' decision-making processes remains invisible</li><li>detailed description of the actions taken and context, involving crystallization (Richardson and St Pierre 2002) rather than triangulation</li></ul>
Ethics	<ul><li>primarily concerned with the role of the researcher and their interaction with the context and actors within it</li></ul>

Researching the craft of pedagogy opens up discrete practices and ways of thinking about practical knowledge that are not as accessible from a scientific perspective. Prioritizing crystallization rather than triangulation acknowledges the diversity and contradictions inherent in the research site, as well as in the role of the researcher. This metaphor works, in that crystals are 'prisms that reflect externalities and refract within themselves, creating different colours, patterns and arrays casting off in different directions. What we see depends on our angle of repose' (Richardson and St Pierre 2005: 963).

Understanding pedagogy as craft, Elbaz (1983) studied a high school teacher (known as Sarah) for a period of two years to obtain a sense of her practical knowledge (including experience of students' learning styles, needs and interests; students' strengths and difficulties; and a repertoire of instructional techniques and classroom management skills). Elbaz (1983) identified five areas of teacher craft practical knowledge: knowledge of self, milieu, subject matter, curriculum development and instruction. She explored how this knowledge was represented in varying degrees of visibility in Sarah's practice. In this process she looked at rules of practice, that is, 'brief, clearly formulated statements of what to do or how to do it in a particular situation' (p. 132). She examined practical principles, that is, 'more exclusive and less explicit formulations in which the teacher's purposes are more clearly evident' (p. 133). Finally, she identified images through 'a brief, descriptive and sometimes metaphoric statement which seems to capture some essential aspect of Sarah's perception of herself, her teaching, her situation in the classroom or her subject matter and which serves to organise her knowledge in the relevant areas' (p. 137).

In his analysis of the study by Elbaz (1983), Fenstermacher (1994) suggests that looking at this same study of one teacher's pedagogy from an understanding of pedagogy as science would move the focus to whether or not Sarah was an effective teacher, how she thinks given this or that theoretical orientation, or whether her actions are predicted by some theory. However, understanding pedagogy as craft, Elbaz is able to tease out and construct Sarah's knowledge of her working world, that which is hidden and hard to know, 'without imposing theory or established methods on the form of inquiry and without structuring Sarah's responses within an existing tradition of academic research' (Fenstermacher 1994: 8). To achieve this requires a study of 'knowledge carved out of and shaped by situations, knowledge and that is constructed and reconstructed as we live out our stories and retell and relive them through processes of reflection' (Clandinin 1992: 125).

The next case example (3.2) provides another example of research methods and approaches consistent with an understanding of pedagogy as craft.

Case example 3.2: Pedagogy as craft: Investigating the development of craft knowledge in beginning university teachers (Guzmán 2009)

Context: A doctoral study at the University of Barcelona of the developing craft knowledge of two beginning university teachers. An understanding of craft knowledge that includes an emphasis on reflective judgement, 'applying a reflective approach to problems, cultivating use of the imagination and showing commitment to the value of words, relationships and experiences' (Guzmán 2009: 327). Pedagogical knowledge seen as related to 'the content of

Case example 3.2

discipline and the application of reflective action on the part of the teacher' (p. 328).

Goal: To 'discover, analyse and understand the process by which beginning teachers start building and developing teaching wisdom, based on their initial teaching practices, in order to improve their students' learning'. To answer the questions: What are beginning university teachers' beliefs about teaching and learning? What sorts of pedagogical strategies do they use in their classes to encourage learning? Do they think that improving their strategies is necessary? How?

Outcomes: Through comparing the two teachers, an understanding of the various ways of being a teacher that includes 'developing an *intuitive knowledge* in the course of giving instruction' (p. 332). Findings indicate that in 'the case of new teachers, institutional support appears to be crucial. Only with great difficulty can their training and development as educational professionals proceed alone and unsupported without specific institutional measures to facilitate the exchange of teaching practices' (p. 332).

Research methods: Qualitative, phenomenological, multi-case-study approach. Generating 'a detailed description and analysis of the particularity, complexity and interactive processes that characterize a specific case over a relatively short period of time ... a detailed description and analysis of unique social units or educational bodies and is aimed at an in-depth understanding of a particular reality' (p. 328). Classroom observations, in-depth interviews with teachers, focus groups and student interviews, with data analysed in an ongoing process throughout, looking for categories and interrelationships in the data using constant comparison.

Understanding pedagogy as craft asks researchers to look at everyday practice in a way that is meaningful and actionable from the point of view of the research questions asked. The practice itself is visible in the classroom (the what), hidden in plain sight. It is why the teacher engages in practice in this particular way that needs exploring. This includes previous experience; planning for and consideration of individual learners as a result of previous interactions; pitch and level of engagement as a part of the emergent relationship between teacher and students; selected content knowledge; enacted pedagogical knowledge; and research- and practice-informed decision-making. Thus, as Shulman (1986) has stressed, teachers have many kinds of knowledge: knowledge of content, curricula, learners, educational ends, plus a mix of general pedagogical knowledge ('broad principles and strategies of classroom management and organization that appear to transcend subject matter' (p. 8), and pedagogical content knowledge, which brings general pedagogic and subject knowledge together. The content of what teachers teach is a starting point for their teaching (subject matter knowledge), but this is transformed into a form that is comprehensible to learners. All this could be considered the sum total of one person's experience of being, becoming and belonging in a community of practice – part history, part present and part future.

Designing sophisticated research methods, which can in different ways represent and interpret pedagogical experience, is at the heart of researching pedagogy as craft. What is hidden here and hard to know is precisely what the researcher wants to represent – the intentionality within the practice and the networks of relationships and interactions that sustain and extend it. Making visible these practices and intentions will require more than **survey** or observation, and asks teachers themselves to explore the sense and meaning behind their day-to-day experiences. This can be messy and confusing, and findings here are often not clear-cut. Pedagogy always carries its own message, so teasing out this message is one of the central concerns for a researcher of pedagogy.

We further explore this idea of intentionality as we turn to discuss pedagogy as art and implications of this conceptualization for research design.

An artistic approach to pedagogy research: Invisible pedagogies that lead by following

Teacher-researchers negotiate the borders of educational practice and research as they simultaneously wrestle with daily dilemmas of practice and employ research-informed decision-making to theorize their experiences. In many ways, this intersection and interaction between the science and the craft can be understood as the art of teaching and pedagogy, particularly when attention is paid to the interactions between teachers, students and stakeholders sharing an interest in this process. Conceptualizing pedagogy as art blurs the boundaries between art, craft and science, but in the same brush stroke effaces from view the particulars of practice we want to make visible in our research.

If we understand pedagogy as science to be about bringing the outside in, in an attempt to understand the world around us, we can then see pedagogy as art as an attempt to bring the inside out, helping those around us to understand. The language of inside and outside is common in writing that theorizes our metaphors for pedagogy, but in this context we do not use 'inside' to suggest something within or intrinsic to the person, but rather the practice itself, and what is invisible even to the insiders of practice. Pedagogy as art involves appreciation of imagination, emotion, expression and creativity developed in the relationships forged in teaching and learning. Invisible to the naked eye, since often what we see in practice is the effects of this process rather than the process itself, this facet of pedagogy is one of the hardest to make visible, know and understand in pedagogy research. Table 3.3 summarizes

Table 3.3 Pedagogy as art: Implications for research design

Nature of questions asked	• what do teachers do? • what is the nature of the relationships and interactions around teaching and learning in a living and live community of practice?
Role of the researcher	• understanding their role as a part of a particular community of practice • explorer of pedagogy through a focus on relationships, interactions, emotion and expression • acknowledging that they may already have emotional investment in the products and process of previous pedagogies

Goal of the research	• knowing why • exploring the relational aspects of pedagogy • exploring the role these relational aspects play in teaching and learning • examining how these change over time through a focus on histories of participation
Methods	• suited to getting at the meaning, structure and essence of a particular lived experience for a person or a group of people • **phenomenology**, ethnography
Data collection	• generating multiple types of data from that learning context that reflect the relationships between different members of the community
Data presentation	• dialogical findings generated from more than just the teacher • depictions of interactions, conversations and relational elements • accounts of complex social relations (agency, power, identity)
Data analysis	• inductive • emergent, driven by experiences and social relations
Meaning of evidence	• understood as produced through and between individuals within a community of practice, where each individual has their own role to play
Measurement	• largely invisible practices which influence and orchestrate teaching and learning
Ethics	• primarily concerned with the role of the researcher and the relationship between the researcher and the participants

some of the implications for designing research consistent with conceptualizing pedagogy as art.

Researching pedagogy as art does not always have an explicit and visible starting point in observed practice, as is often the case when looking at knowledge of craft inherent in the everyday practice of teachers. Conceptualizing pedagogy as art can rely as much on researchers and their willingness to see, explore, question and theorize around practice, as it can on the practice itself. We need, as researchers, to pay attention to how experiences are organized, authorized and produced in complex social relations of power and agency in volatile communities of practice. What is hidden and hard to know from this perspective will remain so, unless the researcher develops and employs innovative and collaborative research methods such as those described in case example 3.3.

Case example 3.3: Pedagogy as art: possibility, creativity and imagination in the early years (Cremin, Burnard and Craft 2006)

Context: A UK study that places the identity and integrity of the teacher at the heart of artful pedagogy. Research focused on creativity, imagination, risk-taking and emotional and personal connection through involving students as co participants and self-directed, agentic partners in learning. Understanding possibility thinking, problem finding and problem solving as at the core of creative learning (Craft 2000, 2001).

Goal: To explore the connections between possibility thinking (including questions, play, immersion and making connections, imagination, innovation, risk-taking and self-determination) and pedagogy.

Outcomes: Findings about the pedagogical features of selected teachers' practices that foster possibility thinking, creativity and imagination including teacher reflection. Highlighting as central to possibility thinking and artful pedagogy the practices of standing back, profiling agency, and creating time and space.

Research methods: Selecting three creative teachers and considering them individually to explore how each employs both professional judgement and personal artistry to develop creative pedagogies that are effective for their students. Data collected through in-depth interviews with individual teachers, video-stimulated review,

Case example 3.3

charting of **critical incidents** and possibility thinking through teacher accounts, classroom recording, researcher classroom observation and whole-group data surgeries. In the data analysis phase, engaging teachers as co-researchers and co-learners sharing, critically exploring, categorizing, coding and synthesizing data.

Considering the research outlined in case example 3.3 in a little more detail, Cremin, Burnard and Craft (2006) explain how the pedagogy employed was a somewhat 'invisible one' (citing Bernstein 1977 and David et al. 2000), as teachers 'positioned themselves off centre stage' as they followed the children's lead in their classroom. Cremin, Burnard and Craft (2006: 11) reiterate Neelands' (2000: 54) observation that 'the true art of teaching lies in the complex tempering of the planned with the lived'. They suggest that the rhythm of learning was 'reminiscent of Woods' (1995) description of orchestration and pattern in the classroom, described by one of the teachers as 'the very opposite of pace – more of a dance' (Cremin, Burnard and Craft 2006: 11). They conclude that within this invisible pedagogy, 'high levels of professional artistry were observed and documented in action' (Cremin 2006: 12), highlighting the roles of reflective tools such as the video-stimulated review (see Chapter 7) and charting of critical incidents as central to a shared reinterpretation of individual professional practice.

It is clear when comparing the three case studies in this chapter that, while some of the findings within the studies have superficial similarities, the researcher journey and the process of research design and enactment were dramatically different in each study. We draw attention to this here to emphasize further the complexities inherent in pedagogical research. Looking at pedagogy as art allows Cremin, Burnard and Craft (2006) to see pedagogical features successful at fostering possibility thinking, just as how looking at pedagogy as science allows Clark et al. to see increases and decreases in teacher effectiveness over time. At first glance there is little difference in the types of claims made in both sets of findings, but understanding the research design of each according to the three metaphors for pedagogy as outlined in this chapter makes visible the fundamental and integral differences between these studies. This laying bare of pedagogy research helps to begin to make visible the many decisions and complexities inherent in researching pedagogy.

Building a framework for pedagogy research

Adams (2011) identifies the classroom, the institution and wider society as three theatres for pedagogy, explaining that each has its own discourse that acts to socialize students, teachers and researchers. Based on this, Adams (2011: 467) argues that we should conceive of pedagogy 'through the prism of the interaction between social, political and cultural forces and that which occurs through classroom practice'. Understanding also the social, political and cultural elements inherent in pedagogy, and by implication pedagogy research, we suggest that alongside these three theatres, the metaphor of art, craft or science offers meaning-laden discourses in which to position research.

Returning to the other metaphor of the plans for our imaginary dwelling at the beginning of this chapter, all three sets of plans (from the artist, the carpenter and the scientist) have something unique to offer and there may be advantages in bringing them together. Similarly, in the moment to moment of our practice, we (teachers and researchers) are at various times and sometimes at once scientist, craftsperson and artist. Researchers have a story to tell about themselves as well as theory work (Carter 1993). If we remember this, then pedagogy becomes 'a dynamic process, informed by theories, beliefs and dialogue, but only realized in the daily interactions of learners and teachers in real settings' (Leach and Moon 2008: 6).

Employing the metaphors of art, craft and science to research pedagogy also offers an interesting method for researchers to begin to engage in **identity research**, a complex theme explored in more detail later in this book (Chapter 6). Returning to Hunt's (2006) belief shared at the beginning of this chapter – that metaphor allows us to negotiate and make sense of the creative space between what is personal and what becomes public in the complexity of identity construction – his claim also makes sense: 'For better or worse, my professional identity has now self-evidently been shaped by my attempts to make these processes public' (p. 238). Making these processes public requires researchers to make visible and explicit their decision-making approaches around the development of their own pedagogy. Understanding pedagogy as art, craft and science extends our definition and understanding of these decision-making processes for both teachers and researchers to include reflection, critical engagement, consideration of the role of identity and experience, consideration of context, relationships and interaction within communities of practice and research-informed decision-making.

Our discussion of pedagogy as art, craft and/or science makes highly visible the complex relationships between theoretical stance, pedagogical context and research approach. We also draw attention to the many ways in which the researcher and those who are researched are always connected to other worlds and histories, and are themselves a part of a shared trajectory that extends into past, present and future experience. Applying what we have discussed in this chapter to pedagogy design will necessitate a consideration of methods that also makes visible these concerns and, in this regard, will facilitate the researcher to question previous experience and so on in the research.

It is not possible in this chapter, precisely because of what we have explored here, to provide new researchers with prescriptions for the instruments and research methods they will need for each unique research situation. Nonetheless, returning to Fenstermacher's (1994) perspective on knowledge, our aim is not to present knowledge or what is known, rather to consider ways of knowing and thus thinking about pedagogy research. Our methodological blend of these central metaphors of pedagogy research, to understand them as a part of the same story, allows cross-disciplinary affordances to the study of pedagogy. It transforms the metaphors themselves into practical tools for thinking about pedagogy, so researchers can begin their research with an understanding of their own role and the role of the context. In this way, this chapter complements and informs the final two parts of our book in which we offer examples of research methods and instruments. This is undertaken in the context of partic-ular studies in which we ourselves have been a part and share some of our dilemmas, based in some part on the ideas within this chapter.

Challenges for pedagogy research: Learning to look and looking to learn

While this chapter cannot offer a 'how to' guide to pedagogical research, it does present some challenges for consideration when deciding on pedagogical research designs. Thus, we conclude with a brief discussion (to be resumed in later chapters) of the simple questions on engaging in pedagogy research posed for readers at the beginning of this chapter: What do we look at? Where do we look? How do we look? What is visible and invisible from different points of view?

Our definition of pedagogy (what we look at) calls for a consideration of value and language in research design. This demands consideration of what contexts, for and by whom and for what period our definition of pedagogy holds. For example, limiting the focus to classroom practice may be too restrictive. The concepts brought to bear on pedagogical practice, and what we need to be cognisant of in relation to possible problems or contradictions inherent in these concepts informs our complex research designs. This ties to our second question, that of where we should look as researchers of pedagogy. This includes how we draw on previous studies and theories and also what sources of information we look at to provide evidence for our research. This opens up questions such as what constitutes a pedagogical text, and how we as researchers generate our own data and evidence in our looking. How we look asks researchers to consider the relationship between instruments, sources of evidence and the nature of findings emerging from the study. Considering what is visible and invisible from different perspectives and points of view offers researchers the opportunities to consider other ways of knowing and approaches to pedagogy research. Finally, the exploration of research methods arising from conceptualizing pedagogy as an art, craft or science is helpful in bringing to the fore the kinds of questions requiring further consideration, for example:

- What do teachers know from their experiences as teachers?

- How do researchers tease out this knowledge?

- What and who constructs knowledge about pedagogy in what contexts and according to what conceptual basis?

- What implications does this have for research design and findings?

- When it comes to the design of our own studies, what will we look at? Where will we look? How will we look? What is visible and invisible from different points of view?

Further reading

Midgley, W. (2013), *Metaphors for, in and of Education Research*, Cambridge: Cambridge Scholars. This book explores the ways in which a number of different metaphors for teaching, learning and beyond can be adapted as research methods and instruments in education research.

Levin, B. (2003), *Case Studies of Teacher Development: An In-depth Look at How Thinking about Pedagogy Develops over Time*, Mahwah, NJ: Lawrence Erlbaum. This book presents four longitudinal case studies (each of fifteen years' duration) of the development of four teachers' thinking about pedagogy. It is recommended here because of its simultaneous focus on method, teacher thinking and decision-making, and changing understandings of the pedagogy of teachers, based on their own experiences.

Mahlios, M., D. Massengill-Shaw and A. Barry (2010), 'Making Sense of Teaching through Metaphors: A Review across Three Studies', *Teachers and Teaching: Theory and Practice,* 16(1): 49–71. This review synthesizes findings from three studies which apply metaphor in a study of teachers and teaching to understand how particular metaphors are reflected in teacher views of schooling, life, childhood and teaching and how these influence classroom pedagogies. Of particular interest is the research instrument included in this review in appendix B.

PART TWO
Researching pedagogy in context

Introduction to part two: Researching pedagogy in context

Part Two's chapters offer three very different but exemplary sites for pedagogical research. The research stories they tell exemplify and extend the conceptions of pedagogy and pedagogical research explored in Part One to show the importance of pedagogical context when undertaking pedagogical research. In each of the settings and various supporting case examples, we trace the journey of how the researchers decide what constitutes a pedagogical text and how they come to understand the nature of pedagogical research data in their own study, setting and context. We consider the implications of researcher decision-making for research design and the selection and application of methods, including reflections on our own decision processes in our pedagogic research.

Chapter 4 explores research methods in pedagogic studies in early childhood settings. We begin our discussion of pedagogic research in particular settings with this because, unlike in other sectors, early childhood pedagogies are highly theorized. Alongside fitting methods to the context, we examine methods fitting the various purposes of overview, comparison, identifying causation, examining effectiveness, exploring and changing practice, understanding pedagogic culture and children's meaning-making, and engaging young children in research. Ethnographic, multimodal and child-centred methods are at the heart of this chapter.

Chapter 5 explores research methods for studying pedagogy in school settings. Focusing on classroom talk, this chapter describes research methods that make visible the complex and often hidden enactment and experience of schooling. We begin with a review and chronology of contemporary perspectives on classroom pedagogy research approaches. We then look in detail at two of these perspectives – first what we term process-product/effectiveness-based classroom interaction, moving to broader and more experiential conversation-based analyses in classrooms. Central to both perspectives is the understanding that language, in use and in situ, forms the focus of study where context, community and intentionality are central to these research approaches. Case examples of research from the United Kingdom and Sweden, along with our own studies, are interrogated to highlight the advantages and challenges of engaging in pedagogical research in school and classroom-based settings.

Chapter 6 acknowledges the complexities inherent in the definition and research of pedagogy through an exploration of pedagogical research completed in everyday, informal and out-of-school settings. We use case examples from England, Australia and the United States and our own research experiences to explore methods to study pedagogy in settings without a formal curriculum or named teacher, such as after-school clubs and people's homes.

CHAPTER FOUR

Researching pedagogy in early childhood settings: Ethnographic, multimodal and child-centred methods

Introduction

Early childhood settings make fascinating contexts to study pedagogy. One reason is that this is a sector where pedagogy is fiercely debated and where the pedagogy (outside the home, at least) is often made explicit. There are education sectors such as further and higher education where there is little theorization, but this is not the case for the early years sector. As Fleet et al. (2011: 18) argue, 'While the idea of theory is threatening to some people, early childhood pedagogy is steeped in theory (both implicit and explicit); much of our teaching has a history of thinking associated with it.' Such history includes engagement of major thinkers in developing theories of early childhood learning, including German pedagogue Friedrich Froebel, Italian educator Maria Montessori, British psychologist John Bowlby and Austrian philosopher Rudolf Steiner. Such work has had a lasting legacy, greatly influencing *pedagogy as specified* (see Chapter 1). There are significant, often holistic, pedagogical movements for the early years sector, such as Montessori Education, the Reggio Emilia Approach, Developmentally Appropriate Practice, High Scope and *Te Whāriki*. Even in countries such as Scotland, where the core body, Learning and Teaching Scotland (2005: 3), acknowledges that 'the term "pedagogy" may feel unfamiliar to some of us', there is an explicit 'pedagogical base' clarifying the deep 'understanding of what is informing our [early years education] practice, and importantly *why* we work in particular ways'.

A second reason for early childhood education being of great interest to pedagogy researchers is that the theoretically informed pedagogies have been researched in a plethora of studies of *pedagogy as enacted*, providing a landscape of evidence and methodological examples for the interested scholar. Much of the research has been concerned with pedagogical effectiveness. Such scrutiny is a reflection of governmental and academic understanding of the early years as the foundation for all later learning. Stakeholders have increasingly recognized that what goes on in early childhood settings has long-lasting effects on academic development and social behaviour, even into adulthood, as shown in the influential longitudinal studies of the High Scope (Schweinhart, Barnes and Weikart 1993; Lynch 2005) and Head Start (Kresh 1998; Zill, Resnick and O'Donnell 2001) interventions in the United States.

Thirdly, researching early childhood pedagogy provides the additional challenge of the learners, who may not perform the role of research participant in the ways of adults or even older children, and who present the researcher with additional methodological challenges if they are interested in *pedagogy as experienced*. There is an extensive methodological literature on research with children, and researching children's lives. It takes a bit of work to translate this into the particular focus on researching pedagogy and we try to ease the burden of this translation in this chapter. Linked to this, the early years sector is one in which the tasks of the (qualitative) researcher and the practitioner may be closely related in that they may share an interest in how young children make meaning and in documenting their learning process. As Learning and Teaching Scotland (ibid.) articulates in relation to making pedagogy explicit, 'Asking *why* encourages the research, reflection and sense of participation needed to ensure that pedagogical approaches develop, evolve and are effective.'

Early childhood settings

The organization of early childhood education is subject to considerable international variation. While early childhood is largely taken to refer to birth to eight years, early years education more often applies to three to eight years, with considerable difference in when children enter the formal education system.[1] There are differences, too, in how ideas about young children's educational and social needs come together, with 'the borders and relations between different types of services' shifting and melding as 'children are being seen as people in their own right, rather than problems to be managed' (Petrie et al. 2005: 2). Supporting the holistic development of young children may be the role of 'pedagogues' in that 'in continental Europe, the word "pedagogy" relates to the overall support for children's development. In pedagogy, care and education meet' (ibid.). Parents may be seen as the first pedagogues, and in this chapter we include research methods applied to home as well as formal settings.

International surveys have been important in illustrating differences in early childhood education at an organizational level and also some pedagogical differences. The International Review of Curriculum and Assessment (INCA, Bertram and Pascal 2002) reviewed the early years curriculum, pedagogical and assessment approaches embedded within a range of frameworks extending across twenty countries (Australia, Canada, England, France, Germany, Hungary, Republic of Ireland, Italy, Japan, Korea, the Netherlands, New Zealand, Northern Ireland, Singapore, Spain, Sweden, Switzerland, United States, Wales and Hong Kong). This resulted in Bertram and Pascal (2002: 21) identifying a strong consensus regarding the curriculum principles for children aged three to six years, including

- child-centred, flexible and individually responsive curriculum;

- the importance of working in partnership with parents;

- the need to offer broad and relevant learning experiences in an integrated manner;

- the importance of play and active, exploratory learning;

- an emphasis on social and emotional development and

- the need to empower the child to be an autonomous, independent learner.

This level of consensus contrasts somewhat to the international picture of pedagogy from the research of Alexander (2000) discussed in Chapter 1; consensus extends to the recommended pedagogical approach:

- This emphasized an interactional pedagogy, where the children and adults operated in reciprocity with one another.

- There was an encouragement of play-based, first-hand, exploratory experiences that provided children with opportunities to talk and interact.

- The provision of opportunities for children to self-manage and self-direct their learning was also encouraged.

- Collaborative, peer group learning was the preferred model, with whole class teaching or circle time being used selectively to support this.

- The role of the adult was generally viewed as being to facilitate and support learning through skilful and guided interaction, adopting a flexible range of teaching and learning strategies according to the needs of the children.

- Some countries specifically discouraged the use of early disciplinary and prescriptive methods of instruction, for example, Italy, Hong Kong, Japan, Singapore and Sweden. (Bertram and Pascal 2002: 22)

Petrie et al. (2005) identify a similar shared script about the principles of pedagogic practice in early childhood, including a focus on the whole child, adult relationships with the child, children's and adults' shared spaces, practitioner reflection on their work and theoretical understandings combined with practical engagement, children's role in each other's lives and development, and working as teams for children. It would be easy, however, to overestimate the similarities in early childhood pedagogy for, as Chung and Walsh (2000) illustrate, while 'child-centred' may be a common term in this context, there are at least forty different interpretations with various emphases on children's interests, participation in decision-making, developmental stages or development of individual potential.

Research methods for early childhood pedagogy

Having set the scene, we begin our discussion of research methods for studying pedagogy in early years settings by looking at the breadth of research methods. We then focus in most detail on particularly well-suited ethnographic, multimodal and child-centred methods. We can think of the range of methods as including

- methods for overview, comparison and causation;
- methods to examine effectiveness;
- methods to explore practice;
- methods to change practice;
- methods to understand pedagogic culture and children's meaning-making and
- methods to engage children in the research.

Methods for overview, comparison and causation

Researchers often choose surveys when wanting to make comparisons. In early childhood settings, one example is work by Pascal et al. (1999) to evaluate the Early Excellence Centre initiative in the United Kingdom. In this, a three-year national evaluation used seventy-two common indicators (of contexts, processes and outcomes) to elicit responses that would allow evaluation of the extent to which these were being achieved across thirty-three pilot Early Excellence Centres. When commenting on this work, MacNaughton, Rolfe and Siraj-Blatchford (2001: 151) observe that 'although most large-scale surveys are aimed at getting a small amount of information from a large number of people, a good deal of the research carried out in early childhood settings involves relatively small populations'. **Questionnaires** may be used alongside secondary sources, interview and observation to help develop a complete picture when answering a complex research question.

Once researchers have made the decision to use a survey, the need for practical advice on applying the method should lead them to generic texts on survey design, sampling issues, methods of dispatch, handling and analysing data. In that any survey is likely to be administered to adults in the early years context, the early childhood focus does not have particular implications for the design. In addressing when and why researchers might choose survey methods in early childhood pedagogic research, we have collated some examples in Table 4.1.

Table 4.1 Purposes for survey methods in early childhood pedagogy

Research purpose	Example of study and context
Getting an overview or making comparisons	How early years educators are prepared for their pedagogic roles, surveying faculty members across nine states in the United States (Hemmeter, Santos and Ostrosky 2008)
Finding out who holds what kinds of pedagogic knowledge and what correlates with that knowledge	What technological pedagogical content knowledge is held by 335 early childhood teachers in Taiwan, adapting an existing survey (TPACK: Schmidt et al. 2009) for a new cultural context (Chuang and Ho 2011)

Determining teachers' pedagogic beliefs For intrinsic interest – a survey may be used in isolation For comparing with practice – combined with observational and other methods Identifying beliefs in common and where variance occurs	How the pedagogical beliefs of early childhood teachers vary across grade level in the United States (Valuti 1999), important because of the relationship of beliefs with pedagogic decisions. Making use of existing survey instruments with reliability analyses: the Early Childhood Survey of Beliefs and Practices (Marcon 1988) and the Teacher Beliefs Scale (Charlesworth et al. 1990; Charlesworth et al. 1993). **Correlational analysis** of self-reported beliefs and practices with observed practice, important because incongruence is associated with ineffective pedagogy
Determining causation Using survey data to make predictions	Use of the Primary Teacher's Beliefs and Practices Survey involving self-report of beliefs and practices related to developmentally appropriate practice. Factor analyses and hierarchical multiple regression analyses to identify classroom and teacher characteristics predicting teacher beliefs and developmentally appropriate pedagogic practices (Buchanan et al. 1998)
Determining the characteristics of effective early childhood pedagogies	Early work and calls to link research data with census, administrative and evaluation data (e.g. Australian Council for Educational Research)

Methods to examine effectiveness

There are many examples of studies of effectiveness of pedagogy and curricula in early childhood contexts. Some of these are long term, such as the evaluation of the Enriched Curriculum in Northern Ireland (McGuinness et al. 2009a,b; Sproule et al. 2009). More well known, and less pedagogically focused, is the longitudinal study by National Institute of Child Health and Human Development

(NICHD) in the United States, which followed 1,364 children from birth, addressing childcare experiences, quality and outcomes (Brooks-Gunn, Han and Waldfogel 2002). In the United Kingdom, the Effective Provision of Pre-school Education (EPPE) Project similarly followed three thousand children from over a hundred preschool centres from three to seven years. The latter two studies are beyond the scope of most researchers, but they provide a data set that demonstrates the contribution of high-quality early childhood provision for children's language and cognitive development that can be used in secondary analysis. Smaller and newer examples are the Competent Children Study from New Zealand (Wylie, Thompson and Lythe 2001), following a representative sample of five hundred children from early-to-middle childhood, and the Longitudinal Study of Australian Children (Gray and Sanson 2005).

In large studies such as these national ones, statistical analyses involving controlled comparisons are used to examine causal relationships and cumulative effects. This is interesting for pedagogy researchers when, for example, different dispositions to learning, sense of agency, motivation and curiosity are explored. However, the methods used in some studies have been criticized in terms of adequacy of sample size, and the outcome measures and appropriateness of statistical tests (Van Horn et al. 2005), with large-scale studies using multilevel statistical techniques being more robust (e.g. Van Horn and Ramey 2003).

Our first example in this chapter, case example 4.1, is a particularly well-known and detailed study of the effects of the kind of pedagogy, practice and curriculum on cognitive and social/behavioural development outcomes, regarded as sufficiently robust to enable prediction. It is a great example of going beyond methods that determine *what* settings are effective, to understanding *why* they are effective. It also shows the utility of combining methods in a case study approach for getting at complexity.

Case example 4.1: Researching Effective Pedagogy in the Early Years (EPEY) Siraj-Blatchford et al. (2002)

Context: An English study conducted as part of the major longitudinal EPPE study. A particular focus on pedagogy defined

Case example 4.1

for the study as 'the instructional techniques and strategies which enable learning to take place ... the interactive process between teacher and learner ... [including] the provision of some aspects of the learning environment' such as the physical environment, family and community (Siraj-Blatchford et al. 2002: 10).

Goal: To 'identify the most effective pedagogical strategies that are applied in the Foundation Stage to support the development of young children's skills, knowledge and attitudes, and ensure they make a good start at school' (ibid.).

Outcomes: Explanations for the statistical relationships found in the EPPE data. Finding that the most effective preschool teachers engaged children in interactions that showed sustained shared thinking, where adults and children work together 'to solve a problem, clarify a concept, evaluate activities or extend a narrative' (Siraj-Blatchford and Sylva 2004: 718); showed a good understanding of the content of curriculum areas; encouraged children to engage with cognitive challenge; drew as appropriate on a repertoire of pedagogical activity (including direct instruction); differentiated the curriculum; equally balanced child-initiated and adult-initiated activities; and had clear behaviour and discipline policies involving children talking through conflicts.

Research methods: Intensive case studies conducted in diverse, 'effective' settings selected based on child social/behavioural and cognitive outcomes from the EPPE project. Detailed documentation of naturalistic observations of staff pedagogy; systematic structured observations of children's learning; interviews with parents, staff and managers; telephone interviews with childminders; **documentary analysis**; literature review.

We have alluded to researchers of early childhood pedagogy making use of the data that other studies have already generated. One example of a method for doing this as part of researching effectiveness is the **best evidence synthesis** or systematic review. This method was adopted by Mitchell and Cubey (2003) in work commissioned by the Ministry of Education in New Zealand. They explain:

> The best evidence synthesis is derived from research that provides strong evidence of linkages to learning opportunities, experiences and outcomes for children. ... Specific emphasis is on evidence related to learning opportunities and outcomes through the provision of professional development for Mäori children, Pasifika children and children from low socio-economic families. An extensive search was made for New Zealand and international material through library databases and contact with researchers and professional development providers. (Mitchell and Cubey 2003: viii)

Critical to this research method is extensive searching for relevant research evidence, deciding which studies meet the quality criteria for inclusion in the synthesis, and analysing and integrating material to answer research questions. The methods at each stage should be explicit, transparent and replicable (Oakley 2002), making the synthesis amenable to updating. Mitchell and Cubey integrated qualitative and quantitative research, providing evidence of programmes, quality of teaching or training and linked in some but not all cases to outcomes for children. They describe their analytic approach as using features from narrative and realist synthesis, but researchers have other alternatives within this overall approach. They stress that educational theory aided them in their analysis and this is important for challenging ideas that systematic reviews are value free.

Elliot (2006) sums up the richness of studies available for researchers employing secondary or **meta-analysis** methods. There are the early studies of the links between quality of care and attachment (the early USA Head Start and High Scope work), then second generation studies of the multifaceted dimensions of quality in settings and pedagogy and the impact on outcomes, and most recently, neurological studies. Across these groups are randomized control studies, deemed particularly suitable for studying effectiveness. We are reminded though (e.g. by Sammons et al. 2002) that cautions have been sounded about the methodological challenge of disaggregating the complex variables that influence academic achievement. This is particularly important for methods seeking to achieve a cost-benefit analysis from the data (Watson, Schafer and Squires 2000).

Methods to explore practice

Researching *pedagogy as enacted* involves getting insights into dynamic practice. Learning and Teaching Scotland (2005) are not alone in seeing how pedagogic insight is of concern to practitioners as well as researchers. In Australia, Fleet et al. (2006: 312) discuss the importance of **pedagogical documentation**: 'a process of gathering artefacts, conversations, ideas, and displaying children's learning, energy and theories'. The concept, being adapted for Australia, comes from the work of educators in theoretically rich environments (Reggio Emilia in Italy and Sweden). The method of pedagogical documentation is of interest to pedagogy researchers as it

> follows children's and educators' thinking and finds ways to make that thinking visible. It is a means of analysing what lies beneath the play experiences to find the questions being asked and the learning that occurs. ... Documentation is not only the process of gathering evidence and artefacts, but also the reflection on and analysis of the collection, and the presentation of that collection, in a way that makes the children's learning visible to the children, the teachers and other adults. (Rinaldi, in Wurm 2005: 8, cited by Fleet et al. 2011: 6)

Pedagogical documentation is useful as it encompasses observation and record-keeping plus analysis and reflection. It therefore informs understanding and action. This fits more with pedagogy (and pedagogy research) as an art or craft than as a science in that this is not a detached or distant process, but an up-close one of being attuned and attentive to what is observed and said. It is a method that fits well with the cycles of action research where the purpose is to enhance practice.

We find pedagogical documentation offers additional potential for the researcher in that it is a collaborative method, with educators, families and children all able to contribute, thereby strengthening the understanding gained. Fleet et al. (2011: 6) comment on its affordances, including providing a new lens through which to see the everyday (citing Strozzi, in Reggio Children 2001: 58), in arguing that 'through documentation, we can show the ordinary to be extraordinary'. They encourage practitioners to use the method to feed their curiosity and their desire to use theory as they craft convincing and evocative narratives with which families and community members can connect. In research terms, it is important in that, in their words, 'In the process we become critical thinkers about children, play and theory and begin to understand more comprehensively the purpose and the impact of our work' (p. 8). Here ethical, meaningful practice and research are interwoven with advocacy for early childhood education. Fleet et al. (2011: 10) explain that 'in letting go of the image of the all-knowing professional expert, being uncertain and unsure allows room for the "other" to also be knowledgeable in particular and equally valuable ways'. This is an important basis for relationships between professionals and families, but it is equally important for research relationships in some kinds of research as we go on to show later in the chapter. This is a method that does not exclude the reader or research user from the conversational process of finding out and making meaning.

Our last point about the value of pedagogical documentation as a research method is that it is a tool for generating evidence of many aspects of pedagogy from the nature of the curriculum to pedagogical relationships, from underpinning theories to pedagogical practices, from practitioner perspectives to perspectives of the whole learning community. The evidence helps to make visible what might otherwise be invisible; it helps us to know the hard-to-know (see Part Three for full discussion on the 'hard-to-know'). This has practical benefits: 'Pedagogical documentation is a way of keeping the process of thinking and the "problem at hand" open and visible to the group of children and adults while it is occurring (Olsson 2009)' (cited by Fleet et al. 2011: 14). Equally important is that in this method evidence and theory are powerfully connected so that reflecting on observations in documenting experiences with children, theories are used, more or less explicitly to aid thinking and enrich the picture being drawn or story being told. The examples Fleet et al. (2011: 20) provide for practitioners are also useful for researchers:

> We might be using developmental theory when we write about children increasing a skill on the jumping boards. Or we might

engage socio-cultural theory when we interpret two children's engagement with ideas about marriage. ... An observation of two children playing in the sandpit can be framed through different theories. We could use maturational theory, seeing the children developing in ages and stages in their ability to manipulate the sand and the equipment. Or we could see a social event, and frame the play through socio-cultural theory, explaining their conversation and play as socially constructed. We could also see it from post humanist theory, where the sand and equipment are active agents upon the children. Or we could see gender theory in action as the children delegate roles in the play according to gender, 'you be the mummy'... . It's also important to note that at any one time multiple theories are in action, and so the above scenario might be written with all theories identified.

Waller and Bitou (2011) reflect on the method of pedagogic documentation and explore the implications of this as a participatory approach. They take a sociocultural perspective in their study of outdoor learning for three- and four-year-olds in a nursery in England, arguing that it is 'meaningless to study the child apart from other people' (p. 7). Waller and Bitou also cite Dahlberg, Moss and Pence (2007: 145) in proposing that pedagogical documentation provides the means for practitioners and others 'to engage in dialogue and negotiation about pedagogical work through making the pedagogy visible'. They relate this to 'learning stories' developed by Carr (2001) in New Zealand in which narrative documentation is built around critical incidents in children's learning, prioritizing the child's input into the account. Pedagogical documentation is an approach that fits with the increasing emphasis on formative assessment. Formative assessment is essentially the process of equipping learners with the information or feedback they need so they can bridge the gap between what they can and cannot do (Black and Wiliam 1998). It involves learners in using feedback to make decisions about their own learning. It is complex and subtle work for teachers because it requires that learners themselves take ownership of their learning. It is aided by documenting pedagogy. Recent work by Carr and Lee (2012) is a good example of the integration of research and formative assessment in the early years.

Other researchers of pedagogical practice have used more directly observational methods. Broadhead (2001, 2006, 2009), for example, has spent a number of years observing young children's play with each other in nursery settings and reception classes within the context of the English Foundation Stage curriculum. She observed the different pedagogical sites of sand play, water play, role play, large and small construction, and was able to identify dominant pedagogies, play types and developments associated with different contexts. She largely acted as a non-participant observer, making detailed notes of action and talk, also opting to take photographs of critical moments, which she annotated to support the analysis (Broadhead 2001). Her 2001 paper shows the method of alternating between observational vignettes and reflective interpretations, which is common in early childhood research of this type; it is particularly useful for its commentary on pedagogy where there is no teacher present.

Once again, Broadhead (2006: 194) connects what it is that researchers do (observation in this case) with what it is that teachers do, when she notes: 'Observation of pupils and interaction have long been staples in early years educators' repertoires, as precursors to effective planning and organization, as integral to individual assessments and in the identification of "children's pathways of learning"' (Nutbrown 1994: 148). The methods Broadhead uses depend on deep observation – she shows how such observations can be followed up in dialogue with children to gain insight into their thinking, understanding and learning, illustrating how the adult perspective can only be partial. Thus, from research observations she develops The Social Play Continuum to support practitioners' use of observation and interaction for formative assessment. Her paper

urges practitioners to see observation and interaction as practitioner research and formative assessment and to recognise the potential for extending their own professional knowledge, especially when engaged in these activities alongside similarly engaged colleagues. This fosters a community of reflective practitioners who, together, are extending their own knowledge and understanding of children's learning processes. (Broadhead 2006: 202)

The pedagogy researcher wishing to use observational methods to study practice has the option to use more structured, systematic methods than the ones described so far in this chapter. Valuti (1999), for example, had quite different expectations of observational methods in wanting to look at teachers' practices alongside their pedagogical beliefs. Here the aim was to gather objective and representative observations and so an existing schedule, The Classroom Practices Inventory (Hyson, Hirsh-Pasek and Rescorla 1990), was applied. A time-sampling method involved researchers noting the occurrence of certain activities and behaviours at five-minute intervals over a one-hour period, allowing calculation of mean frequencies. This kind of observation can be conducted by less experienced observers with specific training to reach target inter-observer agreement scores. In researching pedagogical practice, the choice of method of observation must match the researcher's goals and conceptual framework. Though having obvious advantages, there are disadvantages to the use of predetermined categories and time sampling in capturing classroom practice, and we revisit this theme in Chapter 5.

Methods to change practice

Pedagogy is not static. This is a challenge for the pedagogy researcher, but also an opportunity. Learning and Teaching Scotland (2005: 13) points to the importance of practitioners

> Developing a reflective and enquiring spirit ... [which] encourages the very reflection, discussion, debate and evolution critical to an effective pedagogical base. Where we have a clear vision and a feeling of ownership of our pedagogy, we become more confident, more able to take responsibility and more willing to be thoughtful, to reflect, question, struggle and to celebrate.

This is one of many ways in which the roles of pedagogue and researcher may overlap or merge by joining together in the process of inquiry into practice with the dual aiming of better understanding and improving or changing that practice. Case example 4.2 sums up an example of this from our (Melanie's) experience, which we go on to explore further.

Case example 4.2: Enhancing the communication learning environment of an early years unit through action research (Nind 2003)

Context: The staff of an early years unit (comprising a nursery and two reception classes) of a mainstream school in London and an academic consultant from a local university working in collaboration facilitated by a local authority adviser. A desire to improve children's communication abilities alongside shared interest in not labelling communication difficulties as residing within children – who are therefore deficit in some way, but rather seeing difficulties as pedagogic – residing in a learning environment that is amenable to change.

Goal: 'To develop the communication abilities of the pupils by enhancing our understanding and provision of the best possible communicative/interactive environments for their learning, working together to think about ideas and practice, and trying things out in a supportive and reflective environment' (Nind 2003: 348)

Outcomes: Changes in the unit's communicative learning environment including increased small group work, introduction of child-led 'show and tell' sessions, and practical improvements to support quality, uninterrupted conversations between adults and children. Better understanding of what practitioners needed to support communication and enhanced communication among the children and community. A sharing of the lessons learned with the wider professional and academic community.

Research methods: 'an action research project where we reflect, plan, do, reflect again, plan again and so on' (ibid.). The consultant working as a catalyst and facilitator for the practitioners' active inquiry and as an enabler and critical friend, starting with negotiating with them the project agenda to fit the school ethos, the values of those involved and the lived realities of the unit. The core research tools were observation, reflection and discussion.

Action research is a well-known research approach. This example sees it used in the context of early childhood pedagogy. Melanie was the academic consultant in the project and so we are able to expand more on the thinking about the research methods involved (though much of this is actually explicit in the paper). Melanie reflects:

> I knew that rapport would be everything in this project. Unless we could establish a sense of shared purpose, and trust in each other to keep that focus at the forefront of our activity, then we would not get off first base. This made me work very openly from the start. I shared my expectations on paper and verbally, including all the parts that I could not know, and that we would need to work out together. I laid out my values and theoretical position, but also my openness to learning with and from the practitioners and children.

Often in the qualitative research literature, the message about building rapport does not spell out the actions that need to be taken; the emphasis is on spending time in and around the research participants and becoming familiar. However, in pedagogical research of this kind, what is needed to build rapport is pedagogical conversations. I knew that we would largely be working from what we saw, knew and talked about within the unit, but I also wanted to bring in some outside stimuli – ideas for busy practitioners to chew over and play around with, but were in no way imposed or presented as recipes for action. These would be lenses through which we could critically engage with the observational data from the unit – a means for seeing the familiar in a new light – a vehicle for pedagogical talk and getting to know our own and each other's thinking better.

This process echoed Melanie's own processes in that reading Wadsworth's (2001) chapter, which introduces the concepts of the mirror, the magnifying glass, the compass and the map as methodological apparatus for facilitating participatory action research, helped her thinking and talk.

> I would carry out detailed observations and offer a different perspective on what was familiar to the EYU [early years unit] team. This was Wadsworth's (2001) 'mirror and magnifying glass' work. I would do some of the analysis ahead of our meeting and we would do some of it during the meetings. (Nind 2003: 350)

The first phase of the project involved us negotiating our
agenda and approach. This was the 'compass' work (Wadsworth
2001) of shaping, framing and conceptualising the project. (Nind
2003: 349)

In some ways it was important that we did not have the
answers to all of these [emergent] questions. This helped to keep
everyone involved – in some ways equally – all and none of us
were experts. We had our original compass, our good practice
guide as our anchor and we had our observations and our
dialogue as our tools. (Nind 2003: 361)

The first phase in this project was data collection through observation
and reflection. Melanie did much of the detailed observation, as the
practitioners had little scope to do so within their existing roles.
This included observing the teacher-led sessions, free play and small
group or individual teaching and assessment. It involved capturing a
series of child–child and child–adult communications and the entire
communicative exchanges of one child across a session. Words were
recorded along with proximity, pauses and context, for instance.
The transcripts were prepared for discussion with a basic analysis of
whether exchanges followed an adult or child agenda and involved
open or closed questions, responses or directives. In this second
phase, the stimulus of summarized research papers, for example
about teachers' interaction styles, combined with the team's own
ideas to enable comparison of how the communications matched
to a model of good practice, thereby supporting the creation of a
change agenda for the next exploratory action phase. That phase
would also include observation of each other and critical reflection.
In the third phase, the actions were evaluated and new plans made.
The most complex areas requiring more thought and reflections on
the research process were also discussed and recorded. In this study,
'conversation and action were integrally linked', with conversation
being a core research method, a 'process of inquiry and meaning-
making' (ibid.).

There are many other examples of the action research approach
employed in early childhood pedagogic research. The work in Sweden
by Pramling Samuelsson and Asplund Carlsson (2008), developing
their theory of the playing child, also incorporates action research
in which teachers develop their understanding of play in learning.
They adapt their practice to have fewer whole-group planned

activities to make room for 'improvisation, interaction and listening to the children' (p. 636). This in turn supports their proposal for a 'sustainable pedagogy for the future, which does not separate play from learning but draws upon the similarities in character in order to promote creativity in future generations' (p. 623). This, again, shows the interaction between research methods and theoretical development, how research methods can inform a critique of early childhood contexts as places to promote learning or play separated in time and space, and the importance of methods that tease out processes of meaning-making.

Methods to understand pedagogic culture and children's meaning-making

Many of the methods discussed in the chapter have enabled researchers to say something about the pedagogic culture of various early childhood settings. None of them, however, has achieved deep understandings of culture as their primary aim in the way that ethnographic studies do. Moreover, ethnographic methods are fundamentally different in that they seek to leave the research settings undisrupted (Bucknall 2014). Cultural immersion is one way to understand the culture, but this poses a problem for adults who do not always fit readily into children's learning environments and who have to negotiate their roles as non-participant or participant observers, helpers, playmates and so on. Rogers and Evan (2007) were able to get up-close to the role play of four- and five-year-old children in English reception classes. They were able to draw conclusions about the relationship between the children's play and the quality of the indoor space (including role of interruptions, as in Nind's study above). They could tease out differences for boys and girls and the roles teachers played, and assigned to children, in indoor and outdoor environments.

In ethnographic research of early childhood pedagogy, the balance of observation and talk will depend on whether the researcher is more concerned with exploring the perspectives of the adults or the children. In a study of meaning-making in various early childhood contexts in England, Melanie and colleagues (Flewitt, Nind and Payler 2009; Nind, Flewitt and Payler 2010, 2011) focused on young children identified with special educational needs who were experiencing the pedagogic cultures of home, a mainstream education setting and a special education setting. Understanding their meaning-making necessitated research methods that could tease out the experience for the child within the pedagogic culture of the various contexts. This led to the adoption of ethnographic case studies involving video and **multimodal analysis** to explore multimodal literacy and play events and processes of inclusion as summarized in case example 4.3.

Case example 4.3: Exploring children's meaning-making in different contexts using multimodal video ethnographic case studies (Nind, Flewitt and Payler 2010, 2011)

Context: A UK scenario in which parents of children with 'special educational needs' may choose to combine the benefits offered by mainstream early years settings with those offered by special settings, resulting in children needing to making sense of two pedagogic cultures in addition to the home culture. The settings included a Children's Centre and an Opportunity Group, both with additional specialist resourcing, an assessment unit in an infant school, a parent-initiated playgroup, a 'special inclusive' playgroup and a provision for fathers and their children. For each child, the combination of setting was part parent choice and part dependent on local availability. Little is known about what such combinations mean for children in practice. The researchers' theoretical orientation was towards seeing agency, culture and structure as equally, and interconnectedly, explaining social practice.

Goal: To examine how the children made sense of the differing experiences and pedagogic cultures, including 'how the actors in the various settings constructed the child – how they saw, talked about and treated the child as a particular kind of person. ... [To] listen to the children by reading, observing and interpreting the meanings drawn from their interactions and contexts' (Nind, Flewitt and Payler 2011: 361). 'To look at the interactions between structure, culture and agency' (Nind, Flewitt and Payler 2010: 656).

Case example 4.3

Outcomes: Detailed descriptions of the different ways in which the children and the children's competence were constructed in their different settings dependent on a complex set of interactions, resources and dispositions. 'Our data lend support to the critique that in/competence is very much about context' (Nind, Flewitt and Payler 2011: 369). Demonstration of how the children were 'actively negotiating their positions, moment-by-moment, within micro-cultures' (Nind, Flewitt and Payler 2010: 667). Descriptions of inclusive pedagogy and suggestions from the data, for example that 'inclusive literacy pedagogy requires a clear understanding of literacy as social practice rather than as a narrow set of technical sub-skills required for reading and writing' (Flewitt, Nind and Payler 2009: 231).

Research methods: Case studies of three children and nine settings (one home and two education settings for each child). Review of relevant documentation including the children's assessments ('statements' of special educational needs) and home–school correspondence. Fieldwork observations of the settings by two researchers, generating rich descriptive portraits informed by use of indicators from the Orchestrating Play and Learning Criterion of the Evolving Inclusive Practices Dimension of the Index for Inclusion (Early Years) (Booth, Ainscow and Kingston 2006) and a selection of items from the ECERS-R scales (space and furnishings and interactions) (Harms, Clifford and Cryer 2005). Two periods of intensive observations separated by around three months. In these, the children were video recorded 'to capture the multi-sensory, multimodal dynamism of children's meaning-making (total 2–3 hours' video recording in each of the nine settings, plus 2–3 further hours' general observations in each setting)' (Flewitt, Nind and Payler 2009: 216). Videos were supplemented by field notes and research diaries. In the field, researchers conducted semi-structured interviews and had informal conversations with staff (keyworkers and managers) and parents. Additional data were generated by the parents completing diaries of the children's activities for the observed weeks. 'Data analysis was structured

Case example 4.3

around qualitative, iterative and inductive interpretation ... with cross-researcher checking and discussion of emerging findings. To build up detailed descriptions of how interactions were constructed through multiple modes, the video recordings were viewed many times, with image only, and with both sound and image. The Computer Aided Qualitative Data Analysis Software package Transana was used to identify patterns in the data, to select key episodes for more in-depth analysis and to enhance the systematic, rigorous scrutiny of the complex multimedia data set. ... Observational and interview data were then further coded.' (ibid.)

Multimodal approaches broaden the focus of the research to the different ways in which 'meanings are created not just through talk but through multiple "modes" of communication, such as gesture, gaze, movement, body positioning, words, vocalizations and alternative and augmentative communication systems' (Flewitt, Nind and Payler 2009: 214). Such an approach shaped the conduct of this research. From a multimodal perspective, talk is just one of many communicative modes and may not be the most important one (Kress and Van Leeuwen 2001). The researcher needs to read different 'texts' such as writing, drawing, mark-making or embodied actions such as posture, speech, gaze and movement. Social and cultural processes shape children's (and practitioners') choice of modes. In case example 4.3, categorization of the data focused on the following: the setting; the type of activity within the setting; the resources incorporated; the communicative mode(s) utilized; and whether the interactive space was solitary, social, child- or adult-led, playful, routine, open, closed and so on. Equally, the data spoke of the function or outcome of the interaction, such as shared and/or focused attention, mutual pleasure, conflict, inclusion or exclusion. In this way, the researchers were able to see how some early education settings restricted the communicative space available to the children, whereas in the home setting, literacy activities, for example, even when adult-led, might take on a familiar game-like quality with rhythmic patterns, eliciting richer vocabulary and generating more interest and competence.

Methods to engage children in the research

Through multimodal ethnographic case study, as we have shown, researchers are able to gain complex insights into pedagogic situations in terms of how young children experience and interpret them. Some research methods have been developed to go further and to engage young children more integrally in the research process. Most notable is the **Mosaic approach** (Clark and Moss 2001, 2005) using participatory, visual methods to bring together children's and adults' meaning-making concerning their everyday experience of their educational environment. Whether special child-friendly methods are necessary in **participatory research** is hotly debated (Gallacher and Gallagher 2008; Clark 2011; Nind 2014), with some researchers settling instead on participant-friendly/ participant-centred methods that are not age specific. This is the case in the Mosaic approach in which children and adults generate knowledge, using methods developed to 'play to the strengths of young children, methods which are active and accessible and not reliant on the written or spoken word' (Clark and Moss 2001, 2012) (cited by Clark 2011: 324) and engaging for all. The initial principles of the approach in which young children were regarded as 'experts in their own lives', 'skilful communicators', 'rights holders' and 'meaning makers' (Clark and Moss 2005: 5) are ultimately applied to adults too.

As with pedagogic documentation, described above, the Mosaic approach is about making the implicit knowable – 'for participants to "see" [the early years environment] in different ways' (Clark 2011: 323). Thus, the researcher uses the children's research products (photographs, drawings, etc.) to stimulate reflection by the practitioners and other adults and to create a safe vehicle for so doing:

> The Mosaic approach is a multi-method framework, which combines the traditional methodology of observation and interviewing with the introduction of participatory tools including the use

of cameras, tours and **mapping**. Other tools such as drawing and role-play can also be added. Each tool forms one piece of the Mosaic. In Stage 2 these pieces are brought together with parents and practitioners comments to form the basis of dialogue, reflection and interpretation. The Mosaic, which is made, is a form of documentation, co-constructed by the children and adults. (Clark 2001: 334)

Clark (2001) describes how the Mosaic comprises discussion between children, between practitioners and researchers, between children and researcher, between parents and the researcher, and between practitioner groups and the researcher. This, she argues, is the process of '"meaning making" in which young children play a central role: making sense or interpreting what this detailed and varied material can tell us about their lives' (p. 338).

The Mosaic approach is equally suitable for exploring different experiences of pedagogic cultures and environments, especially considering the argument from Rogoff (2003) discussed by Waller and Bitou (2011: 7) that in 'communities of learners meaning is only established when ideas are jointly understood and enacted within the particular community'. Waller and Bitou (2011), in applying the Mosaic approach to their study of outdoor learning, asked whether using participatory tools engages children, whether the adult agenda changes children's experiences, and about the empowerment process. They were able to establish 'a high level of reflection on the benefit of giving children opportunities to create their own learning environments' and became focused on 'eliciting children's views and perspectives' (p. 10). They concluded that 'photographic and video images do not empower children on their own, it is the shared construction of knowledge around conversations with the children based on their photographs that can enable children's meaning to prevail' (p. 15).

These examples show the importance of intersubjectivity in applying research methods to the study of pedagogy. This can help us to know what is hard to know, and to know it from multiple and interconnected perspectives. Participatory tools cannot expose everything to the researchers, but they can support co-construction of pedagogic knowledge, even when very young children are involved. Waller and Bitou (2011: 17) remind us of the argument made by Gallacher and Gallagher that 'participatory methods should be grounded within ethnographic study and not seen as a replacement for it'. This in turn is a reminder that research methods are only as good as the research design in which they are located.

We finish the chapter with one final suite of examples of research methods for early childhood pedagogy in action. This comes from the work of Bertram and Pascal (2006, 2008, 2014), who have tried to adopt an inclusive, participatory stance in their projects: Effective Early Learning Programme (Bertram and Pascal 2006); Accounting Early for Life Long Learning (Bertram, Pascal and Saunders 2010); and especially Children Crossing Borders research (Bertram and Pascal 2007) and the Opening Windows programme (Bertram and Pascal 2008). Their methodological stance is based on the importance they perceive in listening to children. They describe Children Crossing Borders as a 'major international project that aimed to examine the practices, values and expectations of pre-school practitioners, and the aspirations, expectations and views of parents and children from "immigrant" communities in multi-ethnic cities in five countries' (Bertram and Pascal 2014: 274). Unusually for such a large project, they wanted children's voices included in the dialogues. Therefore they adopted the anthropological approach from Tobin's study, Preschool in Three Cultures (Tobin, Wu and Davidson 1989), positioning preschools as 'key sites for preserving and reflecting cultural beliefs and practices about early childhood education and care' (p. 275).

In their study, Bertram and Pascal used Tobin's video-cued, multivocal stimulus method. This (as with pedagogical documentation discussed earlier in this chapter and video discussed in Chapter 7) was to encourage reflection and discussion among parents, practitioners and children. They facilitated this in **focus groups** in which dialogue was elicited using video material. The participants in each nation saw the same set of videotapes. This design reflected Freire's concept of 'conscientization'; the researchers wanted to stimulate action for change among the groups based on their awareness of inequalities. The Opening Windows training programme and materials are based on this, enhancing the impact of their research by getting practitioners to use exploratory research techniques to achieve the modelled 'symmetrical dialogue' with children (p. 277). Practitioners were introduced to a challenging 'menu of strategies to create and sustain democratic encounters' including 'Video Stimulated Dialogue, Cultural Circles, Critical

Incident Analysis, Story Telling and Naming Your World, Wishing Trees, Map Making, Guided Tours, Focused Observations, Photography and Film Making' (p. 279). This is, in some ways, a kind of methodological research in that these researchers found out about the environmental and support factors that children and practitioners need in order to express themselves, to reflect and to risk adopting a transformational position.

Conclusion

In this chapter we have provided a showcase of some quite challenging research methods for use in the early childhood pedagogic context. The methods reflect in many ways the ambitions of the researchers in what they want to know. Now we provide readers with questions to consider and suggestions for further reading. We conclude by returning to Learning and Teaching Scotland (2005). In promoting reflections on the pedagogical base for practice, this body encourages early years practitioners to consider more deeply a range of questions. These questions, some of which we paraphrase here, are useful prompts for pedagogy researchers to consider, both as potential research questions and in terms of the research methods each would demand:

- What do we mean by children being central to their own learning?

- How does the pedagogical approach recognize and value children's existing capabilities, interests and perspectives, and build on these to provide valuable, coherent and challenging experiences?

- How and why do early years pedagogues interact with children in certain ways at certain times?

- How/is the wider environment, including family and community, taken into account when planning learning experiences and opportunities for young children?

- What is our image of children/childhood in the twenty-first century and how do the values we put on learning – and bring to learning – impact on children?

Further reading

Jeffery, B. (2001), 'Challenging Prescription in Ideology and Practice: The Case of Sunny First School', in J. Collins, K. Insley and J. Soler (eds), *Developing Pedagogy: Researching Practice*, 143–60, London: Paul Chapman. This chapter discusses the methods and findings from an ethnographic case study, and also shows how theory and the radical pedagogy ideas from Chapter 2 apply in an early childhood context.

MacNaughton, G., S. A. Rolfe and I. Siraj-Blatchford (2001), *Doing Early Childhood Research: International Perspectives on Theory and Practice*, Maidenhead: Open University Press. This book provides practical guidance on setting up early childhood research projects, taking into account the multidisciplinary nature of most settings and including some pedagogical examples.

In addition, you might like to follow up on multimodal methods, and a good place to start is the special issue of *Qualitative Research* (2011, 11(3)), edited by Bella Dicks, Rosie Flewitt, Lesley Lancaster and Kate Pahl on 'Multimodality and Ethnography: Working at the Intersection'.

Note

1 Children start school at ages ranging from four years old in the Republic of Ireland and Northern Ireland, five years in England and Australia, to seven years in Sweden, Poland, some Eastern European countries and China, with the bulk, including the United States and India, starting at six (EURYDICE 2013; World Bank 2000).

CHAPTER FIVE

Researching pedagogy in schools: Methods focused on classroom interaction

Introduction

In his Editorial to a new journal entitled *Pedagogies: An International Journal*, Alan Luke comments on how schooling practices are less stable now than in the past. He says:

> Transformation of communications media; globalised flows of discourse, capital, and population; innovations in esthetic and representational forms; the spread of popular and educational cultures; the rapid multiplication and dissemination of scientific knowledge; and powerful claims to indigenous and local knowledge have together placed systems, schools and teachers under increasing pressure to think anew about which knowledges and which practices count. (Luke 2006: 2)

In such a complex world, the 'scientific fixing of pedagogy' (Luke 2006: 2) is inappropriate. An examination of specified pedagogy, as we noted in Chapter 1, is narrow and inadequate on its own to grasp what goes on in classrooms. This is the case whether this is framed in terms of statements of how teachers should teach or what the outcomes of education should be at particular points in time or principles and procedures of 'effective' pedagogy. Understanding these specified pedagogical practices as 'guides to action' (Wenger 1998), however, makes visible important influences on what happens in classrooms and how participants enact and experience their schooling.

Our focus in this chapter is on research methods for making this complex (though often hidden) enactment and experience of schooling more visible, through an exploration of ways of researching interaction and, in particular, classroom talk. The learning theorist and sociolinguist, Courtney Cazden (1988: 2), argues that 'spoken language is the medium by which much teaching takes place and in which students demonstrate to teachers much of what they have learned'. As such, spoken language is of vital importance to the pedagogy researcher. We begin with an exploration of two central and overlapping types of classroom talk/interaction that researchers can focus on in classroom pedagogy research, namely process–product/effectiveness-based classroom interactions and broader conversation-based analyses in classrooms. We then examine various methodologies relevant to classroom interaction and show how different aspects of classroom interaction become visible through their application. Similarly, we highlight the different assumptions underlying each approach and discuss the implications for the dimensions of pedagogy each may reveal.

While the primary purpose of the chapter is to highlight different research orientations and methods relevant to the pedagogy researcher concerned with school classrooms, among other things the chapter offers a review and chronology of contemporary perspectives on the study of such pedagogy.

Classroom interaction research based on process–product analyses

Over forty years ago, pedagogy researchers seeking to ascertain what counts as effective teaching were working on the assumption that process–product studies were needed. This includes the idea that pedagogic approaches or teaching techniques are variables that can be manipulated or held constant in experimental research designs for different types of students, schools and catchments. To recap on our discussion in Chapter 3, in such 'scientific method' behaviour is assumed to be stable and generalizable across classrooms, and researchers assume that teacher and pupil interactions can be reliably and objectively observed. Among critics of this stance, socioculturalist Michael Cole has strongly criticized the assumption underlying some of this research that types of cognition, ability, intelligence, talent are 'species specific' and not 'context specific' (see Cole 1996 cited by Luke 2006: 3).

Among the most widely used research instruments designed to focus on interaction in the process–product tradition was the Flanders System (Amidon and Flanders 1967). As a system it sought to describe verbal interaction fully by logging teacher–pupil speech every three seconds using a ten row by ten column matrix, where the majority of categories referred to the teachers' talk. Types of statements and questions (open-ended, higher order, etc.) could be categorized and statistically analysed to make judgements about the relationship between, for example, types of teacher statements and pupil attainment, where the latter was also captured. The intention of this research was to identify an effective teaching style based on causal explanations. Inevitably, such accounts required aggregated numeric data.

In case example 5.1 we highlight one process–product example, noted because it triggered a major strand of research, especially in primary schools.

Case example 5.1: Observation and Classroom Learning Evaluation (ORACLE)

Context: A series of classroom studies was conducted in England in the mid-1970s, namely Observation and Classroom Learning Evaluation (ORACLE). This series of studies was new and innovative at the time because it was based on observation of moment-by-moment interactions between teachers and learners.

Goal: To shed light on teacher effectiveness.

Outcomes: Because academic progress was measured alongside classroom observation (as is typical in this style of process–product

Case example 5.1

design), the researchers claimed to identify a number of different pedagogic approaches and to establish the effects of these approaches on pupil behaviour and attainment. The nature of the methodology allowed researchers make claims such as whole-class teaching is associated with greater use of open-ended questions and statements, and 60 per cent of peer-to-peer conversations is to do with matters unconnected to the task set.

Research methods: The many observers and researchers would select a sample of target children, matched by biographical variables such as age, ability or gender, and conduct a series of observations to a predetermined pattern of fixed time intervals. While interactions were recorded for later analysis in this systematic way, extended observations of teaching and possibly interviews with the teacher and the learners would also be conducted. In the case of the ORACLE study, which involved a large team of researchers, observations took place in nearly sixty classrooms and researchers followed learners as they transferred out of primary education and into their first year of post-primary education. The dataset comprised large amounts of numeric data (e.g. frequencies, proportions, means and range of open-ended or closed-ended questions and statements) subjected to conventional statistical analyses.

It is interesting to note that other similarly designed pedagogic studies of classroom interaction have tended to confirm previous findings, but studies conducted after the introduction of the National Curriculum in England point to a fall in individual teacher–pupil interaction and an increase in whole-class interaction. Because the evidence concerning classroom interaction could be coded into pre-existing categories, it was presented in the form of tables and charts rather than extracts of classroom talk or action, restricting what could be said to large patterns rather than details.

Research projects such as the ORACLE study and its follow-up in the 1990s suggest trends over time with designs incorporating systematic observation schedules using predetermined categories. Based on a repeat study drawing on the ORACLE research design,

Galton et al. (1999) maintain that the shift in whole-class teaching has been taken up by an increase in the amount of 'talking *at* pupils' and not in 'talking *with* pupils'. They conclude that teaching in today's primary schools is mostly a matter of teachers talking and children listening. While this is not a direct concern of this chapter, we are interested in how scholars investigate classroom interaction and the contemporary issues that have to be attended to. In this regard, we stress (as we have also done in Part One of this book) the importance of one's conceptual framework and its influence on research design and resultant findings. While this is true for all research, we will show how in the case of classroom interaction it is vital.

Researchers who themselves have conducted some of these large-scale studies involving considerable scale and scope of evidence acknowledge the difficulty when different researchers interpret the same 'slice of life' or series of classroom exchanges or the same event in different ways. At a minimum they may use a different coding system (Galton et al. 1999). However, other researchers ask different questions or pose different problems, challenging the assumptions underlying the methods based on predetermined codes and categories.

One of the biggest criticisms of the classroom interaction research based on process–product analyses is that it is not based on interaction that recognizes the grounded reality of its emergence in a particular context. Essentially, a coding scheme collapses a complex behaviour to a number. Many classroom researchers began to challenge the idea of working from predetermined categories of talk and the analyses based on them. In line with developments in learning more generally, researchers wanted to acknowledge in their research methods how all interaction, including that occurring in classrooms, is an activity jointly accomplished by the participants and always context dependent. Researchers became resistant to formal precoding of categories, seeing it as simplistic and reductive, and 'flattening of human behaviour' (Stivers 2015: 2).

Classroom interaction research based on conversation analysis

The focus on early process–product studies was predominantly on the teacher's behaviour, with limited focus on learners' (or indeed teachers') experiences or perspectives on what was happening. By the 1970s and 1980s researchers were turning to other details of classroom life, especially interaction among students themselves. A linguistic turn in classroom research was thus heralded when conversations among peers, interactions, utterances by teachers and learners, and the contexts of their occurrence all assumed significance. Sociolinguistics, conversation and **discourse analysis** eventually became the hallmarks of this move. So, too, did qualitative and interpretative methods although quantitative approaches continued to be used. For some, though certainly not all, the aim was to understand, describe and promote productive ways of supporting learning in classrooms.

One pedagogical pattern of interaction that emerged from the linguistic turn was what is known as the Initiation-Response-Feedback (IRF) sequence of interaction where the teacher initiates a response from students by posing a question and then provides feedback on that response. Sinclair and Coulthard (1975) demonstrated how this pattern was pervasive in classrooms, and research since then attests to its resilience (e.g. Nystrand et al. 2003; Alexander 2001; Mercer 2008). This interactional pattern is much criticized as it is assumed to limit the participation and voice of the learner (e.g. Bereiter 1986).

While one line of research continues to seek evidence and understanding of interactional approaches in various curricular domains with a view to improving interaction for learning, particularly in areas such as mathematics and literacy, another line of research seeks to grapple with how interactions function in classrooms. Thus, one can identify two related types of classroom interaction research and associated approaches: one interested in research geared to the promotion of talk for learning, the other attending to the effects of naturally occurring talk. Both types are explored here and both provide an important alternative to the process–product line of classroom inquiry presented above. Both types emphasize conversation, and they conduct what is referred to in the literature as **conversation analysis** (CA) and/or discourse analysis (DA). These approaches differ methodologically from the earlier, systematic, process–product research in their emphasis on the actual utterances: their verbatim presentation and analysis in ways that are most holistic and that operate from the ground up, rather than from top-down, preset categories.

Next we discuss research methods that are associated with trying to promote more productive, learning-oriented dialogue in schools and classrooms – what could be termed instructional and learning talk.

Researching productive talk in classrooms

The following statements appear in an edited book by Littleton and Howe (2010) about classroom interaction:

- there is certainly a lot of talk going on in classrooms, but seemingly to little effect (Littleton and Howe 2010: 3)

- educational dialogue is typically less effective than it ought to be (Littleton and Howe 2010: 10)

- much of the talk in collaborative activity in classrooms is unproductive (Littleton and Mercer 2010: 271)

- there is value in interaction where children express contrasting opinions in pursuit of joint goals (Howe 2010: 35)

It is not surprising, then, that pedagogy researchers are interested in understanding how to foster the kind of interaction that leads to learning in classrooms. Talk is one of the principal tools for constructing knowledge and this has been well established by several seminal scholars, whose work has given impetus to classroom interaction studies (Nystrand 1997; Wells 1999; Mercer 2000; Cazden 2001; Alexander 2008). The research focus, therefore, is often the search for and promotion of 'learning talk'. Based on their work with groups of learners in classrooms, Mercer (2000) and Mercer and Littleton (2007) devised an analytic framework for looking at classroom interaction relevant to learning. They refer to different types of learning talk, for example, 'exploratory', 'cumulative' and 'disputational'. The first and most well known of these is defined by Mercer (2000: 98) as follows:

Exploratory talk is that in which partners engage critically but constructively with each other's ideas. Relevant information is offered for joint consideration. Proposals may be challenged and counter-challenged, but if so reasons are given and alternatives are offered. Agreement is sought as a basis for joint progress. Knowledge is made publically accountable and reasoning is visible in the talk.

This type of analytic framework has resulted in several studies of classroom talk, especially talk among peers where the unit of analysis is the group rather than the individual. Intervention studies involving close investigation of classroom interaction by Mercer and others have shown that the use of exploratory talk enhances children's problem solving and ability to work well in groups, as well as promoting academic attainment in mathematics and science in the primary school. Much of this work is on learners in groups and how they use talk to think together, as indicated by the title of his book, *Words and Minds: How We Use Language to Think Together* (Mercer 2000).

To illustrate the research methods used in this kind of research, in case example 5.1 we draw on an example of a classroom interaction study that is in line with current, sociocultural understandings of how people learn. The study, therefore, like others in this genre, adopts certain assumptions about talk and learning: that talk promotes learning and that 'learning talk' is different from other, everyday social talk in that it is linked to a discipline or domain of curriculum. The assumption in our example also is that debate, dialogue, sharing and justifying decisions through talk are all important features of learning in contemporary classrooms, especially learning how to argue a point of view.

Case example 5.2: Examining talk for argumentation and knowledge production (Aberg, Makitalo and Saljo 2010)

Context: A study was conducted at the University of Gothenburg with students aged fifteen and sixteen years. The study focused on a panel debate and the planning for it required students to present and argue their case in a public forum where different concerns and imperatives and points of view were at stake. Students had to work in pairs on assigned countries, continents or the European Union.

Case example 5.2

Pedagogically the panel debate, which followed several weeks of project work, was to serve as a context for learning how to argue on sociopolitical issues in a democratic society and was designed to give students some ownership of the process of knowledge production. The researchers were interested in how the students interpret what it means to be knowledgeable in these kinds of educational arrangements. Importantly, from the point of view of the nature of language and dialogue, they adopted the view that learning how to argue cannot be viewed simply as an individual matter that can be learned through following a model. Rather, they saw argumentation as a creative, shared practice dependent on participants, context and the emergent unfolding of actions in the setting. This means that any fragment of conversation or any utterance or claim is assumed to be shaped by and crafted in response to other utterances.

Aims: To understand speaker roles and responsiveness to others in the context of a panel debate on climate change. To analyse how students hold themselves to account to others and what they consider to be acceptable arguments.

Outcomes: The findings are discussed in terms of the pedagogical issues and implications arising from the analysis, especially with reference to the affordances and constraints of the pedagogic approach. The published study incorporates several excerpts from the interactions that occurred, each one faithfully and exactly reproduced, with annotations and a **transcription** legend to help the reader understand the context of the evidence and its detail.

Research methods: The conceptual framing of the study had noteworthy implications for how data would be collected, analysed and presented. In summary, the researchers described the data-gathering and analytic processes they used: ethnographic fieldwork spanning seven weeks, fifty hours of video recording, several target student conversations transcribed verbatim and non-verbal interaction added as comments in transcripts.

Aberg, Makitalo and Saljo (2010: 18) conducted a microanalysis of interaction with a view to answering the following kinds of pedagogy-oriented research questions:

- What stance do the students take to the information they have collected about their country ... (factual, aligning with or distancing)?

- How do they position themselves as speakers in relation to this information (i.e. as assigned representatives of their specific country and/or as students)?

- How do they respond to potential critique and argument from their opponents, that is, how do they rhetorically incorporate such potential critique into their own argumentation?

The transcription legend is reproduced here to give some flavour of the research management and analytic process:

(.)	Shows just noticeable pauses (micro pauses)
(1 s)	Shows pauses over one second
((text))	Gives a description of an activity or something that is hard to phonetically write out in words e.g. laughter
text	Shows when a person is reading out loud or when a person writes and reads out loud what is being written
text	Shows that it is a stretched sound
[text]	shows co-occurring talk where the square brackets indicate where overlap starts and ends
Te(h)xt	Talk with a laughing tone
Text=	Shows that there is no pause between speaker turns.

(Aberg, Makitalo and Saljo 2010: 30)

Aberg, Makitalo and Saljo (2010: 19–20) use the next excerpt, during which two (target) learners are planning their work for the debate, to illustrate how the students are preparing to account to others for the stance they take. We present it to illustrate how evidence is analysed and presented in this kind of study.

101.   ANNIE: we're lucky to at least having the Kyoto protocol that's something good ((keeps on writing))

102.   BENNY: yes

103.   ((Benny changes paper))

104.   ANNIE: ((writes and reads out loud)) *the Kyoto protocol*

105.   (4 s)

106.   ANNIE: ((reads out loud)) *reads the Kyoto protocol* (I s) ((writes and reads out loud)) *since we* ((inaudible))

107.   (8 s)

108.   BENNY: ((stops reading and looks at Annie)) we do have a lot – or we have one fifth of u:hm (.) water power stations as well did we write that?

109.   ANNIE: yea (.) re- so now we have started to realize how eh important it is (.) ((writes and reads out loud)) *how important it is* (.) for the environment ((finishes the sentence in writing)) ((reads out loud)) *started to realize how important it is with the environment* and – wait ((orients towards the printouts and reads))

110.   ANNIE: how important it is with the environment and uhm (3 s) ((contentedly)) our future hm

Interaction studies based on conversation analysis tend to be extremely time-consuming because of the close attention required to precise utterances, their collection and analysis. Moreover, careful selections of utterances have to be made since depth and theory building are often privileged over scale and breadth and aggregated facts. Parks (2011: 220) describes the care needed when collecting (generating) data and the fieldwork involved:

From September to April, I visited Diana's classroom weekly during mathematics instruction. (I also occasionally observed lessons at other times of the school day). During each of these visits, I took detailed field notes, collected student work and teacher lesson plans and audio-recorded the conversations. I relied on these tapes to transcribe all conversations when writing up my field notes which I did within 24 hours of my classroom observations. In addition, I interviewed the teacher formally and many of the children informally ... rather than sitting down at a particular time to question children, I asked the children about their participation at the moment of my observations.

Sampling and interpretation merit particular checks, therefore, to enhance trustworthiness of claims made. This raises the question of how this might happen in interaction studies, where the scope for the portrayal and presentation of conversational evidence is limited in reproducing utterances of sequences of interaction. Our example in case example 5.3 is helpful in addressing this point. We draw on the work of van Drie and Dekker (2013), who consider these issues in their paper, 'Theoretical triangulation as an approach for revealing the complexity of a classroom discussion'.

Case example 5.3: Enhancing trustworthiness of evidence in pedagogic research: Triangulation (van Drie and Dekker 2013)

Context: A study of whole-class discussion in the curricular domain of history, in which the focus is on theoretical triangulation. Theoretical triangulation involves the use of various perspectives when examining a phenomenon.

Goals: The researchers sought to contribute to the search for methodologies to help take account of the complexity of classroom interactions. The research question that guided their study was: How can the quality of a whole-class discussion in history be described when using theoretical triangulation? (van Drie and Dekker 2013: 343).

Outcomes: By using theoretical triangulation, the detailed analysis from three different perspectives (from the teacher's perspective, from the history perspective and from the students' perspective)

Case example 5.3

provides an alternative and complementary take on one excerpt of a whole-class discussion. Through this process the researchers were able to relate the perspectives of the teacher, the students and the domain to each other.

Research methods: Triangulation – the process of drawing evidence from multiple sources or methods, usually to enhance the dependability of that evidence and interpretations based on it (Bryman 2013). A further dimension of triangulation is the involvement of several investigators independently analysing the same fragment of interaction, and then sharing and discussing their analysis. The use of multiple theoretical perspectives (see Miles and Huberman 1984) is a further approach, as elaborated by van Drie and Dekker (2013). They identified and explained three key concepts that were a focus of their attention to interaction, each highlighting a different dimension of the interaction, one of which bore directly on the nature of the discipline in question. The three interrelated notions were

- interactivity of the talk (which focused on the teacher);

- conceptual-level raising (which focused on the learners) and

- historical reasoning (which focused on the domain).

Van Drie and Dekker (2013) generated knowledge about the nature of the interaction and the nature of historical reasoning. They offered a fine-grained conversation analysis of one fragment of interaction from the three theoretical perspectives identified above. They incorporated these theoretical perspectives on the basis that, in their pedagogical view, in whole-class discussions students should be actively involved in disciplinary discourse represented by interactivity of the discourse, conceptual-level raising and historical reasoning. Thus, their focus and analysis incorporated the teacher and the students, as well as the curricular domain.

By using theoretical triangulation they sought to obtain a more holistic picture of the quality of the discussion. The explanation and justification of the theoretical framing in this way provided boundaries to and a focus for aspects of the interaction. Their theoretical framing also provided clarity and justification about the evidence presented and the claims made, based on that evidence.

In another study, Kathy (Hall 2002) considered how different theoretical stances on literacy shape different researchers' interpretation of a small database of evidence on one child (Stephen), as a struggling reader in a primary school. In this research, well-known literacy scholars were each presented with the same slice of teacher–pupil interaction about an assessment task and asked, on the basis of that interactive assessment evidence, to respond to the same four questions:

- What do we know about Stephen as a reader?

- What else should we know about him?

- What should his teacher do to help him as a reader?

- What theoretical perspectives underpin your claims and suggestions?

Unsurprisingly, the theoretical orientation to literacy, learning and assessment adopted by the scholars who were interviewed for the study proved to be highly influential in understanding their interpretations and recommendations. Again, the point of that exercise and of mentioning it here is to highlight the importance of exposing and exploring the fundamental assumptions researchers make about key dimensions of pedagogy, in this case the curricular domain and how to assess it. It is another example of the intertwining of theory and research methods that we have illustrated many times in this book.

We would suggest, therefore, that in a sense different perspectives provide a kind of informal coding (Schegloff 1993), though not of course for the purpose of statistical analysis such as in process–product analyses. Thus, doing coding of a sort is already an inevitable part of the research practice of conversation analysis (Steensig and Heinemann 2015). The key point is that we do not enter any research study as a 'blank slate' – we always come with perspectives, histories and agendas. The important issue for the researcher, then, is to seek to acknowledge that pedagogic research (all research) is perspectival, that what is discovered is inseparable from the knower. There is always a wider context of structures that shape events and interactions. There are, for instance, cultural traditions, norms and expectations for the context, as well as hierarchies and relations of power, which influence what happens though not of course in predictable ways. We develop and illustrate this idea further in the next section.

Representing classroom talk: Methods of transcription

Several approaches to the analysis of classroom conversation have evolved in line with the theoretical stance that learning, language and especially classroom talk are distributed and dependent upon relationships, context, history and agendas. Tannen's work (1984), although not originating in classrooms, provides analytic tools for examining features such as pausing, pacing and overlapping speech, together with words uttered and concepts recruited into conversation. The four modes of classroom participation suggested by Kovalainen, Kumpulainen and Vasama (2002) provide guidance on dimensions of pedagogy bearing on talk in classrooms:

- Evocative mode (asking questions to evoke interest)
- Facilitative mode (re-voicing to integrate and draw ideas together)
- Collective mode (talk geared to the promotion of collective responsibility)
- Appreciative mode (valuing contributions).

We have already reproduced an example of a legend designed to help the reader interpret the utterances in a transcript. A common transcript format for conversations is that developed by Gail Jefferson (see Zuengler, Ford and Fassnacht 1998: 8), where:

Brackets ([or]) indicate overlapping speech

Equal signs (=) indicate talk that is latched or contiguous with the following turn of talk

Numbers in brackets indicate length of pause

A colon (:) after a letter shows a lengthening of sound

Underling and capital letters are used to indicate stress and loudness respectively.

Clearly, the amount of detail in a transcript can never be exhaustive (Auer 2014) and has to depend on the focus of the research and the questions being addressed. (See Chapter 7 for a discussion of more complex multimodal transcripts.) Auer (2014), for instance, suggests that, to be feasible, transcription demands glossing over certain aspects to avoid becoming lost in masses of detail. So the researcher has to decide, for example, how important the following might be: loudness; stress; speed of articulation/tempo; and whether grammatical and syntactical elements need to be decomposed so that modal verbs, pronouns, nouns and so on are indicated. Obviously, the more detail that is put into a transcript, the more demanding it is to read, and so communication may be hindered. However, the level of detail has to link to the focus of the study. The legend reproduced in case example 5.2 might be considered typical of the detail needed for the pedagogy researcher attempting to examine productive talk in curricular domains. It may be that the researcher needs to distinguish between transcription for accessing the recording made, and transcription for the purpose of making certain empirical claims (see Auer 2014 for detailed discussion). If the former, the objective might be searchability and accessibility, while the latter would likely require more fine-grained details of, say, gesture, posture, prosody, gaze and silence.

As a method of data generation, presentation and early analysis, transcription, similar to video and other methods discussed in later chapters, is not an unproblematic capturing of the reality of the lived and enacted interaction experience of participants. As with all methods, it involves the researcher in a series of decisions that will ultimately shape the nature of the recorded transcript. Bucholtz (2000) defines these transcriptional choices for researchers as interpretive decisions around content (what is described) and representational decisions around form (how is it transcribed). Researchers may choose, for example, naturalized or denaturalized transcription and within this make choices about if and how to represent non-verbal communication, rituals and routines, contextual cues and so on. Bucholtz (2000: 1462) suggests that researchers need to consider very carefully their transcription practices and how these are influenced by their own theories and beliefs. She explains that reflexive transcription practice should involve the researcher in dialogue with colleagues, other researchers and participants, 'not to find validation for our own decisions but to discover other ways of hearing and transcribing' that will bring new meanings to our data. As we transcribe, we need to be aware of what Bucholtz (2000: 1440) terms the politics of transcription and how:

> All transcripts take sides, enabling certain interpretations, advancing particular interests, favoring specific speakers, and so on. The choices made in transcription link the transcript to the context in which it is intended to be read. Embedded in the details of transcription are indications of purpose, audience, and the position of the transcriber toward the text. Transcripts thus testify to the circumstances of their creation and intended use. As long as we seek a transcription practice that is independent of its own history rather than looking closely at how transcripts operate politically, we will perpetuate the erroneous belief that an objective transcription is possible. ... The transcription of a text always involves the inscription of a context.

Studies bearing on 'productive' talk have developed understanding of how learning occurs and are highly relevant to educators. By focusing on the language used and how it is used, researchers can give insight into thought processes for, as Roth, Mercer and others have argued, thinking itself is distributed across space and time. As such, thought/learning requires a temporal analysis (Mercer 2008). Bloome et al. (2009) provide some good examples of the kind of interactional research that takes account of time and memory. Kim and Roth (2014: 304) suggest that problems and problem statements 'come into being': they do not exist of themselves. It is not surprising, therefore, that increasingly the focus in interaction conversation-based studies in classrooms is on naturally occurring events and moments of interaction, supplemented perhaps by interviews.

The social turn in the human sciences in general, and in classroom research in particular (Mehan 1979), means that we need to understand the social processes through which pedagogy takes place. This brings us to a related set of research foci and approaches.

Understanding the processes of interaction: Discourse analysis

Researchers continue to seek to understand ways in which the interactions among students influence their opportunities to learn. Many such studies are not necessarily seeking to intervene or even to promote a particular kind of 'learning discourse'. Rather, the intention of many ethnographic studies of interaction in classrooms is to understand from an insider point of view what is meaningful to participants; the intention is to better understand the processes of interaction. Because of this, researchers try to be unobtrusive data gatherers, tending to observe for extended periods, sometimes over many months and even years (see Rex, Steadman and Graciano 2006 for a review of the field). They typically take on the role of participant observer in order to understand what is going on.

Technology for audio and video recording assists this process and, indeed, has been highly influential in all classroom research. The observation of exact utterances and partial words, overlapping speech, pauses, intonations, gestures, posture, gaze directions and other similar aspects of behaviour are rendered visible and audible through technology. We explore this in more detail in Part Three, especially Chapter 9. Evidence that would have been far too difficult to register and record merely by listening or watching a recording repeatedly is now accessible, with the help of digital technology. Researchers can excavate episodes or fragments of interaction to identify participation structures and linguistic frameworks in which individual students are positioned with different rights and obligations for 'initiating, receiving, questioning, accepting, evaluating, and challenging ideas and information in classrooms' (Greeno 2006: 817). Digital technology also allows downloading audio evidence to computers from individual microphones placed on participants, and can by synchronized with the visual data. However, researchers need to be mindful of the impact and limitations of different technological approaches on what can be seen and heard in classrooms. Technological approaches to data gathering need to be considered at the outset of the research as part of the overall theoretical and methodological intention of the project. Zuengler, Ford and Fassnacht (1998: 25) observe that 'while technology never eliminates the need for sensitive, inquisitive, skilled, and dedicated researchers in the field, its intelligent application can open up a whole new world to the researcher of language and interaction'.

Although not neatly distinguishable from the kind of interaction studies described in the previous section, the type of study we next describe is more inclined to attend to the local rationality of classroom life. The kinds of questions posed by investigations seeking to understand the processes of interaction in this line of classroom inquiry include the following:

- How do particular kinds of interaction (including perhaps an IRF exchange) function?

- How are interactions making sense to the various participants?

- What work is being done by the interactions?

- What are the talking norms and conventions in the class?

- What roles and responsibilities do different participants take up?

- Who gets to speak and when?

- Who interrupts or diverts attention to something new?

- Who appears to set the agenda and how can it be disrupted or changed?

- How is control 'handed over' and to whom, when?

Rex, Steadman and Graciano (2006: 745) effectively sum up the central question: 'who can say or do what to and with whom, when and where, under what conditions, in relation to what actions or artifacts, for what purposes, and with what outcomes?' To address such questions, attention is devoted to detailed descriptions and analyses of what participants say and how they say it, including the context of conversation.

Returning to the reference earlier in the chapter to the Initiation-Response-Feedback pattern being so resilient to change in classrooms, Mehan (1979) has argued that this pattern evolved historically to establish order, to maintain particular social relations, adult–child authority structures and gender relations. In other words, it does certain work in classrooms, it is designed to achieve certain effects and it would seem that in many cases it remains a taken-for-granted sequence of interaction. Another form of questioning and interaction in this vein, though less well known, is the 'Designedly Incomplete Utterance' (DIU) described in detail by Koshik (2002) and Margutti (2010). Typically used to encourage student self-correction, and the display of knowledge and understanding, it consists of incomplete utterances produced by the teacher. Like the IRF sequence, the kind of questioning is designed not to ask an authentic question (to which the teacher does not know the answer), but to establish whether the student knows the answer. Such interaction conforms to what Mehan (1979: 285) labels 'known information questions'. Such questioning functions effectively with large numbers of students in a class. For instance, Margutti's (2010) evidence shows that, owing to its versatile features, it can be used repeatedly on any unit in the progression of the teacher's talk and provides for the turn's reversibility when students do not know how to complete the phrase or sentence. What Margutti's (2010) own research shows is the importance of studying how linguistic patterns of interaction achieve their effects, and one of the important effects of studying the way interaction happens is the insight it gives in relation to what counts as learning and success in the minds of all participants, learners and teachers alike. It can provide 'an interactional account of the participants' own views of learning' and how it is achieved (Margutti 2010: 344; see also Koole 2010). To do this, Margutti argues, it is necessary to conduct fine-grained sequential analysis of teacher–student interaction in pedagogic sequences.

An important point to note here again is how the focus of the research, and more particularly the conceptual framework, influences what is 'discovered'. While some might argue that the IRF pattern denies authentic interaction, others (e.g. Heap 1986; Lin 2007) explain how that pattern allows the teacher to shape learners' contribution towards acceptable cultural knowledge and values. Heap's (1986) own work drew heavily on conversation analysis to show 'the point' of a lesson, the local rationality obtaining in a given classroom context.

Case example 5.4 is illustrative of the kind of study that investigates how classroom talk functions.

Case example 5.4: Discourse analysis (Davies 2005)

Context: An investigation pursuing an interest in females' achievement in schools. The database is small discussion groups in secondary school classrooms in England. The context of the study is boys' underachievement in comparison to girls in England. The project examines the processes of pupils' learning through talk-related activities. It explores the strategies girls used to learn, collaborate, maintain friendships and affirm group solidarity.

Goals: To investigate the process of talk and learning, paying attention to ways in which this process connects with identity maintenance and formation.

Outcomes: Davies (2005) found that some linguistic features were far more common in girls' discussion groups than in boys' discussion groups. Crucially, she argued that these features of their discourse contributed to an atmosphere conducive to collaborative learning. Her contention, on the basis of her analysis, was that girls' gendered social and linguistic practices advantage their learning with academic and social benefits accruing to them. Using both narrative and conversation/discourse analysis to probe her evidence, Davies identified excerpts from the discussions to demonstrate the various features characterizing their interaction and which, she argued, explained their success in the tasks set for them. The fragments she presented illustrated how the girls build on each other's statements through adopting the same grammatical and semantic structure. Particular rhetorical devices described included:

The use of pronouns ('we' as a pronoun of inclusion and rejection)

- The use of shared phrases and rhetorical questions (to convey agreement)
- The use of tag questions to elicit positive responses (e.g. 'he'll just like ignore us, won't he'?)
- The use of the present mood ('and I goes ...')

Case example 5.4

- Parallelism in grammatical structure

- Tentativeness and hedges in statements (conveying belonging and valuing contributions of others in the group e.g. perhaps, may)

What this approach to interaction revealed was how the girls were able to combine friendship work alongside the completion of tasks. Academic and social goals were thus achieved simultaneously.

Research methods: Group discussions were audio recorded, and Davies drew on discourse analysis and narrative analysis to help her understand the context-specific nature of the discussions that she observed. Interestingly, she argued that the speech she recorded and analysed was not naturally occurring, since students were requested by their teacher to talk about specific topics within a particular time frame and were aware that their talk was being monitored and assessed by the researcher.

Discourse analysis (DA) is frequently mentioned as an analytic frame in pedagogic research. Along with **critical discourse analysis** (CDA), it can provide a helpful framework for researching classroom interaction in relation to power and ideology. It can help to make explicit issues of authority, legitimation and competence. There are many approaches to the conduct of DA (see Hall and Chambers 2012) with several scholars writing on it as both a method and a theory, as well as applying it in diverse areas to explore what is happening in social settings such as classrooms (e.g. Gee 1999; Lewis, Enciso and Moje 2007; Rogers 2011).

DA is the term given to a whole range of approaches to the analysis of texts. There is no single way to define or do DA. We can think of discourse as words uttered or written but, importantly, discourses are also ways of being, and ways of behaving and acting in the world. Discourses are like mental scripts that we draw on when participating in different activities and situations. They are taken-for-granted ways of behaving, doing and being. People who are 'in the know', that is, who are on the inside of a discourse, view the world from their own discursive lens. In DA, analysts are interested in what the taken-for-granted, insider scripts and discourses are and how they might enable and constrain what is doable, sayable, thinkable in, say, a classroom situation.

Some researchers prefer the phrase 'discourse studies' to 'discourse analysis' on the grounds that what is involved is a combination of theory and method. A major review of the field by Rogers et al. (2005) shows the diversity in approach and method, as well as the range of theoretical and methodological tools that discourse analysts use in their work. We mention just one approach using DA, which one of us (Kathy) applied in a literacy class in order to understand how learning opportunities are constructed, afforded and constrained (Hall 2002). The approach in question drew on a conceptually coherent framework devised by Gee and Green (1997) known as the MASS system, which refers to material, activity, sociocultural and semiotic aspects of discourse. The analytic system assumes that language simultaneously reflects reality (the way things are) and construes the situation in which it is used. The four aspects of a situation are interrelated.

The material aspect concerns such factors as the actors, places, spaces and time involved in the interaction. Simply put, it is about when, where and with whom members interact. The activity aspect is about the specific tasks on which time is spent and on which participants are engaged. The sociocultural aspect refers to the norms and expectations, roles, obligations and identities that seem to be relevant to the situation. The semiotic aspect refers to situated meanings and ways of knowing connected to language, gestures and images. A situated meaning is a pattern that participants in an interaction make on the spot in the course of communicating in a particular context, usually based on conventions and past experience. Examples of semiotic questions might be:

- What situated meanings are there in this classroom?

- What ways of knowing are being invoked in an activity?

- How do these models or discourses frame identities or extend agency for learners?

- What discourses are being produced?

Overall, the MASS system is guided by the principle of contrastive analysis, which allows the analyst to shift between meaning aspects (semiotic), material aspects, activity aspects and sociocultural aspects. Together, these aspects can help to identify sources of influences on observed actions and to understand the way collective and individual actions and identities are socially constructed.

DA is sufficiently flexible to deal with the complexity of inter-action in classrooms, and with differences in curricular domains, therefore it is highly suited to answering the kinds of questions listed earlier. Because it is at once theory and method, it has to be considered in the planning stage and considered in the context of an overall conceptual study framework. DA is well attuned to a sociocultural perspective on pedagogy. It can deal well with context, activity and the 'recognizability' (Sachs 1992: 300) of action on the part of participants. Because interaction tends to be patterned and structured through how participants understand, grasp and orient to the recognizability of each other's utterances, the interested researcher needs to understand what counts as ways of being and acting in contexts. As Nishizaka (2015: 27) explains, one needs to look at interaction in a given instance or context as 'a set of normative rather than factual connections of identities, activities, sequential positions'.

Conclusion

This chapter incorporates a wide range of practical and theoretical aspects relevant to the pedagogy researcher who is investigating life in classrooms. It is far from comprehensive, but we have sought to highlight critical issues involved in investigating interaction among classroom participants. One theme we did not address is the linking of home/community talk and school talk. While other chapters in this book have considered the out-of-school and hard-to-know dimension of pedagogy, it is important to recognize the intersection of home and school talk and discourses, and how one interacts with the other. For instance, the work of anthropologist Shirley Brice Heath, specifically her seminal study, *Ways with Words* (1983), shows how learners enter formal schooling with certain expectations about the world, relationships, entitlements and norms about speaking that may constrain or empower them in school, depending on their alignment with its cultural practices. Her work showed how the interactional practices of the families in each of the three communities she studied subsequently influenced significantly children's interactions and performances in school, as well as the teachers' attitudes and responses to the children. Thus, there is overlap across the out-of-school and the within school, from the point of view of the pedagogy researcher.

Similarly, we suggest that there is no simple distinction across studies designed to investigate productive talk in classrooms and studies that 'stand back' and seek to understand 'the point' or the rationality of classroom life from the perspective of participants. Both lines of inquiry overlap in various ways, not least in the research methods of data collection and analysis deployed. Central to both lines of inquiry is the view that language in use, in situ, must be the focus of study as context is fundamental. Adopting this perspective allows one to investigate the ways in which student identities can be produced, reproduced and transformed within classrooms.

Further reading

Kim, M. and W. M. Roth (2014), 'Argumentation as/in/for Dialogical Relation: A case Study from Elementary School Science', *Pedagogies: An International Journal*, 9(4): 300–31. This study examines argumentation in early elementary classroom. The authors provide several fragments of classroom dialogue to describe and explain how argumentation emerges and develops *as*, *in* and *for* dialogical relations with others. They show how this sets the stage for argumentation to evidence itself later when students are tested individually.

Mercer, N. (2010), 'The analysis of classroom talk: methods and methodologies', *British Journal of Educational Psychology*, 80: 1–14.

Parks, A. N. (2011), 'Diversity of Practice within One Mathematics Classroom', *Pedagogies: An International Journal*, 6(3): 216–33.

We have suggested these articles for further reading as they are excellent examples of how theory and research methodology are intertwined. These papers offer discussion and examples of issues and methods in the conduct and presentation of talk in classrooms. Mercer's paper, in particular, argues how methods are embedded in particular methodologies which are, in turn, based on particular theories of social action, of research orientation and even disciplinary area.

CHAPTER SIX

Researching the everyday and out-of-school: Research methods and innovation

Introduction

Researchers of pedagogy often favour formal, academic or institutional sites of learning that evidence pedagogical practices as described in our previous two chapters in this second part of the book. Acknowledging the complexities inherent in the definition and research of pedagogy, this chapter explores innovative opportunities for researching pedagogy in everyday and out-of-school/academic settings and the research methods that follow. Working from a broad sociocultural definition (resulting in our understanding of the nature of learning) of pedagogy as participation in practice (Hall, Murphy and Soler 2008), an exploration of pedagogy necessitates more than an understanding of teaching and learning in schools and formal settings. The research methods for pedagogy considered in this chapter are applied to research outside of the school gates and within everyday practice and facilitate a study of pedagogy in the absence of a formal curriculum or teacher. They align with an understanding of pedagogy put forward by Hall, Murphy and Soler (2008: ix) as

> what is salient to people as they engage in activity and develop
> competence in the practice in question. ... This deeper and broader
> notion of pedagogy, which is not confined to a particular place,

setting, age or stage, draws attention to the identities which are variously valued, reproduced and transformed as people participate in activity. Whether the practice is in relation to becoming a reader, a learner of mathematics in school, a teacher, an architect, a hairdresser and so on, how the cultural practice is mediated by one's lived experiences becomes significant for one's ability to demonstrate oneself as competent and be recognized by others as competent in a given practice. Pedagogy involves an appreciation of the significance of experiences and meditational aspects as key to supporting learning.

Researching pedagogy in everyday practice enriches the interplay between the role of academic and social contexts in learning, the school and the everyday. Understanding school and everyday practices as porous and connected presents the researcher with multiple sites, methods and approaches, data and perspectives for researching pedagogy. Wenger (1998), who explains the boundaries that connect and mark different communities of practice, argues we should not seek to protect or blend experiences, since communities of practice are themselves rich opportunistic sites for learning and can become spaces of renegotiation and learning of shared practices. Similarly, we maintain that the interplay between in- and out-of-school learning can provide innovative and rich avenues for pedagogic research. To exemplify the nuances of this interplay, this chapter explores three themes central to understanding pedagogy, namely the role of relationships, community and identity in learning.

We present three case examples from England, Australia and the United States respectively, which investigate these pedagogical concerns in out-of-school practices and settings. The stories we tell are of researchers engaging in what are, for them, unfamiliar and sometimes strange contexts for learning and communities of practice. We explore these in detail according to methodological choices made (such as what, where and how do we, as researchers of pedagogy in everyday settings, look and what becomes visible and invisible from these different points of view) to begin to make visible researcher thinking and concerns.

The journey of the researcher in out-of-school research is central to this chapter, as Alicia shares her own experiences through these links to related experiences and dilemmas of researchers within the case examples and other research presented. The focus throughout the discussion remains on the researcher of pedagogy and her experiences, struggles and conflicts (the issues experienced in the practice of research). At the same time, the exemplification of methods in the case examples and related research provide insight into out-of-school and everyday research methods, activities and practice (the planning and design of methodology). Each case example positions the researcher in particular ways and allows an elaboration on the researcher of pedagogy in everyday practice as meaning-maker and voyager in the extension and development of her own identities in different contexts and communities of practice.

Shifting researcher identities: Ethical starting points

Though we have shown in previous chapters that no single size fits all when it comes to research design, researchers in out-of-school settings tend to share an understanding of learning and pedagogy that prioritizes social and experiential aspects – *pedagogy as enacted and pedagogy as experienced*. Research methods for data collection and analysis in these settings centre on meaning, but this meaning may be found in experiences, aspects or documents of the practice that are unfamiliar to the researcher. This contrasts with the experiences of some researchers of pedagogy in institutional or formal settings where, throughout the research process, they retain their expert stance (or, at the very least, familiarity) in relation to what is under study. Pausing briefly here to consider the starting point of one researcher of pedagogy in out-of-school settings exemplifies the understandings, dilemmas and implications for methodological design inherent in beginning research in out-of-school settings.

Alicia's previous research experiences broadly explore the nature of learning in adolescent everyday experiences across a variety of social interactions and settings. Beginning research in an out-of-school setting, the researcher first has to accept that there is no single, objective reality to be captured. All that can be researched is the interpretation of individual experience in a social world. Meaning is central to research design, and researching everyday experiences in out-of-school settings necessitates an inductive and holistic in-depth investigation of natural processes in natural settings, often with a small number of participants. Research questions in out-of-school settings are often experiential in nature and can revolve around, for example, the nature of experiences and resultant evolving and emerging identities for young people (as learners, teenagers, sport players, writers and so on). This sociocultural and experiential focus necessitates a methodological design that can lay bare features of experience in relation to specific phenomena, such as learning or literacy, while also making visible the impact of these experiences on the participants. The researcher in these settings also has to acknowledge and understand that her readings and interpretations of experiences within the study can be coloured by her own history, as she negotiates the meaning of the experiences with the participants.

Participant selection at the start of the research process is deeply important for researchers of everyday practice, as a number of concerns need to be addressed. Researching the meaning of the lived experiences of individuals means researchers select a small number of participants (one, even) to allow immersion in their experiences through approaches such as phenomenology, ethnography and identity work explored in this chapter. Research in these settings is not linear and the researcher becomes a tool integral to data generation and analysis. Because of this, the nature of the relationship between researcher and participants in studies of pedagogy outside of schools/formal settings can have powerful effects on all other elements of the methodology and the process of research. It can also have significant effects on the participants, and researchers need to conduct the research in a way that does not marginalize and that is not detrimental to the practices, community and individuals involved.

Researchers of out-of-school practices often focus their concern on a crystallization rather than a triangulation of experience. As we can never objectively know the world, but only our own social experiences of and in it, crystallizing experience – holding a small moment in time up to the light and examining it from every possible perspective – becomes a central concern of the researcher of pedagogy in everyday settings. Richardson's (2000: 934) crystals, introduced in Chapter 3, combine 'symmetry and substance with an infinite variety of shapes, substances, transmutations [and that] grow, alter and change [as] prisms that reflect externalities and refract within themselves, creating different colours, patterns, arrays, casting off in different directions'. Researchers of everyday out-of-school pedagogies similarly need methods and approaches that attempt to reflect, refract and generate new understandings of pedagogy and learning through multiple data sources and perspectives on practice.

An understanding of crystallization helps us to see the complex methods required in out-of-school pedagogy research where researchers explore communities and practices unfamiliar to them, compelling them to look at pedagogy and learning in different spaces and from alternative points of view. This shift in identity for the researcher from expert knower to inductee in new pedagogical practice requires exploration of the various aims, intentions and agencies inherent in the identity development of individuals through practice, interactions and learning. These messy and intricate experiences of pedagogy mirror in many ways the value Richardson (1994: 11) places on crystallization in that they provide 'us with a deepened, complex, thoroughly partial understanding of the topic'. Richardson argues, 'Paradoxically, we know more and doubt what we know' (p. 11). Phenomenology, ethnography and identity work present three significant, overlapping approaches for researching pedagogy and learning in everyday and out-of-school settings. We explore these three methodological approaches later alongside our three central case examples, each of which focuses on one of these (phenomenology, ethnography and identity work) to exemplify the design, and the resulting research practices and concerns that emerge. Elements of each are present across all three case examples, however, and they are all in many ways integral to a study of pedagogy in out-of-school settings.

Researcher as meaning-maker: Phenomenology, relationships and pedagogy research

Phenomenology asks 'what is the meaning, structure and essence of a particular lived experience for a person or a group of people' (Patton 2002: 104). Van Maanen (1990) defines phenomenology as a process that aims to gain a deeper understanding of the nature or meaning of our everyday experiences. Phenomenological approaches focus on how members of a community make the social world meaningful. Such research centres on the shared experiences of the participants in relation to a given phenomenon (e.g. learning) as the researcher uses methods that create a description of what participants experience and how they experience it (Moustakas 1994). Table 6.1 summarizes a phenomenological approach to research design.

Table 6.1 Phenomenology as method

Nature of questions asked	<ul><li>what is the participant's subjective experience and how is meaning made in the moment of practice as individuals experience the world</li><li>'what is the meaning, structure and essence of the lived experience of this phenomenon for this person or group of people' (Patton 2002: 104)</li></ul>
Role of the researcher	<ul><li>to understand and describe a phenomenon, experience or event from the point of view of the participant</li><li>not to make assumptions about an objective reality, as the focus remains on the participant's experience and their understanding of the meaning of this experience</li><li>to look for commonalities between the experiences of individuals around a given phenomenon</li></ul>
Goal of the research	<ul><li>to describe how individuals construct, perpetuate and understand their own practice and world in communities of practice</li><li>to gain access to the world and practices of an individual</li></ul>
Data collection	<ul><li>in, close to, or about natural sites of social practice</li><li>from a small number of participants</li><li>observational notes written to identify and describe precisely what occurs</li><li>primarily interviews and casual conversations to develop in-depth understanding of feelings of those directly experiencing the phenomena</li><li>participants identify (through action, interaction, description) what is meaningful for them in their own lives in relation to a particular phenomenon</li></ul>
Data presentation	<ul><li>thematic or chronological presentations with quotes from participants made central</li></ul>

Data analysis	• using reflective writing and grounded theory to describe where and how meaning is made in the social practices of participants • seeking significant statements or quotes which evidence the meaning of experience for participants
Meaning of evidence	• the subjective experiences of the participants • subjective realities of individuals undergoing a particular experience
Measurement	• snapshot of the experience of a person or a group at one point in time
Ethics	• general concern with confidentiality, anonymity, design and use of instruments • how to present the practices explored to ensure that they do not marginalize the group or individual in question, or cause other detrimental issues for participants

A focus on relationships is central to pedagogic research in which understanding of learning ensures that teachers and learners are not dichotomized: they share in the processes and products of teaching and learning. Researching learning relationships in school can be difficult, as the authentic aspects of these relationships are often obscured from view. This happens through the dynamics of power relations in which the relationships and experiences at the heart of pedagogy remain hidden and hard to know. In contrast, case example 6.1 centres on the role of educational relationships in pedagogy and learning.

Case example 6.1: Examination of the role of educational relationships in out-of-school activities and their impact on young people's learning (Wikeley et al. 2007)

Context: A comparison of the experiences of out-of-school activities of impoverished young people with those of their more affluent peers in the South West of England.

Case example 6.1

Goal: To explore what young people gain from engagement in out-of-school activities that involve a learning intent, comparing the experiences of impoverished young people with their more affluent peers.

Outcomes: A diverse range of out-of-school activities was apparent and reasons for initial and continued commitment of young people identified. Findings categorizing what and how young people learn in these activities including specialist knowledge and vocabulary, self-control and confidence, learning the importance of educational relationships and agency.

Research methods: The methods involved capturing the experiences of the learners themselves. Participants were chosen from rural and urban contexts and the intended sample size of forty-eight was split between primary and secondary schools. The difference in ages also facilitated the investigation of age-related changes. The young people were asked to map on a sheet of paper how they spent their time in a typical week, when not in school. This map formed the basis for interviews in which the researchers chose two activities for more in-depth exploration, asking about engagement in other activities absent from and present on the students' maps.

Our inclusion of this case example as the first in this chapter serves a dual purpose, as our exploration of its methods simultaneously illustrates some of the values and concerns surrounding the use of out-of-school sites for pedagogy research. For example, the breadth of the diverse organized and spontaneous activities identified on the activity maps in this study provides researchers of pedagogy with innovative and dynamic spaces for research. Organized activities included a myriad of clubs (sport, dance, drama, karate, youth, art), religious groups, Air Training Corps, scouts and guides. Spontaneous activities identified included library visits, cooking, shopping, socializing, (social) media, caring for pets, part-time jobs, hobbies, homework and computer gaming. The method allowed for scoping and fitting the research to the way the young people saw their pedagogical spaces and time.

Defining pedagogical texts in out-of-school research

With the opportunities provided in research sites beyond the school gates also come challenges, as the researcher now needs to redefine what constitutes a pedagogical text, data and evidence, alongside how these can be generated and understood. Crucial questions for researchers of pedagogy arise around what can be looked at, what counts as evidence and the nature of that evidence. If we understand part of the role of the researcher of everyday practice to be that of meaning-maker, engaging with the meaning-making of others, we have first to identify where meaning is practised and perpetuated by the participants in the community of practice we are engaging with. This may involve asking questions, such as around what activities and artefacts and in what ways practice in this community happens. In everyday settings, the conversations, statements, family histories, previous experiences, aspirations and the activities are all imbued with pedagogical value and can be understood as pedagogical texts in their own right, with something to say about experiences of teaching and learning.

One of the first decisions for Alicia, exploring out-of-school settings, centred on what would constitute a pedagogical text in this context. Exploring out-of-school spaces and places means that, in these settings, what is visible to the researcher as evidence of learning diversifies beyond teacher–student interactions. This affords the researcher new and dynamic ways of talking about teaching and learning. The researcher has to consider carefully which pieces of data can be used to bring most meaning to the research questions (both those initially asked and those emerging). As research in these settings is centred broadly on individual experiences, the researcher does not need to focus overly on the trustworthiness or validity of the data selected, as long as she ensures that claims are not made to generalize these experiences beyond the research communities of practice. Immersed in a variety of research sites, physical and virtual, out-of-school pedagogical research requires a discerning flexibility in relation to its presentation of data, which would stand as artefacts of experience and allow the researcher to tell her story.

Examples of other researchers engaging with this challenge in other contexts can be found in interesting research that positions computer games as pedagogical texts and tools for developing our understanding of learning. Gee (2003) explores how, through good game design, deep learning for pleasure occurs in everyday practice. Analysing popular games such as Tomb Raider, Gee concludes that successful ones embed many principles of good learning and afford players the opportunity to experience ways of knowing, doing and being, close to that experienced as people learn similar practices in real world contexts.

The interplay between these kinds of analyses and methods used to study pedagogy in formal settings can be seen in studies such as by Dede et al. (2005), where an online learning environment and game was designed to teach scientific inquiry skills to middle school students in the United States. The main goal in this case was for students to find out why the residents of River City were getting ill. Exploring River City, students were able to learn in the same context in which they have to apply their knowledge to solve the mystery and the game, something that cannot always be said about classroom pedagogies. Pedagogical studies like these have led to the development of new pedagogical approaches and research methodologies. For example, Schultz, Colby and Colby (2008) explored enacted emergent pedagogy, where students completed writing projects informed by the game played and written for other players engaged in the online role-playing game, World of Warcraft. In all of these examples, researchers as meaning-makers expand what constitutes a pedagogical text in a way that allows them to talk about teaching and learning in new ways in informal contexts.

Making visible the hidden and hard-to-know in out-of-school research

Alongside expanding understandings of what counts as a pedagogical text, uncoupling pedagogy from the exclusive discourse of schooling or other formal contexts requires a reconsideration of the relationship between theoretical stance, pedagogical context and resulting methodological approach. Within these new research sites for pedagogy, the researcher has to answer the question of what researching pedagogy could look like in this context, using these particular data sources as evidence. Case example 6.1 provides some guidance on answering this question, as Wikeley et al. (2007) explore the differences between learning relationships in and out of school. In out-of-school activities, power is more evenly distributed. Adults are seen as a part of the activity, and as co-learners rather than as part of the system. There is more equal interaction and young people's active participation in activities is defined by choice. There is more meaningful identity development, more enjoyment, personal intent and motivation compared to school activities, with young people becoming involved for purposes of social connection, pleasure and friendship.

Summarizing the values of out-of-school activities for researchers, Roth and Lee (2006) claim that out-of-school activities provide authentic learning and that their value lies in their difference to in-school activities. Briefly exemplifying this authentic learning, the findings of Wikeley et al. (2007) suggest that in these out-of-school activities the young people learned and employed a language and vocabulary that highlighted not only their developing expertise but the ways in which they were becoming members of a community of practice through this shared vocabulary and practice. Awards, performances and continuation of the activities, even into adult life, provided young people with tangible evidence and trajectories for meaningful identity development. The activities and events became significant life experiences for the young people involved, in ways that are difficult to achieve and make visible in classroom practice.

Thinking about the implications of the methods and findings from the research of Wikeley et al. (2007), we see that the researcher as meaning-maker needs research methods that make visible the role of learning relationships. A methodological focus on everyday out-of-school activities allowed these researchers to make visible the authentic and meaningful relationships, interactions and experiences at the heart of teaching and learning in informal pedagogical practice. In the absence of a formal curriculum and a teacher in the traditional sense, young people showed commitment, motivation, learning and an awareness as they participated in diverse after-school activities. The process of moving from legitimate peripheral participation to full member status in these after-school activities resulted from relationships and experiences in communities of practice that are different from school communities of practice, relationships and experiences. Phenomenological methods capturing this allow researchers to make visible the emergent nature of learning as identity development in communities, produced and producing in different contexts.

Taking a phenomenological approach, by attempting to identify the meaning behind the educational relationships experienced by this group of young people, the data and findings in the study by Wikeley et al. (2007) tell a story of learning in various out-of-school activities for one group of adolescents in England. What this study and setting makes particularly visible is a method of researching teaching and learning that privileges the social aspects of learning, relationships, community, experience and identity. In relation to this, it is significant that where (in- or out-of-school/formal settings) and what (in terms of what constitutes a pedagogical text) is researched directly influences how the researcher develops the study and ultimately what is visible and invisible in the analysis and findings. On all levels and in all ways, the researcher of another community of practice makes meaning of experience in ways that can be positive or detrimental to that community. We bear this in mind when we turn to case example 6.2, which explores a research project in Australia taking an ethnographic approach to a study of students' out-of-school experiences of and with literacy practice.

Researcher as ethnographer: Journeys in communities of practice

Ethnographic studies examine the social order by 'combining a phenomenological sensibility with a paramount concern for everyday social practice' (Gubrium and Holstein 2000: 490). According to Harris and Johnson (2000: 77–8), ethnography 'literally means "a portrait of a people" … a written description of a particular culture – the customs, beliefs and behavior, based on information collected through fieldwork'. This involves the ethnographer participating in, and observing, people's daily lives. The focus in phenomenology remains on the meaning of an experience for individuals, which becomes a collective in data analysis as the researcher looks to distil the essence of this experience for participants. Ethnography, in contrast, makes visible the many ways in which individuals do not exist alone and how their positions and agency in communities of practice influence their experience in these communities. Table 6.2 summarizes an ethnographic approach to research.

Table 6.2 Ethnography as method

Nature of questions asked	● what are the experiences of a culture or group of people in one community of practice? what are the patterns of practice, beliefs, values, behaviour and language and the meaning behind these?
Role of the researcher	● making explicit the tacit and invisible knowledge held by the group under study
Goal of the research	● describing and interpreting the experiences shared by a culture or group of people ● exploring useful dimensions with social phenomena, for example issues of power within a group
Data collection	● participant observation, interviews (including conversations) and document analysis in naturalistic settings ● unstructured and extended time spent in the field ● key informants identified with whom the researcher works more closely than other participants
Data presentation	● narrative ● direct quotes only alongside interpretation of their meaning by the researcher
Data analysis	● often simultaneous with data collection ● categories for interpreting practice are not pregiven or fixed ● descriptions and explanations which may be organized thematically
Meaning of evidence	● portrait of the group of people and how they interact, share their practices, etc. ● portrait emerges from both the descriptions of the participants and the interpretations of the researcher
Measurement	● narrative approach to making meaning of experiences in communities of practice
Ethics	● concern with respect and reciprocity ● openness with participants about nature and aims of the study ● work to ensure that researcher is not compromised as a result of engagement in the community of practice and that community is not comprised either

The following Australian case example 6.2 positions researchers as ethnographers as they visit, observe and interact with students in out-of-school contexts and settings. Engaging with the experiences and lives of their students in this way, teacher-researchers make meaning from these experiences and turn around their thinking about pedagogy and research in many different ways. The effects that their experiences of grappling with everyday practices of their students had on their own pedagogies and identities are evident in accounts of the project from many of the paired early and late career teacher-researchers (Pickering and Painter 2005; Duck and Hutchison 2005). More significant for us in this section, however, is an exploration of the ways in which their thinking as researchers developed over the course of the project.

Case example 6.2: Turn around pedagogies in South Australia and Victoria (Kamler and Comber 2005)

Context: A cross-generational teacher research project in South Australia and Victoria to explore challenges faced by teachers in their daily practice.

Goals: To investigate unequal literacy outcomes in the classroom by exploring student home and family life and experiences, and to develop from these experiences curricular interventions to help at-risk students.

Outcomes: The research showed students not 'in deficit' (Comber and Kamler 2004), but instead having rich potential resources that remained invisible in the school context. Researchers evidenced young people being inducted into important aspects of their cultures (fishing, camping, family practices, etc.). Researchers documented changes in attitude and engagement through pedagogic intervention and these changes were sustained beyond the popular theme or topic into new units of work.

Research methods: A three-year longitudinal study involving twenty teachers (ten early career and ten late career) participating in teacher-researcher networks. Teachers carried out observation

Case example 6.2

in their own classroom and took many opportunities to interview and talk to each other about their experiences of literacy. Early and late career teachers interviewed each other to see what each could learn from the experiences of the other. Teachers then conducted an audit of their own classroom literacy curriculum – what it made available and its effects on different students. They then selected a student (or students) having problems with literacy and sought to learn about them as people. Researchers completed home visits, interviews, informal chats with parents, informal interviewing and surveying of students.

Making the turn: Connecting curriculum, pedagogy and experience

Kamler and Comber (2005) use the metaphor of turning around in this research to identify the pedagogic, curricular and people work undertaken as method to improve student literacy in the classroom. The interplay visible in this study between pedagogy, formal learning intentions (curriculum) and understanding the importance of experiences outside of the classroom is of real significance for methodological design in out-of-school settings. Their use of the term 'turn around pedagogies' to define literacy gains through everyday processes that may not be easy to measure (rather than miraculous and dramatic changes in practice) speaks to a research methodology and an understanding of pedagogy centred on everyday and out-of-school relationships, identities and communities of practice.

The turn within this study is both physical and methodological, based in the world of the everyday and the world of research. In everyday practice, the physical and embodied turn taken by teacher-researchers shifts their understanding of the children and their families in different contexts, as they see them through a different lens. In research practice and methodology, the teacher-researchers shifted their perspective to a more informed and sociological analysis of diversity and literacy. These shifts in their identity and positioning to seeing themselves as differently expert among other participants in a shared practice disrupt the taken-for-granted practices of their classrooms. It makes visible for them, as researchers, the connections between curriculum, pedagogy and experience of in- and out-of-school learning. This moment of insight is explained by two researchers in the study in their own words:

> First we noticed that when teachers recognised their students' expertise and met it with their own expertise as educators, students were able to 'turn around' to literacy. This delicate balancing of teacher and student expertise created new spaces for students to develop a wider repertoire of literacy practices, and also allowed teachers to expand their range of strategies to incorporate children's everyday language and literacy practices as resources for school success. Second, when teachers communicated with parents and carers in ways that opened up different kinds of conversations, they gained insights into the histories, privileges and disadvantages of family lives as well as the children's out of school practices and interests. ... The privileging of traditional school literacy practices was supplanted by a dynamic connection between the worlds of home and school through these new literacies. Videos, CDs, powerpoint animations, e-books and films moved between home and school as literacy artefacts, which had 'currency' in both environments. (Kerkham and Hutchison 2005: 110)

Their out-of-school experiences with young people allowed the teacher-researchers to understand teaching and learning in a new way and reinvent their pedagogical practice. For example, they studied the movie *Shrek* and made e-books, using *The Simpsons* as a resource. They reconnected the refusing male writers by reinventing writing as a social and performative practice, developing technology-rich tasks such as constructing radio programmes and video stores of child-directed films and working with out-of-school knowledge and digital recordings of activities to reimagine writing pedagogy. The teacher-researchers documented how surprised they were about the success of their methodological interventions, sometimes against all odds. Through a small change in perspective and method in an exploration of the everyday experiences of their students, researchers in their in-school pedagogical practice positioned students not as failures, but as successes.

It may be common to think of ethnography in terms of either getting to understand a new/alien culture or getting to know a familiar culture afresh. Alvesson (2009: 159) brings us the concept of '**at-home ethnography,** which is about doing research in our own setting, in which we have "natural access" as an already "active participant"'. In this study, and in this kind of pedagogical research, researchers experience movement between traditional and at-home ethnography as they move in and out of settings that are known and comfortable, from those easy to access to those more challenging to get into. The at-home dimension is relevant in terms of the research questions addressed, which Alvesson distinguishes: instead of 'what the hell do *they* think they are up to?', the question becomes 'what the hell do *we* think we are up to?' (p. 162). In this case, a critical research method is to employ reflexivity, crucial in any exploration of the everyday. While the aim may be to leave the everyday out-of-school cultures undisrupted by the research, it is not to leave pedagogical practice unchanged as a result.

In Alicia's own experiences in out-of-school settings, she understood from the outset the power of investigation of everyday practice to change the experiences and identities of students and of researchers in both school and everyday settings. Engaging with different communities of practice asks the researcher to understand themes under study in new ways as she interprets and develops shared meanings about the qualities of the experiences of her participants through ethnography. This outcome is common in studies that explore out-of-school practices and methodologies, and makes visible the interplay between formal and informal pedagogies and research. The challenge for the teacher-researcher is to decide how to fuse in- and out-of-school experiences together in an organic and meaningful way for their students. This struggle was clearly apparent for the researchers in case example 6.2 as, at times, what was perceived as failure or disappointment in relation to the intervention required a deeper researcher understanding of methodology and a consideration of other lenses that could be applied to understand classroom experiences. An example of this is the experience of some researchers who, though prioritizing out-of-school experience and expertise in their pedagogical design, still expected students to produce written texts to make visible their learning in the classroom (Kamler and Comber 2008).

This difficulty faced by researchers, of how they should represent what they have experienced out-of-school in the development of their own pedagogy, is central to a consideration of out-of-school research methodologies and the journey of every researcher in these settings. It is difficult to extend to classroom practice the diversity of experiences in out-of-school experiences; it requires us to draw on personal experiences beyond that of being a researcher or teacher, but to think about our experiences as a parent or committee member, or part of our many different communities of practice.

An example of a meaningful interplay between home and school worlds is found in the UK Home School Knowledge Exchange Project (Hughes and Pollard 2006). Activities that were understood to bring home into school as part of the methodology included

- children's use of disposable cameras to photograph relevant aspects of their out-of-school lives to link to class topics and to use in writing activities involving parents and siblings;

- children's use of shoeboxes filled with personal possessions and artefacts from home, to support literacy and other activities across the curriculum and

- teachers' inclusive home visits to parents reluctant to visit schools themselves, to develop a trusting relationship between partners in learning.

School was taken into home in this study through

- guidance sheets, booklets and newsletters produced that gave information on the teaching and learning in the school, and that were translated and adopted into community languages, where appropriate;

- showings of videos made and edited in school to parents and family members, and providing copies for family members to watch at home and

- exhibiting student literacy and learning work in out-of-school sites such as the local supermarket, to provide access for parents and family who might not normally have attended such events in school.

In out-of-school research, we may need to experiment with research methods to create such meaningful interplays as those highlighted in the Home School Knowledge Exchange Project. Kamler and Comber (2005) explain that much time is needed to induct researchers into chosen research repertoires, but when successful, as in their project, teacher-researchers may see themselves as agents of change and leaders in their own schools. This is a powerful by-product of engaging in research. Tracing the researcher trajectory from the beginning of an out-of-school research project to its fruition reveals a journey fraught with tension and uncertainty. If, as researchers, we are outsiders to these practices, we have to work against the grain and, contrary to the advice of Van Maanen (1995), we must use research methods that simultaneously make the familiar strange and the strange familiar if we are to develop pedagogical practice in any meaningful way.

Experiences of researchers with out-of-school research methodologies

Cremin et al. (2015), in a newly published book on a recent UK research project, *Researching Literacy Lives: Building Communities between Home and School,* devote a chapter to exploring researcher dispositions. They include some interesting points for understanding in more detail the researcher journey in out-of-school research. Bearing in mind the contexts and stories of research methods explored thus far in this chapter, we introduce some of the more complex issues faced by researchers on their research journeys in these contexts.

Cremin et al. (2015) found it difficult to move from the relative safety of their expertise and classroom practice to the unnatural and unknown terrain of the experience of their students and their families. Anxieties arose for researchers regarding relinquishing power in this shift of territories and discourses, from school to the everyday, from pedagogy to ethnography, and from teacher to learner. Researchers lacked confidence at the outset about entering unfamiliar territory, coping with the openness of ethnographic and out-of-school research methods, and knowing what to look for within (or without) these parameters. They had to develop different kinds of relationships with their students and parents, as called for in the research. As the research methodology developed, so the researchers developed concerns around the nature of research undertaken. These included worrying about their methods in terms of what they should be recording, difficulties experienced listening and making notes at the same time, confusion about what they should do with all the rich data being collected, and concern about the structure and validity of those data. They also reported that the ethnographic home visits (similar to those in our Australian case example) triggered emotions for which they felt unprepared, and in these contexts they did not want to be seen to be intruding or judging the experiences of others. Finally, when it came to writing up their experiences, they lacked confidence again and many worried about 'getting it right' in their representations.

As the researchers visited homes and engaged in the everyday practices of their students, they became positioned differently and, as with any change in position, this both afforded and constrained different aspects of their own identity development and practice. Cremin et al. (2015: 172) conclude, in relation to the journey on which out-of-school research methods take the researcher, that 'research undertaken within the boundaries of their classrooms would not have afforded the same opportunities, nor might it have encouraged the same degree of discomfort, challenge and risk-taking'. They quote Lytle (2008: 373), who explains,

> The real stuff of teacher research isn't safe. It is radical and passionate, deeply personal and profoundly political – richly embedded in situations where the teacher's stance on her own practice and intellectual life matter, and where teachers' work lives, commitments, and relationships are complex and entangled.

Analysing data in out-of-school settings: Identity as method

Out-of-school phenomenological and ethnographic research methods that explore everyday practice often rely on the identity development and learning trajectories of participants to make meaning and build theory. Wenger's (1998) sociocultural *Communities of*

Practice: Learning, Meaning and Identity, though by no means a methodological text, is rich with understandings of the role of concepts such as practice, meaning, community and identity in learning and pedagogical practice. Understanding identity through processes such as participation, reification, socialization, meaning, belonging, negotiation, engagement, membership and the interplay between the global and the local requires the researcher to weigh up the grains and textures of experience in particular contexts, to imagine and define how these experiences add up to produce and reproduce meaningful identities and opportunities for agency for participants in a particular community of practice. This is evident in case example 6.3.

Case example 6.3: The literacy practices of gangsta adolescents in Utah, USA (Moje 2000)

Context: A three-year study undertaken in Salt Lake City, Utah, USA of the complex meanings a group of adolescents made about literacy, gang practices and their lives through their everyday practice.

Goals: To find 'what constitutes alternative or unsanctioned literacy and how adolescents learn and use different literacies at school, at home, and in their unsanctioned social groups. To explore what these unsanctioned literacies accomplish for adolescents' (Moje 2000: 653).

Outcomes: Illumination of how gang-connected youth use their literacy practices as meaning-making, expressive and communicative tools. Their engagement in unsanctioned literacy practice allows them to claim a space and construct an identity in different communities of practice. Understanding that to develop practice, teachers need to provide students with pedagogies that draw on, challenge and extend their own practices in everyday settings.

Research methods: Drawn from a cultural studies perspective, not seeking to present the truth of people's lives but to understand the meanings that people make and examine the complexity and contradiction of everyday practice (Moje 2000). Classroom data

Case example 6.3

collected by spending two days a week in two English classrooms in Utah for the entire school year, along with spending lunch times with students. Students were also interviewed and, in the final year of the study, the researcher 'hung out' with three focus students and became more a part of their social and family practices, such as attending church, going shopping or to the movies and so on. Data sources included daily field notes in and out-of-school, audio and videotape recordings of classroom interactions, formal and informal interviews with students, teachers, parents and school administrators, email communications, artefacts and documents, photographs and a researcher's journal.

Moje (2000) uses the concept of identity as a research and data analysis tool to position gangsta youth as makers of meaning through their literacy practices. As a rationale for this, she explains that if we, as researchers, want to expand our understanding of concepts such as literacy and learning, then we also have to extend our research to ask what experiences in everyday practice *do* for adolescents and how they learn and develop their identities through this practice. Moje's methodology replaces the roles, rules and routines of the school day with graffiti as a way of conveying, constructing and maintaining identity, thought and power, as the young people were extremely motivated to internalize gang writing styles but not conventional ones. In school this had been seen by teachers as acts of resistance, but Moje's out-of-school experiences with these young people show the role of graffiti in the development of meaningful identity.

Acknowledging that these gangsta practices and emergent identities may be reproductive of marginalized positions for the young people in this study, Moje employed a methodology that asks what aspects of these practices may also be empowering and productive. Her participants learned to remain a part of the story, to preserve and produce a meaningful identity. They recognized early on the limitations of school literacies for their own lives and only used these when absolutely necessary. Their everyday practice illustrates the situated and community-based nature of their learning within a complicated hierarchy of gang relations, language, rules and routines. Their manipulation of language and codes betray the learning as Moje makes visible the many different ways in which these young people explore themselves and their world in everyday learning contexts.

Central to Moje's research design is the need to make visible the way in which these literacy practices are taught and learned in everyday practice. Developing out-of-school and identity research projects in an inclusive, rather than a marginalizing, way becomes a central concern and responsibility for the researcher of everyday practice. Some of the research communities of practice in out-of-school settings may be unfamiliar to the researcher, but the researcher must engage with and aim to understand the practices of the communities in which they undertake research (in ways explored in the further reading recommended for this chapter), rather than taking an evaluative or judgemental stance.

Challenges of out-of-school research methodologies

Case example 6.3 throws up many problems for researchers of pedagogy. Moje (2000) positions these young people in their out-of-school practices as successful and motivated learners while reminding us that their classroom teachers would not see them in this same way. Within gang practices, however, Moje's methods show how young people were provided with stories to tell about their lives. Focusing on methods that prioritize and collect details about the identities of participants allowed Moje to make visible how these young people construct emerging identities and become a part of a larger, emergent story of a community of practice. Unlike classroom practice, where they were passive watchers of the stories of others, here they were active agents – and seen to be active agents – in their own agentic identity development. What was said and done really mattered, as it made the young people who they were in very real terms, while Moje's methodological approach made visible their learning practices in terms of identity development. Meeting students in out-of-school contexts allowed

Moje to consider also aspects of identity such as dress, colours, bodily and embodied practices and reactions, and interactions of others to these in everyday and wider community contexts, something which would have been invisible in daily classroom practice and interactions. The out-of-school context also gave Moje scope for her methods. It allowed her to explore tagging (a style of graffiti where buildings, property etc. are 'tagged' or marked with an individual or group/gang name, symbol or 'tag') as an authentic and meaningful tool of identity construction and representation for young people, in a way that would not have been possible in school, as it is risky for students to engage in tagging on school grounds.

This experience contrasted with Moje's (2000) experience of the in-class observation phase of her methodology as she witnessed the students' attempts to keep academic and social practices separate and covert, with code switching between what they felt was acceptable in these contexts. This caused a problem for Moje in her exploration of pedagogy and learning in class, as the young people presented with a 'version' of identity and learning practice. Though Moje experienced similar concerns to those discussed in the previous section on researching pedagogy through ethnography in out-of-school settings, the sophisticated appreciation in her findings for the aspects of out-of-school life that she argues teachers should consider in the development of their pedagogies indicates the value of this kind of research methods. She explains how, as the research progressed, she experienced change in her own identity, and committed herself to be an advocate for these young people in a way that would allow their practices to be understood. This created methodological difficulties around representation for Moje, as she worried about her ability to achieve this aim. As an ethnographer, she shadowed and shared the lived experiences of a number of her participants, but she did this as a trusted adult, and not an adolescent or another 'gangsta'. Because of this, she explains that she does not claim to have the kinds of understandings of the young people's worlds and experiences that they themselves do. The technicalities of her role of researcher also brought methodological concerns, as she employed research tools such as critical discourse analysis, but in a way that would present these analyses as speaking with the adolescents, rather than for them.

Moje (2000) makes the interesting point that, though she is often complimented for her interest in out-of-school practice, she is just as often asked how this research can make any contribution to school pedagogy, curriculum and practice. This signifies a real problem for out-of-school pedagogy researchers, as the implication is that teachers do not have the time to think about these issues. Moje tackles this problem directly in her research and makes visible the many ways in which interplay between in and out-of-school is central to the development of our understanding and practice of pedagogy.

Moje's (2000) out-of-school ethnographic and identity-based methodology presents students who tell stories that allow them ways of being a part of a group that value their experiences. The communities of practice support the young people in an articulation of meaningful literacy practice that develop the shared practice and identities of all the participants. These literacy practices of tagging, rhyming, specialist language and vocabulary, made visible through Moje's methods, evidenced a high level of metalinguistic awareness in wordplay and alternative spelling, but the value of this was obscured from sight in the classroom where the context identified these practices as deviant and resistant. Moje shows that the opposite is true, as in school practices these young people tried to write themselves into the story the only way they knew how, using the practices and literacies meaningful to them. In school practice, what was intended and what was observed just did not match up. Significantly, drawing on the interplay between school and everyday practices and literacies, Moje's ethnographic study illustrates how school practice controlled, silenced or dismissed these young people.

Speaking of the paradoxical power for transformation and tragedy that these gangsta processes have for the young people in her study, Moje (2000) asserts that gangster activity has changed the face of schooling in many ways and this is something that we cannot ignore. For Moje, however, the tragedy lies not in that young people reproduce their own marginalization but that the social spaces these young people inhabit are often devalued and vilified in school and social discourses and methods. Moje argues for a very sophisticated interplay of in and out-of-school methodology and research, whereby we should cultivate methods and pedagogies which should encourage students to begin to see themselves as thinkers and agents of change, developing their own identities (and the identities available to them) through a focus on questioning the value of practice in different contexts in a way that also challenges dominant assumptions about learning and social practice. Applying this research to her own development of pedagogy, Moje (2000: 684) illustrates how she has tried to 'revision existing pedagogies to engage students in action oriented reading and writing projects that teach kids how to use their metadiscursive knowledge to read how the past informs the present and how the present informs the past'.

Conclusion

This chapter has explored methods for out-of-school and everyday research studies keeping central the role, concerns and experiences of researchers and where innovative contexts lead to innovative thinking about methods. The many examples of out-of-school research studies discussed in the chapter offer possible approaches for researchers looking beyond the school gates and can be used as a taster menu of out-of-school research activities and methods to address them. Each study we have included offers examples of what research in these contexts might look like; they pursue and suggest the interplay between in- and out-of-school pedagogic research. Completing research in informal and everyday contexts creates affordances and constraints for the researcher of pedagogy, and this chapter exemplifies some of these through a focus on researcher thinking and experiences. You may want to discuss with peers or advisers from out-of-school contexts any methods that you propose to take outside of the institutional context.

Further reading

Cremin, T., M. Mottram, F. Collins, S. Powell and R. Drury (2015), *Researching Literacy Lives: Building Communities between Home and School*. Oxon: Routledge. This book offers a number of detailed and insider perspectives on completing research in in- and out-of-school contexts.

Moje, E. B. (2000), 'Circles of Kinship, Friendship, Position, and Power: Examining the Community in Community-Based Literacy Research', *Journal of Literacy Research*, 32: 77–112. This article examines various definitions of 'community' as understood in a number of out-of-school research studies, and explores how and why researchers in out-of-school communities and practices must complicate, question and define what is meant by this term.

Wenger, E. (1998), *Communities of Practice: Learning, Meaning and Identity*, Cambridge: Cambridge University Press. This book explores the learning experiences of a community of practice of claims processing workers through themes such as practice, meaning, community, boundaries, identities and belonging.

PART THREE
Researching the hidden and hard-to-know

Introduction to part three: Researching the hidden and hard-to-know

Part Three concludes our exploration of research methods for pedagogy through consideration of the often invisible complexities of pedagogy. Here we focus on elements of pedagogy that are not easy to talk about or even observe, necessitating research approaches and methods that can begin to reach the hidden and the hard-to-know. These are methods geared to that which is discreet, elusive, endemic, obscured, intrinsic and ingrained in pedagogical practices. These chapters centre on the relational aspects of pedagogic interactions and pedagogy research.

Chapter 7 asks the researcher to consider pedagogy as a set of interactions that are always dynamic, fluid, transactional and contingent on the interactive partners and context. Within these interactions, motives and intentions may be obscured and making these visible becomes the primary task of the research approach. Engaging with this task this chapter discusses the ethical issues and vulnerabilities inherent in researching pedagogy as interaction, suggesting that researchers and research gain from doing research *with* participants rather than *on* them. Methods for making the invisible visible in pedagogical research are described and exemplified, including **think-aloud methods, lesson study** and stimulated recall, reflection and dialogue. In examining such methods we also probe their associated technical, representational and ethical challenges. A UK case example of method development in one of our own studies provides the central real life context for this chapter.

Chapter 8 moves the focus onto what is hidden and hard to know in pedagogical research, from the minds of teachers and learners to their bodies and bodily realities. We explore how pedagogy is embodied, and the implications of this for generating and analysing data. Case examples from Australia and Denmark are used to examine how researchers can get up close to pedagogic situations through an understanding of bodies as text.

Chapter 9 continues our exploration of methods to get at the hard-to-know in pedagogical research through an analysis of the role of space in teaching–learning relationships. Here, space as understood in pedagogical research is defined and explained in terms of its physical, social, temporal, experiential and virtual elements. Case examples range across settings in Australia, the United States, the United Kingdom, Finland and worldwide (in the shape of an online ethnography). These exemplify suitable methods for interrogating space in pedagogical research, including verbal, visual, observational, ethnographic, textual, audiovisual, technological and participatory action research approaches/methods. Throughout our discussion here, at the centre is the conception of the various elements of space in pedagogical research as interlinked chains that become a part of the moment in our day-to-day pedagogical practice.

CHAPTER SEVEN

Pedagogy as interaction: Methods for reflecting on interaction and methods using collaborative interaction

Introduction

We begin this final section of the book dedicated to research methods that are suited to the complexity of pedagogic research with a focus on the thinking that lies behind or beneath pedagogic interactions. It can be useful to think about pedagogy as a set of interactions: between teachers and learners, teachers and teachers, learners and learners, teachers, learners and the curriculum and so on. This, though, leads us into the realms of the complexity associated with researching interactions as interactions are always dynamic; they are fluid and transactional, contingent on the interactive partners and context. As we discussed in Chapter 5, researching interaction and classroom talk asks researchers to make many different decisions (e.g. on methods for collection and recording of data, analytical frames, researcher actions, interpretation, representation, etc.) and the decisions researchers make will result in contrasting elements of pedagogical interactions, intentions and practices becoming more or less visible in the research field. Examples of research in earlier chapters have similarly illustrated that we cannot necessarily just see or capture what is going on in pedagogic interactions, or have the people involved describe them to us. This is because what is going on in those interactions is part of what is hard to know about pedagogy: the motives, for example, may be elusive; the teacher intentions may be obscured; the common-sense assumptions may make the pedagogic knowledge being applied inaccessible, even to the teacher involved. In Chapter 5 we attended specifically to interaction as talk; in this chapter we acknowledge and discuss interaction as involving all engagements among the classroom participants as well as the meanings of those engagements for the participants. This requires tuning in to evidence and insights that are available to us through our senses and, crucially, through our sense making.

As soon as researchers start examining people's interactions, ethical issues come to the fore. Interactions are part of people: they belong to them; they reflect them and reflect on them; and they bring their thinking to life, with or without their conscious control. Therefore, to examine those interactions is to make people vulnerable, it is to position them as the subjects of our professional gaze. One way to avoid this, or to address the power dynamic that makes such research uncomfortable for some of us, is to examine pedagogic interactions *with* teachers, learners or both. In this chapter, therefore, while we explore methods that focus on interactions for their value in teasing out the more elusive dimensions of pedagogy, we go on to explore the ways that these research methods can become inclusive, collaborative or dialogic.

Interaction: The seen and unseen of pedagogy

Chapter 5 illuminated research methods that focused on what the researcher can see and especially hear in classrooms. Here we enter further into what looking and listening can tell the researcher (and teacher and learner) about what is going on between people. We focus, moreover, on methods for researching why pedagogic interactions are unfolding as they are – about what cannot necessarily be readily seen or heard. In researching pedagogic decision-making, for example, methods are required that make maximum use of our human capacities to sense (utilize our senses) and to make sense (utilize our ability to reflect). As with previous examples in the book (e.g. the action research and pedagogical documentation discussed in Chapter 4), methods that work for teachers' purposes and methods that work for researchers' purposes often overlap or blend. In this chapter these methods often involve using video as a reflection tool.

Pedagogic approaches that consciously foreground the quality of the interactions and the reflections informing this have fostered particular kinds of research also. Melanie and colleagues (Nind and Hewett 1994) developed *Intensive Interaction* as a pedagogical approach for fostering learning in people with profound and complex learning disabilities. The approach is characterized by regular, frequent interactions between practitioner and learner in which the primary concern is the quality of the interaction rather than any task or outcome. It is based on evidence and theory from research on caregiver interactions and involves practitioners being playful, making micro-adjustments to their interpersonal behaviours and to the tempo and rhythm of the interactions, imputing communication significance to learners' behaviours and responding contingently to put them into the role of leading the interaction.

Researching this pedagogy necessitated a close look at the interactions to inform how it is enacted (Nind and Cochrane 2002; Kellett and Nind 2003) and to know whether it is effective (Nind 1996). The whole approach requires the practitioner to reflect on what happened, what was significant and how it felt (Nind and Hewett 2001), and to use video to help with this. The teacher cannot be a technician in this process; she or he needs subtlety, empathy and skill to enhance the sensitivity of the contingent responding, the matching of the tempo and mood, the playfulness and the judgements. In *Intensive Interaction*, teachers (and other practitioners) are acting like action researchers in a microcosm, continually gathering and analysing data, interpreting and reflecting on the data to plan and adapt their next moves and so again and again. Researching what is happening – the process – has involved combining microdata gleaned from video with microdata from real time observation and with reflective data. Researching the learning as process and product has involved methods to gain the same kinds of data, but systematically over a prolonged time and within some kind of **quasi-experimental design** to retain the naturalistic context yet deal with the research threat of extraneous variables.

Melanie (Nind 1996) used a multiple baseline across subject interrupted **time series design** (Cook and Campbell 1979). This involves capturing data at multiple data points rather than just before and after an intervention, and allows the researcher to measure changes (e.g. in the learners' interactive behaviours) against their own individual baselines (in terms of level and trend). Replication logic applied to the evidence generated by doing this with different learners moving from baseline to intervention at difference points strengthens any claim that the intervention was the most plausible cause of change in the learners. This is an interesting way of using data about interactions, and what can be sensed and inferred, within a more positivist framework. Melanie chose this approach as a robust one for the research to be able to say something about the efficacy of the pedagogy. She could equally have used **practice-based inquiry** or action research approach in that, with fellow practitioners, she was developing the pedagogy by applying theory from the interactions between caregivers and infants (not traditionally seen as pedagogic, but powerfully fostering holistic learning) to a new pedagogic context, continually learning about and adjusting the practice. The action research methodological choice, though, would have suited a different research purpose to the one of making causal claims connecting process and outcome.

Video Interaction Guidance (VIG), like *Intensive Interaction*, is an approach that makes use of the power of interaction and reflection on that interaction. It is described as an intervention where interactive partners are guided to reflect on video clips of their own successful interactions. They become active in working towards better relationships with others by interaction 'guiders', who are themselves guided by the values and beliefs of respect and empowerment (Kennedy and Landor 2015). Again, this is not an approach that is intended as a research method, but one that has affordances for researchers with a transformational orientation. Interaction involves performance, and its various aspects can be subjected to scrutiny and review.

Pedagogically, the intention of VIG is to share and discuss meanings and effects of those aspects under scrutiny. There is considerable overlap with researcher intentions to understand how meanings are shared and how effects are accomplished. The person facing challenges in their interactions and relationships chooses what they see as a successful interaction for the video recording. The person guiding them chooses small, positive parts of the video to discuss. Echoing aspects of action research, the approach works by using micro-moments of attuned interaction as building blocks for wider interaction patterns, with parents or practitioners helping to observe, reflect, review and make changes. This is not so much about learning to interact better, but building the relationships in which helpful interactions naturally occur. In pedagogic contexts, the approach has been adapted into video-enhanced reflection on practice (Kennedy, Landor and Todd 2015) aimed at making a significant contribution to professional development.

Methods such as these explored thus far allow researchers to examine interactions and generate evidence about pedagogic processes and products. However, an understanding of the hidden and hard-to-know in pedagogical research also demands methods that foster active engagement with participants through the evocation of embodied (see Chapter 8) and sensual responses. As Vesterinen, Toom and Patrikainen (2010: 183) remind us, 'It is not easy to explore the pedagogical thinking of teachers by using traditional observation methods.' Ethnographers may use participant observation to gain insights into why teachers teach and interact as they do, and **autoethnography** may offer insights into motivations underlying practices. As Dempsey (2010) concludes, however, researchers applying these methods can be frustrated, for example, by the function of not being able to remember that may come into play when informants retrospectively describe their pedagogic interactions. This frustration is about the challenge of getting inside the interactions and inside the heads of the interactive partners in the pedagogic (or whatever) encounter.

The methods may need to allow asking participants to feel again how they felt, and to share it with the researcher, making visible the hard-to-see and hard-to-know to which we have been alluding. Even for the participant, this can be new territory to be sensed and made sense of, because these hard-to-know pedagogical elements have not been seen or known by them either, rather just felt and experienced from moment to moment. It is only through the research process itself that particular elements of the pedagogical encounter can become seen or known, dependent on the research method in place in ways we explore throughout this book. Dempsey's (ibid.)

answer to the conundrum he poses is the research technique of the stimulated recall interview, which 'brings informants a step closer to the moments in which they actually produce action. It gives them the chance to listen or view themselves in action, jog memories and give answers of '"I did", instead of "I might have"' (p. 350). We discuss this research method in detail later in the chapter, but first we expand on what it is that we, as researchers of pedagogy and pedagogic interactions, might want to make visible and knowable through a focus on sensing and sense making.

If we temporarily limit our attention to teachers rather than learners, there is a component of educational or pedagogic research related to teacher expertise that Shulman (1986) influentially argued was missing. He drew the attention of researchers to questions of how teachers formulate explanations, decide on content and how to represent it, and how they interact with the mis/understanding of learners. Researchers were already aware of the importance of teachers' various forms of applied knowledge of content, curricula, learners and educational 'ends'. Shulman though, highlighted an unstudied form of teacher knowledge – how knowledge of the content to be taught is transformed into a form that is comprehensible to learners. This, he proposes, involves mixing general pedagogical knowledge – the 'broad principles and strategies of classroom management and organization that appear to transcend subject matter' (Shulman 1987: 8) – and (more elusive for the researcher) pedagogical content knowledge (PCK) – pedagogical knowledge specific to the subject matter. Since Shulman introduced the idea of PCK, the concept has taken hold in teacher education with adaptations (Kind 2009). The challenge for researchers, however, is how to develop research methods that can elicit this crucially important PCK.

It is not the case that teachers can simply tell researchers about the basis of their decisions to present ideas in particular ways, choosing particular analogies and examples over others. This, Kind (2009) argues, is active know*ing*. It is the 'craft knowledge' we discussed in Chapter 3 – the practical wisdom that interacts with theoretical knowledge. Such knowledge is tacit, practical and situated (Traianou 2006). We cannot make it visible just by observing teaching, or through interviewing teachers about their teaching. Developing PCK involves the complex interaction of dynamic forces that, if identifiable, teachers can reflect on to transform their pedagogical practices for the better (Özmanter 2011). This has led researchers to seek methods to glean insights into PCK associated with particular pedagogical practices, to make it visible through a combination of observing and interviewing involving **video-stimulated recall** and reflection (Nind, Kilburn and Wiles 2015).

'Gaining access to the thoughts and decision making of others is intrinsic to the endeavour of many social scientists' (Calderhead 1981: 211), but in pedagogy research this takes on practical importance. Calderhead (ibid.) argues that observation itself, whether systematic or participatory, leaves gaps in our knowledge of teaching processes; with teaching being a goal-directed activity, some researchers of pedagogy seek to understand the thinking behind it. Examining teachers' pedagogical thinking has been a part of pedagogic research since the 1980s and there are many examples of studies of it in the United States (e.g. Clark and Peterson 1981; Shulman 1986) and the United Kingdom/Europe (e.g. Powell 2005; Trianou 2006; Vesterinen, Toom and Patrikainen 2010). Pedagogical thinking, knowledge and decision-making are important unseen dimensions of pedagogical interactions. There is a considerable literature on the importance of metacognition and of making thinking processes explicit and therefore more accessible and usable (Morgan 2007). Often, for a researcher of pedagogy, there is a desire to combine data about participants' actual behaviour and the thinking that comes with that behaviour. The latter can be complex, automated and difficult to access (Lyle 2003), and together the two necessitate a combination of methods (Fox-Turnbull 2009).

Methods for making pedagogical decision-making visible

Following Shulman's (1986) powerful argument that to understand the actions of teachers, we need to study their thought processes, evaluations, problem solving and decision-making, we now turn to research methods specifically designed to explore beneath what researchers can readily see in pedagogic interactions. We focus on

- think-aloud methods to research pedagogical thinking in the moment;

- lesson-study methods to research advance pedagogical thinking as it is enacted; and

- stimulated recall, **video-stimulated reflection** and video-stimulated dialogue, to look back at pedagogical thinking soon after the event.

Think-aloud methods

Starting with pedagogical thinking in the moment, Lyle (2003: 861) notes that the 'desire to collect data during the decision behaviour itself has prompted a long-standing and continuing debate about the extent to which "think aloud" techniques provide access to introspective, higher order mental processes'. Such techniques are well suited to artificial situations such as microteaching in professional development and experiments in problem solving. Indeed Thackray (2013) provides a good example of probing physiotherapists' clinical reasoning, using think-aloud techniques in a simulated environment to inform educational strategies for teaching this skill. The research allows her to identify the knowledge acquisition, knowledge storage and retrieval, information processing, cognitive skill development, metacognition and reflection involved and to embed these within a simulation learning strategy in an undergraduate physiotherapy programme. As Lyle argues, however, think-aloud techniques are inappropriate in research of naturalistic teaching situations involving significant verbal communication, real-life problem solving, high levels of interaction, emotive contexts or dynamic actions. It is simply impossible not to disrupt the pedagogic interaction if the teacher is seeking to verbalize the thinking going on (O'Brien 1993).

In the United States, Carson, Weiss and Templin (2010) have used the method of **ecological momentary assessment** (EMA) to capture the emotional states and behaviours of teachers over time. Using handheld personal digital assistants allowed the teachers to enter accurate data at convenient times for them, rather than wait to reflect back, thus avoiding 'retrieval distortion' (p. 165) and eliciting temporal patterns. This method is a form of experience sampling (Larson and Csikszentmihalyi 1983). In contrast to think-aloud methods, it works in recording phenomena as they happen in everyday life situations (Stone and Shiffman 1994). This is helpful when we face the reality that pedagogic interactions are transient in nature, which adds to the challenge of capturing them. In ecological momentary assessment, data are assessed at a moment in time in the field (in our case often the classroom), but there are many repeated data points. Carson, Weiss and Templin (2010: 166) argue that 'this data-gathering method allows researchers to address how phenomena fluctuate and progress over time rather than as a stable arrangement of "typical" experience often acquired in conventional one-time measures'.

The decisions the researcher using EMA has to make include: times for data collection (fixed, random, particular events); frequency of data collection and duration; nature of the data trigger; framing of the questions as about now, or since the last interval; and choice of instrument and software (Carson, Weiss and Templin 2010). There are ethical considerations in relation to the extent to which this might intrude on participants and what it might demand from them. The complex and extensive data generated often require sophisticated multilevel statistical analysis to allow researchers to 'simultaneously estimate effects at and across the moment (within-person), subject (between-person), and group (between-group) levels (Raudenbush and Bryk 2002; Reis and Gable 2000)' (ibid.: 168). Most powerful, perhaps, is the potential of this kind of method to connect teachers' behaviours and emotional states with things going on with learners or within classrooms. The method is relatively new in educational research, but Carson, Weiss and Templin (2010) found that teachers liked using it and readily engaged with it. The problems with missed data did not interfere with its viability, yet they propose there may be value in combining EMA with supplementary journaling by teachers in a mixed methods design. From our perspective (see our definitions in Chapter 1), the approach of EMA focuses strongly on the experience of the individual at a point in time, rather than on the dynamics of the relational. The emphasis is on the person's thoughts, experience and feelings – the intrapersonal, rather than necessarily the interactional and relational and interpersonal.

Think-aloud techniques can be categorized as a verbal report method within a group of process tracing methods (Shavelson, Webb and Burstein 1986: 79), which work to gain data on thinking processes in decision-making and problem-solving situations. The problems that Lyle (2003) raises have led researchers to seek alternative process tracing methods that take a retrospective rather than an in-the-moment approach, accessing the same in-class thinking but after the lesson. Indeed, as we discuss later in the chapter, researchers have applied this retrospective approach to tease out the thinking of learners while they are learning, as well as teachers while they are teaching. Marland and Osborne (1990, cited by Vesterinen, Toom and Patrikainen 2010) have referred to eliciting data that describe both interactive and post-interactive thinking. Other verbal reporting to the classic think-aloud self-revelation includes self-report on general principles and actions, and self-observation reporting on one's own action in a specific situation (Gass and Mackey 2000).

Lesson-study methods

Lesson study is a quite different approach that brings together thinking in different moments in time. This involves detailed thinking about a lesson (known as a 'research lesson') in the form of a detailed lesson plan, followed by detailed observation of how that teacher's planning and thinking is enacted, and further reflection in a post-lesson colloquium. These are the characteristics of the lesson-study method from Japan, where it is used as a 'teacher-led system for improvement of teaching and learning' (Cerbin and Kopp 2006: 250), which has become popular in the United States and has been adapted for research. Lewis, Enciso and Moje (2007: 3) describe lesson study as 'observation of live classroom lessons by a group of teachers who collect data on teaching and learning and collaboratively analyze it'. They explain that the observed research lessons are regarded not as an end in themselves, but as a window on the larger vision of education shared by the group of teachers, one of whom agrees to teach the lesson while the others make detailed records of the learning and teaching as it unfolds. Unlike the various stimulated recall methods we discuss in this chapter, the focus is on live observation with a video recording only for future, further review. In common with them, though, is the concept of making thinking visible; in this case it can be to make 'students' thinking visible ... open[ing] to observation and analysis' how they learn, thereby fostering PCK (Cerbin and Kopp 2006: 251).

The lesson-study method has been interpreted for research purposes in various ways. For example, the observers of the lesson may or may not see the detailed lesson plan in advance; data may take the form of impressionistic notes or structured observational records; and the relative emphasis on reflection or debate differs (Lewis, Enciso and Moje 2007). Messiou (2013) and colleagues across Europe have employed lesson-study methods within an action research framework to develop teachers' responses to diversity. They form research groups to discuss diversity, learning and teaching, then plan, teach and analyse research lessons, and draw out implications for future practice. Throughout the applications of lesson study, the evidence generated is meant to capture 'the complexity of actual teaching and learning' (Cerbin and Kopp 2006: 252). Cerbin and Kopp (2006) advocate lesson study for making the individual processes of planning and teaching more collegial, allowing teachers' knowledge to be accessed and used by others. The method is interesting for the way in which researchers study the thinking and practice of a lesson in tandem. It is often used in research that seeks to improve practice, in which the emphasis in on what is effective in the lesson and why. This allows researchers and teachers to glean pedagogical features worth replicating, but replications are conducted with meaning rather than superficially focusing just on the aspects that are visible. Ainscow, Dyson and Weiner (2013: 3) explain: 'Under certain conditions such approaches provide interruptions that help to make the familiar unfamiliar in ways that stimulate self-questioning, creativity and action. In so doing they can sometimes lead to a reframing of perceived problems that, in turn, draws the teacher's attention to overlooked possibilities for addressing barriers to participation and learning.'

Lewis, Enciso and Moje (2007: 5) discuss the transformational potential of the lesson-study method, addressing the thinking (or in their terms conjecture) that 'lesson study improves instruction through the refinement of lesson plans' and alternatively that lesson study strengthens the pathways to instructional improvement of 'teachers' knowledge, teachers' commitment and community, and learning resources'. The process, rather like the action research discussed in Chapter 4, involves honing pedagogical practice while building theory and understanding about that practice, and in the US design-based research cycles it similarly involves repeated 'cycles of design, enactment, analysis, and redesign' (Design-Based

Research Collective 2003: 5, cited by Lewis, Enciso and Moje 2007: 6). The research data comprise lesson plans, lesson study meeting transcripts and sometimes video recordings and interviews.

Of particular interest to researchers of pedagogy are the debates about evidence, causation and proof surrounding lesson study. In Japan, lesson study has been used for a century without 'summative evaluation' of its effectiveness, whereas in the United States there are calls for randomized controlled trials as part of the preoccupation with studying 'what works' (Lewis, Enciso and Moje 2007: 6). This reflects the tension between deep understanding of what works in local contexts (as in lesson study, case study and action research) and the more abstract understanding of generic pedagogic principles (as in large-scale, centralized and synthesis research). Lesson study is a method in which teachers discuss pedagogy in relation to specific examples of lessons, sometimes leading to a reshaping of their practice and sometimes to critical research data and changes rolled out in repeated cycles of lesson study. In designated research schools, transferable pedagogic principles are demonstrated and discussed, but on the data regarding teachers and learners their interactions are always 'fine-grained and collected from very small samples and without formal attention to inter-observer reliability' (Lewis, Enciso and Moje 2007: 7). The pedagogical learning through lesson study spreads, grassroots style, through refining ways of seeing and practising. Instead of researchers demonstrating 'proof', it is a process of teachers judging value and researchers aiding them in this process of establishing and evolving 'local proof' (Lewis, Enciso and Moje 2007: 8). This, argue Lewis, Enciso and Moje (2007), makes the end point of research not the causal claim, but the transfer of local teacher knowledge to new contexts.

Methods of stimulated recall, reflection and dialogue

In another set of methods, researchers use various forms of stimuli from a lesson to stimulate recall and reflection about that lesson. The dataset here includes the stimulus itself, but the focus of the analysis is on the data generated from using that stimulus. This as an approach that is particularly well suited to researching pedagogy, as it draws the attention of the participants to the details of the pedagogical interactions and then leads them further into the less visible elements underlying those interactions. The stimulus can be learner generated, as in the example of a study of technology in the primary classroom (Fox-Turnbull 2009) in which the children photographed their practice and selected the images to be used in discussion with the researcher about their learning (autophotography). Of key importance here is that the 'autophotographs prompted children to recall and discuss aspects of their total practice that might not have otherwise been apparent or visible' (p. 213). Moreover, the children had some ownership of the process. This can be a variant of using the visual as an elicitation tool (Harper 2002; Bragg 2011). Mahruf, Shohel and Howes (2007), in a study of transition from non-formal primary school to high school in Bangladesh, found the young people barely engaged with traditional interviews, unable to articulate their experience and tacit knowledge without photo elicitation in which researcher-generated 'images acted as memory triggers, reflective opportunities, connection facilitators and potent reminders of the students' school experiences' (p. 54). Other stimuli that can be used include audio recordings (Bloom 1953) as well as, most commonly, video recordings. We discuss in some detail the many variations in these methods, but first we summarize the overall approach in Table 7.1.

As is so often the case with research methods, the set of methods for stimulated recall, reflection and dialogue has emerged to meet a research need. Moyles, Adams and Musgrove (2002: 470), who used stimulated dialogue in their Study of Pedagogical Effectiveness in Early Learning (the SPEEL project), identify this need as being about the 'difficulties for practitioners in surfacing and articulating pedagogical values and beliefs'. Vesterinen, Toom and Patrikainen (2010), who used stimulated recall to study the use of technology in classrooms in Finland, refer to the need to elicit pedagogical thinking. Powell (2005), in a study of active learning, needed to be able to make explicit teachers' tacit assumptions as they engaged in an active learning pedagogic approach. For Melanie and colleagues (Nind, Kilburn and Wiles 2015), studying the teaching and learning of advanced research methods, the need was about understanding the PCK particular to teachers of social science research methods and fostering a pedagogic culture in an area dominated by an instrumental discourse of capacity building. In this chapter we

Table 7.1 Stimulated recall, reflection and dialogue methods

Nature of questions asked	• what is going on in the pedagogical interaction? what is going on in the teachers' minds? what are the learners thinking and feeling? what decisions were made and why?
Role of the researcher	• facilitating participants' (teachers' and/or learners') account of a lesson or pedagogical moment from their perspective • using the stimulus to elicit recall, reflection or dialogue • using what can be seen to get at what cannot be seen
Goal of the research	• understand how individuals make decisions in pedagogical situations • gain access to thinking processes within specific pedagogical moments
Data collection	• from naturalistic situations, usually lessons of some kind • generating stimuli such as photographs, audio or video recordings accompanied by researchers' observational Notesinterviews or focus group discussions to generate data in response to the stimulus
Data presentation	• foregrounding the themes important to the participants and including their reflections in their own words
Data analysis	• usually inductive • seeking insight into participants' thinking during and since the pedagogic encounter such as pedagogical content knowledge
Meaning of evidence	• the subjective experiences of the participants • the meaning-making of the participants
Measurement	• no measures taken, usually non-judgemental
Ethics	• concern not to be judgemental about the pedagogical actions and decisions • care to boost rather than undermine the confidence of teachers and learners through the process

dwell on these and other examples to illustrate how the approach meets these needs.

Moyles, Adams and Musgrove (2002) worked from the idea that practitioners understood effective practice and that the research methods needed to probe their implicit theories, values, beliefs and thinking underpinning their pedagogy. **Video-stimulated reflective dialogue** was their research tool for doing this, enabling the researchers to extrapolate practitioners' perspectives on quality in their pedagogic processes, and with this to generate in-depth understanding of effective early years pedagogy. Comparing video-stimulated reflective dialogue with ordinary interviews, the researchers found that, in the latter, while 'expressing links between beliefs, knowledge, thinking and practice was challenging' but worthwhile, the 'reflective dialogue resulted in different kinds of knowledge emerging' (p. 472) in which descriptions of pedagogic principles in practices could begin to be substantiated and highly complex pedagogy could be identified.

Vesterinen, Toom and Patrikainen (2010) discuss the tendency for video to prompt discussion that focuses primarily on the teacher's performance during the lesson. In their study of technology in lessons, combining the stimulus of video with the stimulus of student-generated concept maps helped to focus the discussion more on the students' learning processes. Powell (2005) used the video stimulus to facilitate teachers in a reflective dialogue process. This method generated data about their intentions as facilitators of active learning, their perceptual and self-awareness, and technical and practical reflections. Powell was able to find how teachers couch active learning 'in terms such as learner autonomy, the empowered learner, and learners learning to learn and stimulating each other's learning' (p. 415). He concludes that the 'teacher emerges as the facilitator of the conditions in which learners take more control of their learning. Teachers recognize the importance of positive affective responses from learners, as active learning is a complex, holistic process' (p. 415). The account provides nuanced descriptions of each teacher's approach and thinking and the resources they call upon, such as Emma's 'deep well of personal and professional experience' (p. 415) and Isabella's strong belief in peer support. Thereby

these teachers' pedagogical decisions are influenced, in part, by their personal learning preferences which become their teaching strategies. ... The evidence suggests that video-stimulated reflective dialogues enabled teachers to articulate their thinking and feelings about active learning. Video sequences provided teachers with a sharply defined focus and context for inquiry into dimensions ... of their professional practice. (Powell 2005: 415)

The examples show some distinctive features of stimulated recall, which is now an established method for helping teachers to reflect on their practice (e.g. Lyle 2003; Moyles, Adams and Musgrove 2002; Moyles et al. 2003), a newer method for helping students to reflect on their learning (e.g. Powell 2005; Morgan 2007), and a newer method still for teachers and learners to reflect together (Nind, Kilburn and Wiles 2015). One important feature is that the video (or photograph or audio recording) is not the primary subject of the analysis; it is the talk that is generated that is analysed. The method is in keeping with the guidance from Alexander (2000: 269) to 'talk with whom we watch'. Vesterinen, Toom and Patrikainen (2010: 184) cite Bloom (1953: 161) for an early explanation of the method: 'The basic idea underlying the method of stimulated recall is that the subject may be enable[d] to relive an original situation with vividness and accuracy if he is presented with a large number of the cues or stimuli which occurred during the original situation.' Thus, the technique depends on the researcher presenting 'authentic stimuli and cues to research participants' and further seeking 'their thoughts concerning the original situation' (ibid.). It can be thought of as an advanced interview method (Alexandersson 1994) or an introspective method enabling people to observe their internal mental processes (Gass and Mackey 2000). Vesterinen, Toom and Patrikainen (2010) note that during the rise in influence of behaviourism on education, such approaches and thinking diminished in popularity, but that it rose again in reaction to the reductionism of behavioural thinking.

Although something of an oversimplification, we can think of the set of methods as evolving from an emphasis on stimulating recall and then extending to stress stimulating reflection and dialogue. Thus, video stimulus is less often used now to probe just what happened and why, and more often to probe the cognitive and affective aspects, and increasingly to generate new understandings from dialogue about the reflections, thereby coming to know pedagogy more deeply. Regardless of the stress on recall, reflection or dialogue though, the distinctive element is that this involves a 'close-up' (Nind, Kilburn and Wiles 2015) examination of a specific lesson or pedagogic interaction. Dempsey (2010: 350) sums up the value of this:

> In typical retrospective ethnographic interviews, ethnographers tend to ask informants to remember, in the abstract, actions that they have taken and the values or strategies that they use in general when dealing with particular kinds of social situations. The technique described here [stimulated recall interview] presents informants with an opportunity to discuss their strategies for interaction while they are directly confronted with recorded examples of themselves engaging in interactions.

Moyles, Adams and Musgrove (2002) see their video-stimulated reflective dialogue as doing what Dempsey describes, but enriching the method by putting more control into the hands of practitioners, who select the episode of teaching for examination and discuss it with others. This approach, they say, draws on aspects of action research, stimulated recall, cognitive interviewing, reflective and evidence-informed practice. The dialogic component is about social rather than individual reflective thinking in a two-way, scaffolded discussion between research partners. In common with action research, there is concern with 'the improvement of practice; greater understanding of practice by practitioners; and improvements in the situation in which practice occurs' (p. 464). The 'ethical stance [is] that it is the practitioners who should guide this process' (p. 464) and the collective stance is that 'synergetic pooling of information ... extends understanding of the concepts explored' (p. 465). Morgan (2007, 2010) calls this kind of method video-stimulated recall dialogue, while Nind, Kilburn and Wiles (2015) refer to video-stimulated recall, reflection and dialogue.

We turn now to some of the practical challenges associated with research methods involving a video stimulus, addressing in particular the decisions that the researcher has to make such as: What video capture and playback equipment to use? How to use the method ethically? When to schedule the recall and reflection? And who selects the video excerpts?

Technical matters

Any kind of video stimulation method requires the researcher to capture video for use later. This can be particularly challenging for teacher-researchers working in their own classrooms as Dodd (2014) found when she wanted to use the method with her pupils. For researchers working in other teachers' classrooms, some of the challenge is making the video process as unobtrusive as possible. Moyles, Adams and Musgrove (2002) took the camera into some lessons before doing any video recording so that everyone could become used to its presence. Cameras that are compact and lightweight can be mounted inconspicuously in convenient areas of the teaching rooms (e.g. on suction-cup mounts) to reduce potential stress on participants. A boundary-style microphone suited to recording group discussion may also be needed. Researchers also need to decide what the camera needs to 'see', with choices between wide-angled and more direct lenses. 'Factors such as camera angles and recorded soundscape emphasize and even manipulate the experience, which the students, teacher and researcher are sharing' (Vesterinen, Toom and Patrikainen 2010: 186–7). Marland (1984) combined a fixed wide angle camera focused on the class and a manned (sic) camera with zoom lens on the teacher. Nind, Kilburn and Wiles (2015) used two unobtrusive wide camera angles, again with this dual focus. For the video playback to focus groups of teachers and learners, the aim was to show these different perspectives simultaneously by combining the camera angles into a single video. A high-powered laptop was needed to capture video synchronously from two separate cameras and to allow a choice of 'picture-in-picture' or 'split-screen' formats. (For a more detailed discussion of technical matters, see Kilburn 2014).

Sharing the video

Technology requires human judgement in its use, and a key area of decision-making in this approach surrounds the choices involved with selecting video excerpts and the time and process of sharing them. Even when much video footage is recorded, only some of it will be useful for prompting pedagogic discussion. Nind, Kilburn and Wiles

(2015) found that the video did not always do the job they expected it to. This was probably at times because the quality of the video/sound inadequately captured the action. Sometimes memories of the lived experience were acute, making the video stimulus, which could not capture the feel of the moment in the same way, redundant. Moyles, Adams and Musgrove (2002: 469) found that initially teachers less used to watching themselves teaching 'may be embarrassed by their own habits and behaviour as well as surprised by the students' actions and learning processes', and so 'they can become aware of their own teaching in a new way'. The researchers used the 'pause' facility to focus on just one frame of pedagogy at a time, to explore underpinning concepts and pursue deeper understanding.

A simple fact of this set of methods is that the amount of data grows too large at an astounding rate (Vesterinen, Toom and Patrikainen 2010); this necessitates both choosing particular parts of the video data and focusing the questioning in relation to it in particular ways. Nind, Kilburn and Wiles (2015) chose clips themselves, during the day of recording, on the basis that the three researchers present found them to represent key, provocative moments for discussion, to mark a critical point or illustrate an interesting pedagogical event or strategy. They also invited participants to suggest episodes they would like to see. Powell (2005), studying active learning, asked teachers to identify a learning and teaching session that involved active learning and, following filming, gave the video to the teacher to identify three extracts as the focus and stimulus for their reflective dialogue. As with the study by Moyles, Adams and Musgrove (2002), the teachers had potential prompts for thinking provided, alongside the video. Another possibility again is to give pupils the option to select video clips, as Morgan (2007) did in a study of information and communication technology in the classroom. Although the teacher chose the lesson to be focused upon, and owned the video, in a revised project methodology the researcher and children studied the video without the teacher, with the children being asked to identify 'a part of this video where you were doing or thinking about something interesting'. Lyle (2003) advises using a stimulus that is powerful, arguing that the power can be enhanced if the participants are involved in its selection.

Linked to decisions about who selects the video stimulus are decisions about the timing of the stimulated recall, reflection or dialogue. Lyle (2003) argues from experience that presenting the video stimulus as soon after the event as possible is important for accurate recall, as long as that does not mean that the participant is too tired to recall. Marland (1984), Mackey and Gass (2005) and Fox-Turnbull (2009) all emphasize the importance of immediacy, building on the information processing idea that cognition can be verbalized only when it still is in short-term memory. Close timing is particularly important when the aim is to approach as close as possible to what teachers (and/or learners) were thinking at the time. When the aim is to get the participants to reflect on the video stimulus, immediate follow-up is less important than time spent with it to consider it (perhaps privately), alongside reflective prompts (Morgan 2007). Hence, Challen (2013) made the decision to allow participants to view the video in their own time, selecting episodes for discussion and gaining a sense of ownership as well as authentic dialogue. Alternatively, careful questioning and prompting can partially compensate for lack of reflection time (Moyles et al. 2003).

Ethical challenges

One of the ethical challenges that we have already alluded to in terms of technical matters is to avoid putting participants under stress. Often researchers tackle this by involving participants in the process, giving them some power over it. Nind, Kilburn and Wiles (2015) stressed to their participating teachers and learners of research methods that the research team was concerned with collaborative exploratory probing of pedagogical practices, and not with making evaluative judgements about them. Moyles, Adams and Musgrove (2002) worked on building relationships with their participating teachers, recognizing Dadds' (1993) argument that practitioners are vulnerable when reflecting on their pedagogic practice, especially when this leads them into challenging and rethinking their constructs and practices. Becoming research partners helps with the dynamic of feeling in control and not under criticism, instead making valued contributions. There are benefits for participating teachers and learners in reflecting on their own work, as we discuss in case example 7.1.

Case example 7.1: Researching the teaching and learning of research methods (Nind, Kilburn and Wiles 2015)

Context: Research in England conducted as part of work on building advanced social science research methods capacity for the National Centre for Research Methods. A 'close-up' component focused on pedagogy as enacted and experienced, to complement an expert panel method.

Goal: To enhance pedagogic knowledge 'by engaging teachers and learners in pursuing pedagogical understanding with us', seeking 'a balance between not wishing to "distort, destroy or reconstruct" (Fenstermacher 1994: 11) that knowledge and wishing to inform rather than merely illuminate knowledge and practice' (Nind, Kilburn and Wiles 2015: 2). To co-produce knowledge by bringing researchers, teachers and learners into dialogue, working with primary data and analytic units that teachers and learners could connect with specific lived experience.

Outcomes: 'Three-way dialogue and a feeling of the challenge of teaching and learning research methods being something we were all in together' (Nind, Kilburn and Wiles 2015: 9). Constructive discussion of pedagogic decisions about structure, timing, group work, balance of activity, the teaching purpose of questions, interaction of learning in and outside the session. Some identification of pedagogical content knowledge. Checks on the individual readings of the training event by each party, from hearing the perspective of others.

Research methods: Video-stimulated recall, reflection and dialogue in focus groups. Each focus group discussion of around fifty minutes followed (after only a short break) a recorded day's training event in advanced social research methods. Between one and three teachers, and between three and thirteen learners took part. The option of separate focus groups for teachers and learners, which may have elicited comments that were more candid, was rejected in favour of open, non-judgemental and constructive dialogue all together. Opening questioning steered teachers to reflect on the

Case example 7.1

challenges they perceived in teaching that day's content, including what guided the approach and any innovations. Questioning then invited learners to discuss what was challenging to learn. Video clips chosen by the researchers were used to stimulate reflection on particular moments, and teachers and learners were invited in turn to identify events in the training that they would like to review on video and reflect on. Prompts focused on what teachers and learners were thinking and how they were feeling. The discussions were audio recorded and transcribed, and the transcripts were thematically analysed by two researchers using computer-assisted and freehand coding in a complementary fashion. Features of grounded theorizing and constant comparison were used to identify and develop themes iteratively from the ongoing data collection and analysis; these themes were discussed among the research team, and with teachers and an advisory group.

The ethical issue of the potential for participants to become anxious about their practice, in the light of the researchers' goal (Calderhead 1981), did not arise in case example 7.1, in part perhaps because of the sense of a shared goal. Similarly, Moyles et al. (2003) constructed their research as collaborative inquiry between the teacher and researcher as research partners; it was intended to bring to the surface only the teachers' thinking and feelings about specific, classroom episodes that they were comfortable with reflecting upon. There was space for the partners to use the video – and each other – as resources to extend and develop their pooled thinking. Thus, we can think of the process in ethics terms as relatively safe with the reflections both scaffolded and supported. When used in these ways the reflective dialogue becomes a tool for professional development (Powell 2005), somewhat like the lesson-study method, and not an intrusion or destructive force. This is more feasible in reflective dialogue in which the teacher 'controls the focus and pace of the prompts' (Moyles, Adams and Musgrove 2002: 465), feeling a sense of ownership rather than being someone that has something 'done' to them.

When approached with ethical concerns foregrounded, the video-stimulated dialogue method can mean an intertwining of knowledge *in* action and knowledge *for* action in that, as Shulman (1987) argues, pedagogical practices both reflect and stimulate thoughtfulness. There are disadvantages, however. Nind, Kilburn and Wiles (2015: 7) found that video can lack the power the researcher wishes it had to bring a pedagogical situation back to life, reflecting: 'It may just be that the ephemeral is just that; video can record and translate experience but it cannot replace or recreate experience.' Atmosphere and context are not necessarily replicable in the video, and researchers cannot intensify the moment for viewers in the way that filmmakers do. Even when the video does engage, the strangeness of the situation of picking over video can be hard for some teachers and learners. Under stress, with inadequate research relationships, 'teachers may produce convincing stories about their thinking processes without knowing what really happened' (Vesterinen, Toom and Patrikainen 2010: 187, after Gass and Mackey 2000: 5–6), reverting to general narratives rather than specific analysis. If, however, the goal is to make visible the aspects of pedagogic interaction under investigation, or to enable practitioners or learners to express their ideas about specific practices, the potential of this approach is worth pursuing. It can, at the very least, alert researchers to 'discrepancies' between what they thought was evident and the participants' explanation (Challen 2013). One practitioner sums it up:

> So, having got the horrible bit out of the way of seeing myself on the video ... it was very interesting, very revealing, and made me think, because the camera doesn't record the layers that are going on in the mind. So, there's sort of layers and layers of thinking going on, and sort of snap decisions and reasons why I'm doing this, that and the other ... and where I intend to go with the activity. ... Watching the video, you don't see the thinking, but the thinking is there. (Moyles, Adams and Musgrove 2002: 470)

If, as Shulman (1987: 6) maintains, 'teachers themselves have difficulty articulating what they know and how they know it', then the researcher's job may be to find a method that helps them with that.

Conclusion

This chapter has ranged widely, addressing matters of technology, technique, values, meanings, beliefs, thinking, action and ethics. A major theme has been the attempt to capture what is difficult to access, what is usually hidden and elusive. A theme throughout has been the ways in which researchers seek to make thinking visible and, indeed, reveal thinking that is no longer available to the conscious mind since some of our behaviours and actions are so deeply taken for granted that we struggle to remember what happened, why it happened or what the rationale or thinking was for certain actions. We conclude by reiterating (1) the intertwined nature of pedagogical interaction and the methods to research them, and (2) the overlapping and blurred nature of methods of teaching and learning and methods of researching. Methods for each are not synonymous; they do not form an exact fit, but insofar as our purposes as professionals are to understand and enhance the how, what and why of learning, so, too, we are in the realm of seeking tools for investigating pedagogy.

We conclude by acknowledging also what we might call the pedagogy of memory. As teacher educators as well as pedagogy researchers, we have encouraged our students to understand their own (and others') practice by attending to their own memory and past experiences as learners. We have operated on the assumption that the idea of memory and the past can be a productive learning space for the present and the future. The past impacts on our pedagogy and so memory can be a tool for constructing, deconstructing and reconstructing what we do as teachers, teacher educators and researchers (Mitchell, Weber and O'Reilly-Scanlon 2005). Since pedagogy involves the personal, the social, the affective and the cognitive, all of which imply the relational, then our research methods inevitably have to align. Whether you pursue the approach of lesson study, think aloud or stimulated recall, you will want to plan your research methodological approach to offer faithful, ethical representations and analyses of events and thinking.

Further reading

Hart, L. C. and J. Carriere (2010), 'Developing the Habits of Mind for a Successful Lesson Study Community', in Lynn C. Hart, Alice Alston and Aki Murata (eds), *Lesson Study Research and Practice in Mathematics Education*, pp. 27–38, New York: Springer. This short chapter offers a case study of a group of primary teachers in the United States as they embark on the process of learning about lesson study as a vehicle for accessing and discussing their pedagogy. The research reports on the group of teachers as they use data collected at the beginning and end of a year-long process of applying lesson study.

Rowe, V. C. (2009), 'Using Video-stimulated Recall as a Basis for Interviews: Some Experiences from the Field', *Music Education Research*, 11(4): 425–37. This paper shows how video-stimulated recall methods can enrich a multi-method design. For more practical matters pertaining to using video cameras in pedagogic research you will find useful, Kilburn, D. (2014), '*Methods for Recording Video in the Classroom: Producing Single and Multi-Camera Videos for Research into Teaching and Learning*', NCRM Working Paper. NCRM. Available online, http://eprints.ncrm.ac.uk/3599/.

CHAPTER EIGHT

Pedagogy embodied: Methods of analysis for embodied practice

Introduction

In this chapter, we retain the theme of researching pedagogy as researching something that is complex and hard to know. While in Chapter 7 we focused more on methods to reach what is in the minds of teachers and learners, in this chapter our focus is more on their bodies and bodily realities. Pedagogy is not just interactive, it is lived. By entitling the chapter 'Pedagogy Embodied', we wanted to draw attention to pedagogy as embodied practice and the implications of this for the methods of generating and analysing data. While the idea of pedagogy as prescribed, enacted or experienced may have resonated easily with readers, for many teachers/researchers this concept of pedagogy as embodied will be quite new and they will have given scant thought to the use of bodies in the practice of teaching. For teacher/researchers of children who are very young or who are disabled, however, the idea of using the body will have more resonance, not least through sitting in chairs that are too small, going home with aching backs, and knowing that teachers and learners actually touch. Jordon (2001), recalling a lecturer who interrupted long sessions with requests for students to move from their chairs to stand and stretch, observes how rarely teachers acknowledge the body. Embodied pedagogy, she argues, recognizes the importance of the body to both students and teacher.

Embodied pedagogy is central for the making of athletes, performers, craft experts and professionals. Craft learning in, for example, masonry and carpentry, alongside sport, dance and other skilled physical activities, depends heavily on observation and repeated exercise, and less on the spoken word (Marchand 2008), although the role of talk should not be denied in these processes (see Chapter 5). We argue here that, for the pedagogy researcher, an understanding of embodied pedagogy opens up new avenues for understanding what is going on. Indeed, the chapters in Part Three – addressing the mind, senses, body and space in pedagogy – really need to be read together.

Bodies and pedagogy

We begin with some basic concepts before moving into more challenging theoretical terrain and to research methods fitting for this embodied reading of pedagogy. First, proxemics: embodied pedagogy 'begins by acknowledging that the location of our bodies affects our interactions with one another' (Jordon 2001: 98). The study of proxemics is the study of the use and perception of personal and social space; for researchers of pedagogy it includes analysis of the position of teachers and learners in relation to the layout of the classroom or learning environment (see Chapter 9). We recall making basic drawings of such in the early, observation days of our teacher training. Second is the concept of whether the use of the body is implicit or explicit, conscious or unconscious, in the process of teaching and learning. Jordon (2001: 99) may be unusual when she discusses her conscious use of proxemics when teaching theology: 'I feel most comfortable and effective as a teacher when I am standing and moving. I find that I need to be physically close to my students, walking around the room, looking them in the eye … . I hope this communicates to the students that I want to connect with each and every one of them.' She even draws on research evidence showing that the distance between teacher and students is crucial to the communication process. Teachers, it has been shown, can improve students' attitudes and readiness to participate by moving closer to them (e.g., Banbury and Hebert 1992).

A third basic concept is body language and the non-verbal messages we continuously send through the way we use body posture, gestures and facial expressions. Fourth is kinesics, the systematic study of interpersonal communication through body movement. Researchers have needed to get up close to pedagogic situations, using video cameras and observation windows to gain insights into these aspects of the body in teaching and learning. However, much pedagogic research goes beyond this to connect use of the body with sociocultural readings of classrooms as places of dynamic power relations. Jordon (2001: 99) illustrates this by citing the reflection in Goldstein (1996: 48): 'In the classroom, I rarely stand and I vary my place in the circle each meeting so that no one gets used to thinking of my chair as the center of the room. I once explained this reasoning to a class, and a student said, amused, "Wherever you sit, that is the center of the room."'

The cultural situation of pedagogical encounters affects the reading of bodies in space, just as much as the cultural background of the actors. This, as we go on to show later in the chapter, means that as pedagogic researchers we need not only to see what is going on, but to sense it using our senses holistically, and to make sense of it.

A more complex concept is that teachers and learners are 'fundamentally embodied, biological creatures' (Granger 2010: 71). The argument, developed by Granger (2010) and based on the work of Dewey, is that our 'principal means of interacting with the world is through the body ... and it is by virtue of this interaction that the body, as the primary medium of habit, is also the primary medium of meaning in experience' (p. 71). Thus, habits are 'essentially embodied meanings' (p. 71). Habitual bodies, moreover, frame 'a spatiotemporal context for action and interpretation' (p. 73). In this way, by turning our attention to what we see through reading the bodies of teachers and learners, we are not departing from reading what is in their minds.

Returning to the question of the pedagogic context, Foucault (1980) reminds us that the body is an unremitting instrument of power and the site of social and political struggle. Bodies are integral to teachers establishing authority through their physical presence and their gaze (Holland, Gordon and Lahelma 2007). Teachers are also subject to students' gaze, which can evaluate or humiliate them, often leading women teachers to opt consciously for a relatively neutral display of their bodies (Kehily 2002). By studying pedagogy as embodied practice, then, we can study issues of hierarchy, equity and justice. hooks (1994) reflects:

> I have always been acutely aware of the presence of my body in those settings that, in fact, invite us to invest so deeply in a mind/body split so that, in a sense, you're almost always at odds with the existing structure, whether you are a black woman student or professor. But if you want to remain, you've got, in a sense, to remember yourself – because to remember yourself is to see yourself always as a body in a system that has not become accustomed to your presence or to your physicality. (cited by Kazan 2005: 379)

Reflecting on her first day as a teacher, Kazan (2005:380) recalls using her body wrongly when she sat down with her students, who did not immediately recognize her as the teacher: 'Though physically present, my body was not read as a teacher's body. I looked too young; I did not look sufficiently "other."' She goes on, 'To be recognized as the teacher, I felt I needed to move to the front of the classroom (the physical position of authority) and use language to stabilize my identity as "teacher"' (p. 381). In this way, she introduces the idea of the bodies of teachers and learners in classroom as corporeal pedagogic texts.

As researchers of pedagogy, we can learn to read bodies as texts that say much about individuality, identity, power, genre and so on. Kazan (2005: 382) notes, 'I use Bakhtin as my primary lens to understand the body as a basis for epistemology that acts in dialogic relationship with other bodies.' There are all kinds of ways of theorizing the body, of course, and these are all a revelation if we have not considered the notion of the body in pedagogy at all. We think it is useful to explore where seeing pedagogic interactions as embodied pedagogical acts takes us as educationalists and methodologists. It helps us to see the complexity involved in reading bodies, necessary from Kazan's perspective for successful pedagogy, but necessary for some kinds of research, too. She explains:

> Institutional spaces discourage us from thinking about ourselves as bodies. Teachers need to be aware of these erasures; otherwise, we condone them. ... Granted, we do not have the power to

control how bodies are made intelligible in our culture. But we do have the power to monitor whether and how bodies are read and responded to in our classrooms and whether students are as active, vocal, and mobile as the teacher. (Kazan 2005: 394)

Here, we see the concept of embodiment as more than just the body, but as the body in context (just as we can think of pedagogy as teaching and learning in context). As teachers and learners doing what we do, we embody a range of practices and ideas. Kazan (2005: 401) illustrates this point with an example:

When students work in groups and have ideas and answers to share, we must get them at the board holding the chalk. This is such a simple move, yet I am always struck in first-year writing and introductory literature courses when students look at me as if I've asked them to do something for which they are unqualified. But in some cases, they *are* unqualified (or at least feel so), as holding a piece of chalk and writing on a blackboard is not the same activity as taking a pen to paper, is not the same incorporated activity.

If pedagogical research takes us towards researching a set of relationships, interactions or encounters, it must also take us to researching a set of embodied relationships, interactions or encounters. Dixon and Senior (2011: 475) point to the work of Estola and Elbaz-Luwisch (2003), which focuses on 'the teacher's body, their physical body and the physical work of teaching; how their body is seen by students and teachers' consideration of students' bodies'. Dixon and Senior note how Estola and Elbaz-Luwisch speak of 'relationships [which] are also embodied and teachers carefully read one another's body messages', such as 'I sensed it on my skin and saw it on their faces' (p. 710). They also draw on the work of Moje (2000), who takes us into the realm of unconscious embodiment, talking of embodied practices 'such as dress, body image, and personal habits' (p. 34), whereby 'our bodies spoke what our mouths refused to speak' (p. 35). The implication for research methods is the need to use our human sensitivities, in that 'seeing is the involvement of reading with body and emotion, that is, reading with the whole body' (Dixon and Senior 2011: 475).

Another implication of the ideas in this chapter for the pedagogical research is the need to attend to the space between people. This might mean attending to the body, but also to 'the body reaching beyond its apparent borders' (Dixon and Senior 2011: 476, referring to Estola and Elbaz-Luwisch 2003). Thus, bodies reach out into affective connections (Zembylas 2007), linking together our bodies, feelings, histories and minds (McWilliams 1996, 1999). For Dixon and Senior (2011: 477), this is about matter-energy, joining teacher and learner in ways that are 'both experienced and palpable' and necessitating microanalysis. We can illustrate this with case example 8.1. We recommend looking at the marked up images discussed in this case example in the original paper. This will help in reflecting on the authors' conclusion that

> our gaze registers the embodied nature of pedagogy. Deep in the forgotten and un-said we give word and image to embodied learning/teaching and pedagogy. ... an embodied pedagogy that crystallizes the relational 'teacher' and 'student' and refuses the distorted normalising gaze of teacher reflection and student observation. (Dixon and Senior 2011: 483)

Case example 8.1: Using images to discern the embodied pedagogic moment (Dixon and Senior 2011)

Context: A three-year study of an arts-based teaching project in pre-service teacher education in Australia. The project exploring a new arts-based pedagogic approach 'generated opportunities for students and the authors to engage with each other, with objects/ artefacts, and opened up the possibilities of bodily engagement. As teacher educators we moved from the academic linguistic discourse of lecture – workshop and discussion mode – to teaching in embodied ways of art making in core theoretical courses' (Dixon and Senior 2011: 474).

Goal: To explore the notion of the 'indwelling midst' (Pinar and Irwin 2005); to use images to discern 'the relationship between' in embodied pedagogy.

Case example 8.1

Outcomes: Perception of intricate relationships and of language, conversation and interactions in embodied ways. Evidence of 'matter-energies between bodies' – of the 'bodily between' – the pedagogical relationship between self that is not just metaphorical but bodily. Descriptions and visual images of, for example, how a teacher 'anchors the pedagogical affect by encompassing the students watching the [basketball] play on the far right' (Dixon and Senior 2011: 480), and how in another image the 'contour line traverses the shoulders of the three involved in this embodied moment and embrace all without privileging one over the other' (p. 482).

Research methods: Researchers deployed images in the form of still photographs of fourteen to fifteen year olds, their classroom teachers and a number of pre-service teachers. These were 'taken at random by any of a number of the participants to record the teaching and learning experience' (p. 477). Each of the researchers engaged with all the images, drawing 'lines of flight' on each one to trace 'the shape or contours of embodied pedagogy' (p. 478). There followed a moderation process using Mitchell's (2005) suggestions for reading images. They shared and discussed the marked images with groups of teacher educators, education researchers, pre-service teachers and practising teachers. They teased out fluid connections felt and seen by others.

While Dixon and Senior (2011) make visible embodied pedagogical relationships, Bourne (2004) focuses on the notion of visible or invisible pedagogy itself. She explains: 'Visible pedagogy is explicit in acknowledging responsibility for taking up a position of authority; invisible pedagogy (whether progressive or "emancipatory") simply masks the inescapable authority of the teacher' (p. 65). In visible radical pedagogy, teachers combine the visibility of their authority with creating a new space for connecting with students. This is important methodologically, as Bourne was able to demonstrate the emerging radical visible pedagogy of the teacher in her study involving a black woman of African–Caribbean origin, who was politically engaged with raising achievement of the disadvantaged students. Based on video-recorded observations of the teacher at work together with interviews with her group of learners, Bourne concludes that the teacher in question inducted students into the discourse of school English necessary to them transforming their life chances while still valuing their discourse contributions. She argues that 'this [pedagogy] was realized through an overtly highly regulated discourse but one in which the tenor of the prevailing relationships between teacher and students was established multimodally by means of gaze, gesture and movement, which both softened and controlled as required' (p. 67). Multimodal methods of analysis were essential to her forming this view, and it is to these methods that we now turn.

Visual, audiovisual and multimodal methods

As we have shown already in this chapter, there are times when researchers of pedagogy need methods that are visual – for generating and analysing data and even for communicating findings. This may be because of their theoretical stance or because they are interested through choice or necessity in data that are additional to, or instead of, verbal data. Going back to researching the *Intensive Interaction* pedagogic approach with people with profound intellectual disability (Nind and Hewett 1994) discussed in Chapter 7, the use of video was central to mapping where and how communicative engagement between student and teacher were evident and changing (Nind 1996). Melanie recalls her thinking:

> We had swiftly learned the power of video in developing this pedagogy. Teaching teams pored over video looking for the moment of connection. We also looked to find the cues we had missed and all the times when we talked too much, did too much, failed to slow down and tune in. When it came to researching the effectiveness of the approach we had painstakingly developed, it was clear to me that I could not do this without video. I needed a design that would allow the minutiae of changes in body language, orientation, posture, gaze, sound making and so on to be recorded and compared week-on-week. I opted for a mix of

observation in real time and via video. I also opted for a structured approach in which the number of occurrences or amount of time in various coded behaviours could be measured and plotted on a timeline. This was nuanced up to a point, but looking back there is some crudeness to the approach too. This was the early 1990s and I did not know about multimodal analysis back then. Nonetheless, this was an exploration of embodied pedagogy that relied heavily on audio-visual analysis.

Research on preschool learners similarly often demands the use of video. Bragg (2011: 94) reflects on how 'Flewitt's [2006] audio-visual recordings of pre-schoolers show how visual data can draw attention to body language and gesture, focus and direction of gaze, and relations between learners, and thus counter the bias towards spoken and written language within education. This may reveal, for instance, that a child considered to lack verbal skills was in fact able to communicate with ease non-verbally.' Such methods then can be inclusive of the kinds of learners that might otherwise be excluded from research. It allows accounts of their pedagogic interactions that might otherwise elude us.

In most uses of visual and audiovisual methods, there comes a point of translation or reduction of what can be seen and heard (and sensed and felt – something we come back to later in the chapter) into the written word or even numbers. There are many reasons for this. One is simply about the supremacy of the written medium in academia. Another is that the digital media options for making audiovisual data readily accessible are relatively new and publishers have not yet caught up with the potential. There is also the reason that there is a great deal of discomfort and sensitivity surrounding showing images of children (Bragg 2011; Wiles et al. 2008). The ethical principle of retaining the anonymity of research participants presents huge challenges for the visual researcher. Flewitt (2006: 33) notes that 'digital technology has made possible the obscuring of on-screen images, such as "fuzzing" participants' faces to protect identity in the public domain, or using a relatively simple technique to obscure onscreen images by reducing pixel count'. Equally, the researcher can use drawn sketches of video stills to show body positioning and direction of movement without showing the individual. Depending on the importance of the visual to communicating the research, however, the researcher may pursue the option of not anonymizing the participants. This may seem dangerous to some readers, but the arguments about the ethics and practicality of protecting anonymity in research are anyway shifting in the digital age and in the context of moves towards participatory research (see Tilley and Woodthorpe 2011).

Bragg (2011: 98) argues that 'our capacity to generate visual data far outstrips our capacity to analyse them'. It can be argued that it also outstrips our capacity to present or communicate them within studies. One of the first challenges in this process is the transcription of audiovisual data (as opposed to audio data discussed in Chapter 5). Flewitt (2006: 34) makes that point that:

> All representations are misrepresentations. (Stake and Kerr 1994: 2) Any kind of transcription, whether of audio or video data, is by definition a process of transformation, where complex, richly situated phenomena are reduced for the purpose of analysis. ... Although this process is traditionally referred to as 'transcription', the term 'representation' is a more fitting description of the interpretive processes involved in the transformation of visual, multimethod data resources into the written forms required by academic writing.

The researcher of pedagogy is able to capture on video camera the eye contact, body movement, facial expression and the manipulation of objects involved in a pedagogic encounter. The challenge becomes how to make sense of the ways in which these subtly intertwine in the purposes that they serve.

Multimodal researchers can help us in that, from a multimodal perspective, 'meanings made with language are interwoven with meanings made in other modes, highlighting the interdependent assemblage of different semiotic modes' (Flewitt 2006: 28). Therefore, using video helps with coming to know 'the multimodal dynamism of classroom interaction, giving new insights into how children and adults coordinate different modes as they negotiate and jointly construct meanings in different social settings' (p. 29). Consequently, multimodal researchers are experimenting with ways to present these modes at work including and moving beyond adding other modes to the transcription of words. They work towards a way of representing 'a new multisemiotic dynamic' (ibid.). Flewitt argues that transcripts in this context are dynamic texts that reflect 'the temporal, spatial and kinaesthetic nature of visually recorded interaction but also the multilevelled interpretive processes of the researcher, participants and readers' (p. 35). Being able to portray co-occurrence of modes and events is essential, as is finding formats for this that are not too cumbersome to interpret. Table 8.1 shows various transcription models drawn from Flewitt (2006) and Cowan (2014) including transducting, that is, remaking meaning across modes.

Table 8.1 Multimodal transcription models

Model	Character and examples
Adding gestures, gaze, descriptions and video stills to historically established discourse analysis transcription	Transducting visual and embodied modes into linguistic forms (used by Norris 2002 when studying children playing a computer game)
Grids with outline sketches of stills combined with extracts from book texts, oral transcripts, descriptions of action and pace/tone of utterances	Partially transducting visual and embodied modes into linguistic forms (used by Jewitt 2002)
Grids with verbal descriptions of movements, gaze direction, vocalization and oral transcripts	Transducting visual and embodied modes into linguistic forms (used by Lancaster 2001 studying a two year old's interpretation of an illustrated written text)
Interweaving (perhaps with notes in brackets) into a traditional orthographic transcript features such as gesture, facial expression and laughter	Transducting visual and embodied modes into linguistic forms (discussed by Erikson 2011)
Conversation analysis style transcript with grammatical signs, symbols and typography to systematically record features of speech alongside the speech showing pauses, emphasis, pitch and volume	Transducting visual and embodied modes into linguistic and symbolic forms (ten Have 2007; see Chapter 5)

Tabular **multimodal transcription** where the columns and rows invite temporal and non-temporal reading of the ways in which vocalization, actions, gaze etc. come together (the first column may show the mode that the researcher values most, often speech, while the white space on the page may represent the silence or absence of action)	Transducting visual and embodied modes into linguistic forms (Cowan 2014 notes how a short section of video quickly becomes a dense tabular transcript)
Timeline-based multimodal transcription with time shown on a continuous horizontal line, left to right, with lines beneath representing different aspects, allowing options for how to read what is going on sequentially or simultaneously (visual stills can be added to written description to make information about the interaction known economically by visually depicting, e.g., distance, posture)	Transducting visual and embodied modes into spatial, linguistic and visual forms (Cowan 2014 notes researcher has to decide which modes to include and how to represent them)

Flewitt (2006) outlines the process she goes through to produce a multimodal transcript. It begins with logging the video recordings including time codes, diagrams of positioning and outline descriptions, and watching the videos without and then with sound. Next, she targets utterances with a traditional transcription generated using online digital transcription software. Repeated viewings at varied speeds feed into the process of creating the multimodal record, which might take one of the forms presented in Table 8.1. Readers who question whether this effort is worth it might heed Flewitt's argument, that it has allowed her to 'produce a well-documented argument about *how* and *why* children make and express meaning in different modes and how institutional settings directly and indirectly both impose constraints on and offer possibilities for children's access to learning in different modes' (p. 44). Bourne and Jewitt (2003) similarly argue that looking in this way at role of gaze in secondary school classrooms enabled them to use bodily and sensory modes as data in pedagogic situations where affective issues are central.

Sensory methods

Multimodal methods of analysis and transcription rely heavily on their theoretical basis in social semiotics. This informs the emphasis on modes of meaning-making. We can relate other theoretical orientations to pedagogy, and these will lead to other research methods and approaches such as **sensory ethnography**, which we examine next. First, though, we cite Thomson (2011: 104) on the importance of sensory engagement within schools and pedagogy:

> Visual and auditory senses dominate schools. Children are expected to look at the board, their books and the teacher. They are watched to see that they do not get into any mischief. Children must listen carefully to instructions in lessons and speak only when it is appropriate and in acceptable ways. (Dinner and toilets smell, but this is to be ignored.)

Thomson shows (most of her chapter is in photographs) how children's movement is highly regulated: they 'must line up for class, stand when visitors or the head teacher enter the room, move around only with approval, play games according to set rules' (ibid.). Their urge to 'touch, fiddle, push, poke or stroke' (ibid.) is regulated except in the yard at playtime and in creative learning. This reminds us that not everything to do with the body and senses is about making meaning, but it can all be meaningful to the researcher of pedagogy.

Visual anthropologist Sarah Pink (2007: 240) points us to 'sensory embodied experiences'. While not focused on education, she nonetheless describes methods that can be used in pedagogic research. For instance, for her a walk together with a video camera is a method that is 'an exercise in experiencing and imagining', 'continually comparing our present sensory embodied experiences ... with potential others' (ibid.). As with many of the ideas in this chapter, the link between embodied experience and spaces recurs here. Classroom and other learning environments are physical spaces, and vested with memories and meanings accessed through textures, smells and so on, experienced at a bodily level. Pedagogy is embodied in people, practices and places. Social anthropologists see *walking with* as one way of the joining in the social world of participants, and readers may want to think about other equivalents suited to joining in the social world of teachers and learners.

Ethnographers have certainly started to think more now about not just visual ethnography but sensory ethnography (Pink 2007, 2009, 2010). This reflects a concern with systematically reflecting on the 'embodied and sensorial nature of their research experiences ... often describing how they came to moments of realisation about other people's meanings and values serendipitously through their own seemingly "same" sensory embodied experiences' (Pink 2007: 244). With sensory approaches emerging as a form of research practice, there is greater awareness of this concept of 'shared corporeal experiences' (ibid.) for ethnographic filmmakers and the like.

Pink (2010) argues that sensory ethnography incorporates 'innovative methods' that extend beyond listening and watching and using multiple media, and beyond the use of writing in ethnographic representation. This, for her, is not a matter of multimodal transcripts but of looking towards arts practice. Various disciplines have taken a sensory turn to become interested in how sensory experiences are connected, rendering a conventional focus on observing, listening and writing/reading insufficient. Moreover, Pink points out, the turn towards public engagement in and with research demands **sensory methods** to engage non-academics and wider publics with research findings. This helps them to know in practice what is being communicated, not necessarily via words. We might opt to involve teachers and learners in participatory filmmaking or to engage them through the film (or other) product. Pink also refers to engaging people through sensing with them (walking, eating, etc.; we would add learning); it can be useful, therefore, to rethink the interview as a multisensory 'event' and expand on the 'serendipitous sensory learning of being there', in our case most often in the classroom. It can also be useful to think of the researcher/ethnographer as a sensory apprentice, learning the skilled practices of others and joining in their embodied activities. Pink's sensory apprentice idea that 'it is through actually engaging in the activities and environments we wish to learn about that we come to know them' resonates well with some of our pedagogical thinking.

Pink (2007) expands on what video offers in terms of enhancing our capacity to learn about multisensory forms of experience. Video provides a tool that enables embodied communication about, and empathetic understanding and representation of, people's perceptions of their environments. It offers 'a process through which people, things and sensory experiences are drawn together' (p. 245). In a doctoral study of children's sense of belonging in school and class, Child (2014) reflected with the children on the videos they made and friendship maps they drew, sensing their realities with them. This fits with the idea that the primary audience for video recordings might be the people in them (Pink 2007), so that any commentary generated from this is co-produced.

Sensory analysis can rely on visual (and other seemingly single sense) artefacts as well as audiovisual ones. In their study of transition from non-formal primary school to high school in Bangladesh, Mahruf, Shohel and Howes (2007: 56) found that 'concrete situations framed in the photographs' made by the researchers of the children's non-formal schools generated emotion, nostalgia and sense of loss. This was often for bodily or sensory things, such as the beauty of the decorations they made, the process of making them, and the links with feelings and activities of home. The photographs elicited pupil comments about the bodily experience of learning in school, such as:

> Looking at this image, the way he is writing is not easy and at the beginning of my primary school days, I felt back pain. Over the time, though the pain went away, I didn't find it easy to write bending on my back and writing on the slate. And then when I begin high school I found it difficult to sit on a low bench and write on high bench and my handwriting became terrible. Now I have adapted to the bench. (Mahruf, Shohel and Howes 2007: 58)

The authors reflect on how, within the context of shared cultural symbolism, images can help elicit memories, feelings and sensory experiences that illuminate connections between the personal and the wider social structural context.

Degerbøl and Svendler Nielsen (2015) relate some of the ideas from sensory ethnography more directly to education. Their approach to embodied learning takes a 'multisensuous perspective' (p. 60). They draw from the work of Andrew Sparkes as well as Sarah Pink, and build on their wish to challenge the status of sight at the top of a hierarchy of senses and to regard sensing as a cultural, social and historical phenomenon. For these educational researchers, ideas and values from narrative inquiry, visual anthropology and sensory ethnography merge into a method that favours the multisensory presence and that extends into dissemination through an audiovisual narrative.

We have referred already to films and photographs as outputs from research. This may be comfortable territory for teacher-researchers in that, as teachers, we are familiar with such multisensory display of our students' work. Degerbøl and Svendler Nielsen (2015) favour video representation as a coherent whole for communicating the research to others. They describe a research strategy 'inspired by videographic participation and ethnographic filmmaking' and 'influenced by the sensory and reflexive turn' (p. 62). It is this strategy and the methods within it that form our next case example (8.2).

Case example 8.2: A videographic participation approach (Degerbøl and Svendler Nielsen 2015)

Context: A year-long study of embodied learning at a national school for contemporary circus in Denmark involving six young people aged sixteen to twenty-three years, learning the art of circus performance.

Goal: To answer the research question: 'What is embodied learning and how does it manifest itself in praxis?'

Outcomes: An academic video essay using primarily audiovisual means to convey how embodied learning is manifest in the circus school. Understanding of pedagogic encounters centred on interdependency.

Research methods: The students were followed for two-week periods three times (totalling 240 hours) over one academic year;

Case example 8.2

twenty-one hours of audiovisuals were gathered. The researchers created films in a process departing from the ethnographic tradition of not using close-ups or editing recordings. Instead they used moving cameras to follow and home in on the lived experiences of the student: 'to capture the joy, which makes the eyes bright and shiny, the fingers shaking because of fatigue, the hands around the arm of the partner to find the right position, the feet repeatedly making the same steps to adjust the run up for the lift and so on' (Degerbøl and Svendler Nielsen 2015: 62). While the ethnography was done with a video camera, the researcher being bodily present on location was equally important. Together this became videographic participation, which allows the researcher to focus on experiencing the situation with the whole body, enriching the analysis and interpretation of the audiovisual data. The researcher was acting as 'human instrument', taking into account the embodied resonance of the viewer who will watch the audiovisual narrative. The researcher's own multisensoriality in situ was there also, to support the process of embodied resonance when sharing the videograph. The video was not left to speak for itself – it was not seen as raw data – but an audiovisual narrative was created.

The authors stress that in this method of videographic participation it is crucial that the researcher is 'present and multisensuously aware, and therefore, has a wider angle than the camera' (Degerbøl and Svendler Nielsen 2015: 65). They cite Pink's (2009: 120) point that 'analysis does not just happen in our heads, but involves all our corporeality'. Being multisensuously attentive, they argue, the researcher is able to notice dimensions in the pedagogic situation that the camera cannot, including temperature, odours, atmosphere and emotion. Their paper records some of the researcher's decisions and reflections:

The handheld camera makes it possible to place myself wherever needed and gives the opportunity to capture the complexity of the teaching situation or to get close to the one(s) in focus. The handheld camera makes it possible to move around with the students, but it contains the risk of losing sight of the entity of the situation because of the involvement with the chosen ones. (pp. 65–6)

[Occasionally the students] come over asking if they can watch the audiovisuals ... being present and visible ... allowed the students to take part in the research by suggesting what could be recorded. By so doing, the students somehow became co-creators. (p. 66)

It is important to be explicitly aware of one's preunderstandings to be able to bracket them. An implication of this is to explicate what situations attract one's attention and why. The researcher's subjective standpoints and preunderstandings certainly influence the gaze, but first and foremost the research question guides the videographic participation. (p. 66)

The analysis process in this example begins with the researcher noting sensory aspects in the context (the noise, the cold concrete floor on bare feet). The systematic part follows and this involves viewing of the audiovisuals in their entirety, recording impressions, logging factual events and evocative parts. Then reflection on the evocative parts begins: 'What is it about? Why this particular sequence? What does it reveal about embodied learning?' (Degerbøl and Svendler Nielsen 2015: 67). Words are chosen to describe the theme of the part (e.g. interdependence) and quotes are selected and videos cut down to call attention to the theme and what can be said about it. Lastly comes the editing, which serves to make the central themes visible and the audiovisual narrative engaging to watch.

'A multisensuous approach means listening to the bodily responses while watching the audiovisuals, and ... [including those parts] which insist on telling you something' (Degerbøl and Svendler Nielsen 2015: 68). This may be because of their intensity or their ability to stimulate curiosity, but they cause bodily responses; the method allows these bodily reactions to guide the selection and analysis. (Reading about this has prompted Melanie to reflect that during the day's filming as part of her video-stimulated dialogue method discussed in Chapter 7, the selection of video clips to review was probably informed by bodily responses in ways the individuals were not aware.)

The case example illustrates how a videographic participation approach might work to 'bring the researchers and their audience closer to other people's multisensory experiences' (Degerbøl and Svendler Nielsen 2015: 64). This is body-to-body communication. We can see echoes of this in the way in which the *Intensive Interaction* research (discussed in Chapter 7) could not have influenced other practitioners as much through just the written word. Seeing the results of the intervention helps, but more than this, people have been able to *sense* the effects of the pedagogic approach through the medium of video combined with narrative. In the videographic participation approach, the video and narrative are further melded. Degerbøl and Svendler Nielsen (2015) are careful to note that it is not that we cannot, as researchers, express ideas about embodied learning in written or verbal language, rather that audiovisual narrative helps.

Touch and pedagogy

So far in this chapter we have not dwelt on touch, despite this being 'the channel through which physical co-presence is most directly embodied' (McDaniel and Andersen 1998: 194). Ordinarily in education, touch is taboo. There is a moral panic about early childhood classrooms in particular as 'precarious spaces ... potentially dangerous and threatening to children' (Robinson 2008: 125). This has led to panoptic surveillance and regulations about 'when, how and how often, adults can touch children' (ibid.), even to schools becoming 'no touch zones' (Johnson 2000; Piper and Smith 2003: 879). This reflects some of the cultural preoccupations of the United Kingdom, United States and Australia, in particular. Yet multimodal researchers are discussing touch, which, for them, becomes a communicative mode if in its social use it is 'a semiotic resource' fulfilling a communication need (Bezemer and Kress 2014: 78).

For researchers of pedagogy, an interest in pedagogic touch may be limited to pedagogic interactions involving young children and disabled learners, where touch may still be an everyday occurrence within learning environments. Nonetheless, these researchers face the challenge that touch is one of the senses that is most tacit and difficult to describe (Bezemer and Kress 2014). If research transcripts are 'transducted and edited representations through which analytical insights can be gained and certain details are lost'

(Bezemer and Mavers 2011: 196, cited by Cowan 2014: 7), then we can only imagine how much is lost when attempting to transcribe touch interactions. Our multimodal transcripts as 'noticing devices' (ten Have 2007: 95) need to include touch. Hewett (2007: 116) uses description combined with reflection on his own response to try to articulate the touch he observes among learners with profound and multiple impairments:

> I saw three young women and two young men hoisted and lowered into a large, soft corner area. They were placed very close to each other. In a slow-motion fashion, they started to roll to pat and stroke and prod and push each other. They became vocally noisy. I did not feel in any doubt that they were having a wonderful time together

Touch may carry communicative meaning for the person touching and the person being touched, but it carries meaning for the observer too. The literature, however, tends to focus on the benefits or dangers of touch (Piper and Smith 2003) rather than its role in teaching and learning and how this can be researched.

Flewitt, Kucirkova and Messer (2014: 108) note the capacity of touch to 'render human experience communicative, sensory and embodied'. They are less concerned with touch between people than with touch 'as part of the corporeality of the body and the objects humans interact with, giving rise to embodied lived experiences where the materiality of the physical world becomes entangled with the minds and bodies of individuals' (ibid.). For them, learning involves reciprocal relating between learner and the things in the learning environment that have particular affordances and offer particular opportunities. In their study of the literacy learning opportunities offered by touchscreen technology (iPads) for disabled learners, Flewitt, Kucirkova and Messer (2014) used familiar research methods: video recordings, field notes and interviews with the teachers. Thus, focused mostly on observing digital touch, they were researching about touch but not through touch. Touch-based research could be a new arena of research methods for pedagogic researchers to explore.

Before drawing this chapter to a close, we remind readers of the importance of using research methods that are fit for purpose. While the new technologies have expanded the potential of the researcher to explore pedagogy, especially embodied pedagogy, more deeply and at first hand, we emphasize throughout the need to develop and understand, as a pedagogy researcher, the lens through which one looks. One final example to emphasize this point is work on craft apprentices conducted by Trevor Marchand (2008) who, originally an architect, became aware of the significance of embodied pedagogy in seeking to understand his participants' growth and development as skilled craftsmen and women. His research approach was anthropological, based on long periods of fieldwork with minaret builders in Yemen, mud masons in Mali, and fine-woodwork trainees in East London. He observed how eyes, ears, hand and tools were central to understanding their participation and identity shift over time. His description of his research integrates both his approach and his own embodiment in the process:

> I train and labour over long periods with communities of craftsmen, and establish a solid rapport with my fellow workers. In this exchange of 'toil' for 'ethnographic knowledge' (as well as craft skills), my physical contribution offers me privileged access to my co-workers' practices and their expertise. A regular schedule of long hours, and engagement in what are often repetitive manual tasks, permits repeated observation leading to a more detailed understanding of both artisan techniques and the modes of communication involved in teaching and learning skills. ... Most on-site communication is non-propositional, and relies more immediately on an intercourse of visual, auditory and somatic information. This coerces me, as researching participant, to become corporeally and sensually immersed in daily work activities with my colleague-subjects, allowing for reflection upon my own learning, mistakes and progress, as well as the pains and pleasures that accompany physical labour. (Marchand 2008: 248–9)

His approach and his sociocultural conceptual framework, based on situation and relationships, allowed him better to understand the ways in which craftspeople 'silently' learn their skills 'on the job', and how the acquisition of these skills is bound up with their emerging social and professional identities.

Conclusion

Recognition of pedagogy as embodied encourages the researcher to view people as inscribed or shaped by the policies, practices and structures of the institution of which they are a part. These structures include spaces, timetables, movement, furniture, classroom design even down to lesson plans, teaching methods and assessment approaches (Dixon 2011). All such structures work to make the bodies and to produce identities. Adopting research methods that examine these processes allows the pedagogy researcher to glimpse compliance or resistance, affordances and constraints of pedagogical approaches. Bodies take on patterns of behaviours in classrooms and workplaces, for instance the act of writing, reading, building a bridge and so on, and as these acts and their actors are regulated and monitored so they take on ways of knowing and behaving in the world. You might find it helpful to discuss the ideas in this chapter with a mentor as they can be quite unsettling. Arguably, to date, pedagogy researchers have marginalized the body, emphasizing instead conceptual knowing in formal schooling. Yet, many have argued that it is with bodies, and not merely words, that people learn, express, interpret, improvise and negotiate – in a word, 'craft' – their ways of knowing in the world (Harris 2007). Thus, the body, embodiment and space are aspects ripe for research.

Further reading

Pink, S. (2009), *Doing Sensory Ethnography*, London: Sage.
Perry, M. and C. L. Medina (eds) (2015), *Methodologies of Embodiment: Inscribing Bodies in Qualitative Research*, Abingdon/New York: Routledge.

If this chapter has got you interested then we recommend spending some time with these books as they will help you to appreciate more fully the role of the body in the act of researching, which you can apply when thinking about researching pedagogy as embodied.

For more infor mation on the ethics of visual methods see: Wiles, R., A. Coffey, J. Robison and J. Prosser (2012), 'Ethical Regulation and Visual Methods: Making Visual Research Impossible or Developing Good Practice', *Sociological Research Online*, 17(1): 1–17, or Wiles, R., J. Prosser, A. Bagnoli, A. Clark, K. Davies, S. Holland and E. Renold (2008), *Visual*

Ethics: Ethical Issues in Visual Research. NCRM Working Paper. http://eprints.ncrm.ac.uk/421/.

For CAQDAS (computer-assisted qualitative data analysis software) that can handle and manage multimedia data enabling new forms of transcription, look at Transana, NVivo, Atlas.ti, MAXqda, HyperRESEARCH and QUALRUS via http://caqdas.soc.surrey.ac.uk.

CHAPTER NINE

Pedagogy as space: Pushing methodological boundaries

Introduction

We conclude Part Three with an exploration of the role of space in researching teaching–learning relationships. Focusing on the hidden and hard-to-know, this chapter examines how a consideration of space in research methodology can aid researchers in reaching that which is elusive and discreet, inscribed in the spaces surrounding and encompassing practice. We begin with a definition of space for pedagogy research. We offer a rationale for a focus on space in pedagogy research methodology alongside exemplary research methods and case examples that focus on pedagogy research in a variety of contexts and spaces. Exploring physical, social, temporal, experiential and virtual spaces with a learning intent, this chapter examines verbal, visual, observational, ethnographic, textual, audiovisual, technological and participatory action research approaches and methodologies that can be adapted and employed in a study of space in pedagogy research.

Interactive spaces: Scripting the physical, social, temporal, experiential and virtual

Space provides interactive scripts, shared resources and points of intersection for teachers and learners. It has physical, social, temporal, experiential (and possibly virtual) dimensions and designing methodologies around different places (school, classroom, out-of-school, online) and their possible interactions requires much more than a consideration of the physical aspects and material artefacts of the setting of the research. In pedagogy research, space is 'not a receptacle, a vessel that can be filled and emptied of its contents ... space exists only as it is inhabited – it is created by the act of occupancy' (Buchanan 1992: 1).

Fielding's (2000) study of teachers who share a classroom and a group of students evidences very well the social and experiential aspects of space. This is as classes with different teachers (but with the same students and in the same room) create for students many different possibilities for movement, interaction and engagement. Tracing the movement patterns of one girl in the same place and with the same group of students, but a different teacher – first a female teacher and then a large, suited male teacher – the researcher shows the extreme difference in the spaces experienced by this young girl through the participation and opportunities afforded to her. Extending our understanding of space, McGregor (2004a: 16) defines the concept of spatiality, as evidenced in this study as 'an interactive relationship between physical and social space'. Understood in this way, spaces are socially practised places (Agnew 2005), temporally, and constantly under construction through processes of participation and reification (Wenger 1998); they are experienced differently by their inhabitants. These spaces require a nuanced and balanced approach to designing methods that can make visible particular aspects of practice that remain hidden and hard to know within these multidimensional and interactive spaces at the heart of teaching and learning.

When we consider the spaces in which we research, and in particular the interaction between their physical, social, temporal, experiential and virtual aspects, we understand space as porous and connected to other places, spaces and time through its participants and their shared and non-shared histories of participation. Understanding the spaces we inhabit as dynamic and both shaped and shaping our experiences across time and space allows us, as researchers, to bring into focus some of what is hidden in pedagogical practice, as we explore through this chapter's case examples of in-school, out-of-school and online spaces. These case examples illustrate some of the different ways that research is enhanced through a consideration of the various dimensions of space in pedagogy research.

Our case examples explore pedagogy as a spatial practice where physical, social, temporal, experienced and virtual spaces shape, afford and constrain pedagogical practice, teaching and learning in a variety of ways. As our purpose in this chapter is to present a variety of methods for conceptualizing and researching different pedagogical spaces, we have selected five case examples, each of which focuses on one particular aspect of pedagogical space. In this way, we make visible particular research questions, methods and tools for exploring these particular aspects of in-school, out-of-school and online pedagogical spaces. However, as our previous definition of space makes clear, research spaces and sites are porous, and are at once physical, social, temporal and experiential, and they have virtual links to other spaces and times. Though our case examples mainly address a single particular aspect of pedagogical space, each space is at once physical, social, temporal, experiential, and links to online and virtual spaces. This is significant in light of the embedded nature of spatial pedagogical practice. To understand pedagogical space, researchers need to work to make visible and untangle the myriad chains of events, people, experience and settings that make up pedagogical practice, as suggested by Higgins et al. (2005: 35), 'The relationship between people and their environments must be complex, and therefore any outcomes from a change in setting are likely to be produced through an involved chain of events. It is the defining and understanding of these mediating chains that is the key.'

The physical chain: Visual methodologies for researching material spaces

At the most simplistic understanding of space as physical and material, the location and place of the research site (urban, rural, surrounding area and community) as well as its nature (in-school, out-of-school, online) will have implications for the research process and researcher. Tools and language used by researchers need to reflect and connect with the lived experiences of participants. Established and traditional research methods such as interviews, case studies and surveys need careful consideration if they are to allow participant engagement and understanding.

Researching the physical aspects of space, researchers can pay attention to, for example, the architecture and design of the space, furniture, material artefacts, atmosphere, lighting, heating, the challenges of the physical and material spaces and artefacts, and the wider area in which the research site is located. They may address the personal space of participants and organization of the space and bodies, as we discussed in Chapter 8. Understanding space as porous, it may also be interesting for researchers to consider how other physical spaces and material artefacts (e.g. home geographies and artefacts) are represented, included, excluded or valued in different pedagogical spaces and practices. Researchers may also like to consider the temporality of space and the effect of this on pedagogical practice. Examples of this include a consideration of issues such as timetabling and room allocations, beginning and ending of school or college day, time and duration of class periods, and how these influence the physical and material spaces of teaching and learning.

Many classroom rating scales allow researchers to explore the links between pedagogical practice and the physical and material aspects of the learning environment. One such widely used instrument is Sanoff's (2001) *School Buildings Assessment Methods*. This manual comprises a selection of survey and discussion tools (e.g. **photo questionnaires**, building surveys) to explore the physical features of school buildings, but can be adapted to other sites and settings. Sanoff's *Six Factor School Building Checklist: A Walking Tour*, for example, highlights six areas that researchers of physical space should pay attention to when researching school or classroom spaces. These include context (the school building's setting); massing (of the parts to give meaning and form to the whole); interface (meeting point of the inside and outside of the building/room); wayfinding (the ability of teachers and students to find routes, movement patterns, etc.); social space (how the environment supports diverse human needs) and comfort. Researchers, participants (or both) can complete another tool, Sanoff's *School Building Observation Form*, to reflect on various aspects of the physical buildings of a school or university. Sanoff's *School Building Rating Scale* allows evaluation of space according to categories understood as important for meeting the demands of optimum learning spaces (including physical features, outdoor areas, learning environments, social areas, media access, transition spaces and circulation routes, visual appearance, safety and security and overall impression).

Moving more towards research tools for participants, Sanoff (2001) includes examples of photo questionnaires to elicit information on their understanding of the role of physical spaces in learning. Wish poems about what my school should be like and group interaction approaches are offered as tools for asking participants to reflect on the physicality of their learning spaces. Sanoff's manual also gives careful consideration to particular classroom and learning spaces and includes, for example, a space assessment worksheet (including consideration of spatial layout, seating, physical attributes, furniture, floor plans and a pictorial representation of the space) that can be adapted and given to participants who can then consider their own physical spaces. These scales, which are all included in Sanoff's (2001) manual, can provide researchers with ready-made tools or creative starting points for the development of their own tools for researching physical and material pedagogical spaces.

The 'Connections between Learning Spaces and Learning Outcomes: People and Learning Places' project undertaken at Deakin University (Blackmore et al. 2010) offers possible areas for **spatial research** and methods for studying these. Blackmore and colleagues list the methodological characteristics of studies, which help move towards a deeper exploration of the pedagogical practice and intent of physical learning spaces:

- Visual ethnographies that observe different uses of different spaces such as open/specialist (e.g. time lapse, video recall)

- Longitudinal studies that look at patterns of use of buildings, specific spaces and changes in pedagogical practice linked to specific learning outcomes

- Teacher and student reflection on meaning-making, sense of self, learning and space (visual methodologies, self-reporting, etc.)

- Student and teacher action research exploring use of space and time, that is, focus on ongoing inquiry and problem solving

- Organizational and policy analysis that addresses how contextual changes in policy, resourcing, system support and demography impact on use of spaces

- Case studies that explore relationships between school cultures and organization pedagogical practices in use of space, and student outcomes
- Identification of the types of professional development and supports that are most likely to lead to productive use of new learning spaces
- Geospatial mapping technologies
- Exploration of the range of assessment tools that could be incorporated in ways that fit with our conceptual framework and that could be used also as research tools.

The bibliography that Blackmore et al. (2010) include with their project report is over a hundred pages long. It lists and summarizes a wide range of theoretical and empirical papers and studies that focus on the relationship between spaces, teaching and learning, and which are useful to the pedagogy researcher. Traditional methods employed by researchers of physical spaces highlighted in the majority of these studies include physical tours of the spaces, plans and blue print analysis, survey, interview, observation, ethnography and case studies. Some of this research focuses on the physical spaces themselves, but does not include in this analysis a consideration of what is done in, afforded and constrained by, the spaces in question. When researching the physicality of pedagogical space, as researchers we need to understand this space as both active and interactive. In applying this understanding to research design, a focus on student voice makes these active and interactive dimensions of physical space more visible.

Fisher (2004: 36) highlights deep spatial silences encountered in students in his critical ethnographic study of an ABC (asphalt, brick and concrete) high school, suggesting ways in which space impacts on the people within it and the social dynamics between them. Exploring student voice and experiences around hidden curricula inscribed in classroom practices and spaces challenges researchers of pedagogy to make visible the hard-to-know aspects of pedagogy hidden in the plain sight of classroom spaces, artefacts and activities. A recent Australian report (Blackmore et al. 2013) highlights innovative and technological visual methodologies that allow the researcher to pay particular attention to student voice in exploring spatialized pedagogical practices in school settings. We look at this in case example 9.1.

Case example 9.1: The embodied pedagogic voice: Exploring methodological approaches to investigating spatialized pedagogical practices in innovative learning environments (Blackmore et al. 2013)

Context: A study exploring the pedagogical spaces of twelve innovative primary and secondary public schools in Victoria, Australia.

Goals: To investigate a number of methodological opportunities for exploring 'associations between spatiality, temporality and the embodied and lived experiences of teaching and learning' (Blackmore et al. 2013: 1), particularly visual research methodologies that focus on student voice and experience and the way that students and teachers use and engage with each other and physical (and other) pedagogical spaces.

Outcomes: Main findings indicate that methodologies that focus on student voice offer very different perspectives on pedagogy, space and time. For example, the places noted by students as most pleasurable and conducive to learning were not seen as learning spaces by the teachers in the study. Evidence that spatial methodologies provide teachers and researchers with different ways to reflect on practice and visual methodologies allows researchers to work with and alongside students as active participants in research.

Research methods: Researchers spent five days in each of the twelve selected schools developing case studies that explored the nature and effectiveness of the twelve primary and secondary school sites, self-identified as innovative learning environments. Extending traditional case study approaches, this study employed a series of innovative and technological visual research methods, including interview-infused participatory photographic observation, drawing, mapping and photography that foreground student perspectives (and specific techniques that we outline next).

To choose their sample, Blackmore et al. (2013) asked schools to apply to be participants in the project, making clear why their practice and learning environments were innovative in design. The researchers decided on this purposive sampling method to ensure information-rich informants. Many of the methods they employed are highly technological and innovative, but are also most accessible and adaptable for other researchers of pedagogy. In Table 9.1 we outline some of these digital and visual tools with their uses, but readers should go to the original report for further detail and examples of how these were employed in the study.

Table 9.1 Digital and visual tools used by Blackmore et al. (2013)

Vidi – annotation software programme that allows researchers to annotate directly onto their research videos and tag particular parts for searching and locating	Can be used by participants to reflect on aspects of their experience recorded on video or as an alternative to transcription, to allow researchers to stay close to the original multisensory data
Pencasting uses Smartpen technology (pens that synchronize sound and written recordings) to create a file where researchers can see the written drawings/notes and hear the audio interview/discussion around this simultaneously	Blackmore et al. (2013) used pencasting to ask participants collectively to draw school maps, fill in features of the space and indicate their own favourite spaces (for learning, working and being) including themselves, their friends and their teachers and suggesting the activities they do in these spaces. As they engaged in this activity, participants also described to the group what they were drawing and further discussion on this was encouraged. Later, the researchers could access any point of the audio recording by tapping on the corresponding piece of drawing. This is also useful in the interview/focus group, as researchers can bring participants back to a piece of the map visually and aurally immediately

Motioncapture tracks the movement patterns of students and teachers but requires much preparation and the installation of a bird's eye view video camera	Blackmore et al. (2013) employed MotionLab to capture how students and teachers move around classrooms and school buildings in their daily practice
Nearmap is an application, similar to GoogleMaps, which allows researchers access for analysis and material for research activities and discussions to aerial photographs of schools and their surrounding areas over the course of a year	Blackmore et al. (2013) made screenshots from Nearmap aerial images for three participating schools in the project. These screenshots could then be analysed in a number of ways for example allowing researchers to chart changes in these images over time or explore student use of space in terms of spatial dynamics
Paperstories allows participants to edit PowerPoint presentations using digital pen technology	Blackmore et al. (2013) engaged students in taking digital pictures of spaces and producing PowerPoint presentations on these for them to review with the researchers.

Blackmore et al. (2013: 14) highlight many advantages to the final method, in particular: 'The data in this process is being analysed by both the researcher and the participants as it is being produced with an agreed upon story and themes. The process takes the coercive power away from the researcher and gives it to the participants. The resulting data is immediately available as viewable text within the project.'

Deciding on their research design, Blackmore et al. (2013) selected traditional case study methodology and enhanced this by including the innovative spatial and visual research methods described. Explaining this in their report, they state:

Most case study approaches require researchers to interview adults, usually the principal, the teachers and often parents, sometimes students, to elicit understandings, validated by documentary evidence, as to what happened and with what effects (Stake 1995). For that reason the focus is on organisational structures, cultures and discourses, and on teachers and their pedagogic practice. ... When students are included in research, these are largely premised upon text based renditions of interviews which often position the student as a passive object of teaching and research (Rudduck and Flutter 2004). This report argues that such approaches do not fully capture teachers' and students' 'lived experiences of space', the multiplicity of ways of seeing and feeling, and how students in particular are active participants in their learning (Cook-Sather 2006; Burke 2008; Prosser 1998). (Blackmore et al. 2013: 2)

To get to the heart of these lived experiences of physical spaces, researchers need to consider the many pedagogical activities (communicating, decision-making, sharing, giving and receiving feedback, questioning, etc.) occurring in the space and time of teaching and learning, and how physical spaces and material artefacts afford and constrain different pedagogical activities. Employing methodologies and methods that prioritize student voice as well as explore physical settings allows researchers to pay attention to ways in which physical spaces hide, perpetuate and generally organize practice and participation.

Next, we look at ways to explore the social dimension of pedagogical space, which offer other ways of getting to what is hidden and hard to know in the lived experiences of pedagogical spaces and learning worlds.

The social chain: Exposing power and agency through video methodology

Researchers examining the social aspects of space can attend to, for example,

- how teachers and students organize themselves and the space for interaction (dialogue, pair, group, etc.);

- grouping and seating of students (according to gender, friends, etc.);

- intentional and non-intentional opportunities for the development of these social spaces in community activity;

- hierarchies of power and the influence of this on individual agency, social purposes and functions of different spaces (staffroom, classroom, hall, etc.) and

- relationships, distance and closeness in relationships, emotional geographies. (Hargreaves 2001)

McGregor (2004a) highlights the importance of space in understanding the hidden and hard-to-know in classroom-based pedagogy research, and in particular the exploration of social and power relations and agency, as she explains:

> The silences around space allow it to be organized to produce and reproduce practices which maintain persistent and unequal power relations. Understanding space as socially produced reveals current social arrangements which maintain and ossify such power relations, but which can then be contested and changed. ... Space hides things from us, through our lack of understanding of it as constructed and contestable ... [and] has a taken for granted quality that blinds us to fundamental ways in which the school is spatially constructed. The almost ubiquitous orderings of classrooms, laboratories, staffrooms and playgrounds in secondary schools thus obscure the way in which the setting is active in sustaining certain power relations. (McGregor 2004a: 13)

As McGregor (ibid.) proposes here, paying attention to the dynamics of social spaces enables researchers to make visible aspects of power and agency in teaching and learning relationships hidden in daily taken-for-granted practices. Considering the physicality of space, she explains that 'school buildings are inscribed with educational ideologies and practices, and the fabric is a chronicle of change and use resulting from the network of relations, local and global, which comprise "the school"' (p. 14). She offers the example of the teacher's desk, a symbol of authority and point of surveillance, as a space that students may not touch, while teachers freely move articles in and around the desks and spaces that the students themselves occupy. In this example, McGregor considers possible meanings for not only the physical but also the kinetic, social and experienced aspects of the space occupied by the teacher's desk.

McGregor's (2004b) understanding of space as social, interactive and relational influences all aspects of her research design. In a study looking at the spatiality of teachers' workplaces in the United Kingdom, she foregrounds 'the mutual implication of the social and the material in the construction of the everyday interactions that constitute the school' (McGregor 2004b: 348). In answering the question what is a school, she reveals how the lives of teachers and students are shared with objects, which 'help configure and define their work and identity, and are a part of spatially constituted subject subcultures' (p. 349). While this study makes visible the interaction between the physical and the social in researching pedagogical spaces, case example 9.2 clearly relates the power contained in the social spaces of pedagogical practice to limit agency and learning opportunities for young people covertly and insidiously.

Case example 9.2: The acquisition of a child by a learning disability (McDermott 1993)

Context: A study of the learning biographies of a group of young children in the United States.

Goals: This study aimed to locate the young children 'thinking aloud' and make visible the ways in which classroom activities exist and are interrupted by spaces, times and tasks that 'never quite stand still' (McDermott 1993: 270). Trying to locate the learning disability assigned to one young student (Adam), the researchers seek to understand the social spaces which surround his engagement across four different settings.

Outcomes: Evidence of the experiences of Adam and of how the social interactions constructed around him, and those of which he finds himself a part of, work to create him as learning disabled. McDermott argues that Adam's learning disability exists in, and is perpetuated by, his social spaces, rather than being understood as a condition of deficit on his own part. For McDermott (1993: 273), this study shows that 'there is no such thing as LD [learning disabled], only a social practice of displaying, noticing, documenting, remediating and explaining it'.

Case example 9.2

Research methods: Three researchers collected a series of video tapes from a classroom of eight- and nine-year-old children in four different settings (everyday life, cooking club, classroom lessons and testing sessions) over a two-year period. Analysing these video tapes, the researchers share the very important understanding that what was available for analysis in terms of the physical recordings and interactions simultaneously hid aspects of pedagogical space from the researcher's view, as these were 'sequenced in the experience of persons in the lived world' (McDermott 1993: 270).

The analysis and subsequent understanding of the power within social spaces to afford or constrain learning opportunities within McDermott's (1993) study resonates with our focus on social pedagogical spaces, as spaces where power and agency are openly and covertly negotiated, claimed, afforded and constrained. Developing a methodology that makes visible some of these power struggles, researchers need first to recognize where and how power is constituted and distributed in and across pedagogical spaces through social interaction. Employing analyses that look at these spaces in more depth, such as those explored in Chapter 5 in relation to classroom talk, allows researchers to make visible the ways in which taken-for-granted practices and positions in teaching–learning relationships are constructed, organized and maintained across social and interactive pedagogical spaces.

Video methods, as we showed in Chapter 8, allow researchers to experience, record and relive experiences; they facilitate the study of learning through visual representations and images of the world of the participants. Video methods are suited to researching social spaces as they capture very well the content and context of interactions. They offer a visual representation of spatial and social relationships, but this representation is not unproblematic; it cannot be read as or in any way more factual or truthful than ethnographic field notes or participant reflection. Videos do not capture reality, but rather make visible how place and space are made in everyday, sensorial engagements with material and social spaces (Pink 2008).

As researchers, we also need to be aware that, to make meaning from these created social artefacts and visual texts, we need also to consider the many contexts that are perhaps not visible in the video, but which are central to the interpretation of experience in this methodology. Therefore, using video may need to be part of an ethnographic approach that also allows time for the researcher to observe, spend time with and talk to participants in the research site. The need for this connection between the researchers and the research site was evident in case example 9.2, as an awareness of the different contexts surrounding Adam's practice allowed researchers to understand how certain pedagogical tasks were obscured for him by the social work required. Other experiences forced researchers to question in how very many different ways Adam and the teacher misunderstood each other in their pedagogical interactions. McDermott (1993: 291) notes how:

> Looking for Adam's LD has become something of a sport in Adam's class … . His every move is designed not to have LD again ascribed to him, and, as such, his every move confirms and recreates the possibility that the label of LD will be available in the classroom for anyone to ascribe to Adam. Where is the LD? Behaviourally, the answer is clear. It is all over the classroom as an interactional possibility. Everyone stands in some relation to it. Everyone is part of the choreography that produces moments for its public appearance. LD is distributed across persons, across the moment, as part of the contextual work members do in the different scenes. Neither Adam, nor his disability, can be separated from the contexts in which they emerge.

Increased availability of video technology (including small handheld camcorders and video and cameras on tablets and mobile phones) brings more opportunities for researchers to engage participants in video-based activities. As we discussed in Chapter 8, there are ethical and moral considerations involved in this, particularly in relation to using digital media with young people. When asked either to be recorded or to make recordings, participants need to understand the natural spatial boundaries surrounding the research and where and in what contexts recording is deemed appropriate and inappropriate. Recording classroom experiences requires school and parental approval, and may require additional protocols to be put in place, for example questioning what parts of the classroom will be recorded, how students will be recorded and when the camera may have to be turned off during the course of the research.

The *Guidelines for Video Research in Education: Recommendations from an Expert Panel* (Derry 2007) provide a useful starting point for planning, developing and organizing video-based methodologies in pedagogy research. Sample documentation is included together with common transcription choices (see also Chapter 8). Other sections consider video-recording strategies, methods of data selection, analytical frameworks and practices, technologies and practices for reporting and sharing video research, how people learn from video, and ethical considerations in collecting, analysing and using video data. Researchers interested in using video methods will also find further real life examples and case studies in *Video Methods: Social Science Research in Motion* (Bates 2014), which explores a variety of different methods including video diaries, time-lapse videos, mobile device videos and ethnographic documentaries.

The temporal chain: Temporal links through talk and observation in pedagogical spaces

If we, as researchers, decide to use video methods to make particularly visible certain aspects of social practice, we must also be cognisant that classroom interactions and experiences do not exist in a vacuum. They are connected through individuals to other spaces and places, and they point to past, present and future experiences. In any learning environment, formal or non-formal, the change in participation of individuals as a result of experience (learning) is not an end point but rather a set of coordinates on a learning journey or trajectory that spans many different spaces and times. Looking at the temporal dimension of pedagogical spaces challenges the researcher to make visible the past, present and future (anticipated and actual) practices of participants and make meaning from the stories these tell. Here, the researcher may employ video alongside other research methods such as intervention, observation or ethnography. In case example 9.3, Mercer (2008: 2) exemplifies a research design concerned primarily with the temporality of classroom talk as it is 'used to represent past shared experience, carry ideas forward from one occasion to another, approach future activities and achieve learning outcomes'.

Case example 9.3: The seeds of time: Why classroom dialogue needs a temporal analysis (Mercer 2008)

Context: An applied, interventional research study in the United Kingdom that explores the temporal nature of classroom talk in a number of primary schools.

Goals: Understanding learning as happening over time and occurring through dialogue, the study aimed to explore the same dialogue over time to investigate how learning happens in primary school settings. Mercer wanted to make visible the connections to previous and future interactions and activities, and to explore which practices and discourses individuals draw on to guide their interactions and experiences in the present time and space.

Outcomes: Illustration of how classroom talk has historical aspects (personal, institutional and cultural context) and dynamic aspects (talk is emergent and unplanned). An argument that to help make meaning of classroom talk, researchers should include in their methodological considerations ways to make visible the shared history of the participants, the temporal development of the dialogue, the trajectory of the event and the educational outcomes of the event.

Research methods: Draws on data from an applied research intervention in a number of UK primary schools. Methods used include video recording and transcribing of classroom dialogue over a period of four months, the selection of both teacher–student and student–student talk about a related series of pedagogical events and analysis of transcripts with a focus on sequence, coherence, continuity and discontinuity in learner experiences.

Case example 9.3

Mercer (2008: 7) acknowledges that there is little methodological guidance for researchers who study the temporal dimension and development of talk, but highlights ways of looking at this aspect by citing questions posed by Gee and Green (1998: 141), such as 'What sorts of connections (intertextual ties) are proposed, recognized, acknowledged, and interactionally made to previous or future interactions (activity) and to texts, to other people, ideas, things, institutions and discourses outside the current interaction? Which processes, practices and discourses do [speakers] draw on from previous events/situations to guide the actions in the current situation (e.g. text construction)?'

Classroom dialogue has many functions, ranging from management to reflection to inspiration and encouragement. Researchers interested in the temporality of pedagogical space may also use video or aural recordings and classroom observation, and look at transcripts of observed practice to identify temporal statements and examine the purpose and design of these utterances. We may consider the time given to different activities in class and to their sequencing, the longitudinal and holistic experience of engaging in learning about a particular unit of work, the learning trajectory of students as individuals or as a group, the connections between classroom practice and past, present and future in and out-of-school practices and experiences.

A focus on the temporal and on learning as a trajectory or journey allows researchers to make visible through video, observational and ethnographic methods the continuities and discontinuities of classroom and learning experiences for individuals. However, this does require creative and careful management of time and resources on the behalf of the researcher, who has to decide how to collect and represent this longitudinal learning journey. Mercer (2008) selected a manageable time frame for the research, but one that would allow sufficient time to highlight continuities and discontinuities in practice.

Focusing on the temporal aspect of classroom space, Mercer (2008) establishes in his methodology that each interaction has a historical and a dynamic aspect. He explains the historical aspect in terms of how the interaction is located within the personal, social, institutional and cultural histories of participants. Interactions are also dynamic, because they are emergent and not planned; they happen in the moment to moment of practice. Looking for patterns in this historical and dynamic classroom talk, Mercer explains that these patterns, repetitions, recaps and so on make visible the many ways in which the talk of the lesson may actually be understood as a part of one long learning conversation between the participants. Understanding his data as an extended text, Mercer (2008: 31) applies discourse analysis and coding to find 'temporal evidence of this class developing through educational dialogue a shared vocabulary for talking about educational dialogue'. An interesting understanding for the researcher of temporal pedagogical space explored here by Mercer is the notion of the significance of repetition in classroom interactions and that 'the same act repeated cannot be assumed to be "the same" act in repetition, because it builds historically on the earlier event. This insight applies as much, of course, to the consideration of verbal acts – and so problematizes the use of atemporal coding schemes for studying the educational functions of discourse' (Mercer 2008: 7).

Holland, Gordon and Lahelma (2007: 221) employ spatial and temporal ethnographic observation in a study following teachers on their 'time-space paths in schools, from corridors to staff rooms to classrooms and breaks'. Focusing on the teachers rather than the students or the places, the researchers ask how space both limits and controls teachers' movements and the use of their time–space paths. Their comparative ethnography of one UK and one Finnish second-ary school follows teachers' movements through the school day to explore how different spaces carry differentiation, connection and negotiation processes for teachers and students. The researchers highlight staffrooms, for example, as spaces that physically, spa-tially and aurally exclude students (and some adults such as trainee teachers or the researchers themselves) from their practices, where invisible rules govern interactions. They observe and analyse school rituals surrounding time and movement, such as entering and exit-ing classrooms, as moments in time where teachers exert control and territorialize the classroom as a place within their control.

Though Holland, Gordon and Lahelma (2007) understood stu-dents in their study to experience immobility and a slow passing of time spent waiting in classrooms, they saw teachers as rushing and mobile in their classroom practice. In this way, temporal spaces become spaces to contest movement, time, voice and so on. Break-time, they argue, marks a different kind of engagement for teachers and students, and always threatens the chaos that teachers manage and subvert through their practices across various dimensions (physical, social, temporal and experiential). Emotions such as fear, stress and anxiety are tied to these spaces for teachers as unconscious structures (Kehily 2002), set in motion as time moves on in their daily practice. These feelings and unconscious structures play a role in teacher and student experiences at various points in the school day where 'whilst students may feel that "my arse gets numb, I get all sweaty", the teacher may feel that she is running around "like a bunny"' (Holland, Gordon and Lahelma 2007: 234).

Temporal analyses such as these can shed light on how young people's experiences, attitudes and learning emerge, change and evolve. They have at their heart a consideration of the emotional and experiential aspects of pedagogical space that we focus on in our next section.

The experiential chain: Action research methods for exclusive spatial practices

Researching the experiential aspects of space, researchers can pay attention to, for example,

- the embodied practices of teaching and learning (as explored in Chapter 8);
- lived experiences of participants and how these compare and contrast;
- embodied pedagogies, feelings and emotions;
- subjective experiences, memories and previous histories of participation;
- expectations and
- markers of identity (gender, race, social class) and their implications for engagement and experience, participant feelings of belonging.

In case example 9.4 we present a study that focuses clearly on the experiential aspects of pedagogical space, exploring how, through a mix of action research and a consideration of contrasting experiential perspectives, the researchers managed very well to keep their participants central to their methodological design and process. This is an essential aim when exploring experiential pedagogical spaces.

Case example 9.4: Youth clubs as spaces of non-formal learning: Professional idealism meets the spatiality experienced by young people in Finland (Kiilakoski and Kivijärvi 2015)

Context: An exploration of Finnish youth clubs as spaces of non-formal learning from the perspectives of the youth workers and the young people.

Goals: To contrast 'the professional accounts of youth workers with the spatiality experienced by young people' (Kiilakoski and Kivijärvi 2015: 48), asking what factors tighten youth club spaces for some young people resulting in them not attending these clubs.

Outcomes: This study shows that youth clubs are often tight spaces for many young people. The young people who attend particular youth clubs often share similar backgrounds and societal positions. The researchers suggest that youth clubs are not experienced by young people as spaces for group-based non-formal learning in the same way as understood by youth workers. They identify interior (intentional regulations and unintended implications of youth work, control and the club culture) and exterior (rumours, inadequate knowledge of the needs of youth groups, poor locations of youth clubs) spatial practices as influencing the experience of young people in these tight pedagogical spaces. Kiilakoski and Kivijärvi (2015: 59) challenge youth workers to 'solve the contradiction inherent in the pedagogical ideal of a loose space'.

Research methods: Action research, interviews, multisite observations, questionnaires and document analysis. Through

Case example 9.4

individual and group or pair interviews with youth club workers, the researchers attempted to reconstruct the professional discourse on youth clubs. They contrasted this with questionnaires and observations of young people in relation to their spatial practices. Thus, Kiilakoski and Kivijärvi (2015: 50) state that 'by combining the different sets of data, we aimed to contrast the two perspectives on youth clubs and their ability to promote non-formal learning'.

This study explores learning and pedagogical practice in the non-formal spaces of youth clubs in Finland, explaining that youth work is seen in the research literature to promote non-formal learning, as contrasted against the more formal learning in school systems and environments. What is most different for researchers of pedagogy in non-formal settings (see also Chapter 6) is that these pedagogical spaces are visible predominantly through conversations between young people under the guidance of youth workers.

Kiilakoski and Kivijärvi (2015) explore the interplay between looseness and tightness in these pedagogical spaces. They define loose spaces as 'open for negotiation and alteration ... [with] adaptable learning opportunities or an emphasis on communal negotiations instead of rigid rules or curricula', while tight spaces 'in an extreme form ... can be used only by certain types of actors and for predetermined purposes' (p. 49). Formal learning environments, they argue, can be considered 'prime examples of tight spaces with hierarchical structuring and pre-planned schedules. Ambivalence, differences and unexpected incidents have little room in tight spaces' (Kiilakoski and Kivijärvi 2015: 49). Employing an action research approach, Kiilakoski and Kivijärvi (2015) discussed their interpretations and conceptualizations with participants throughout the study. This meant that the research process itself also involved researchers having informal discussions, exchanging emails and giving lectures to youth workers so that the results of the study would be intelligible to participants, thereby allowing a dialogue between researchers and participants on the practical implications of the findings. Kiilakoski and Kivijärvi (2015: 51) explain action research as operating on three levels, the aim being to 'transform sayings, relatings and doings (Kemmis 2009)'. For the purpose of this study, they made the decision to focus only on the first of these three aims, to focus on sayings, for two important reasons central to their aims: 'First, making the often implicit and obscure pedagogies of youth clubs explicit meant that work in Finnish youth clubs could be conceptualized. Second, by focusing on what was said and actually done, the "gaps" between discursive ideals and actual spatial practices could be examined' (ibid.).

The virtual chain: Virtual ethnography and adapting research methods for online spaces

Online and virtual worlds provide new spaces for pedagogy research, as it becomes more and increasingly difficult to separate online and offline lives. Researching virtual and online aspects of space, researchers can attend to the different pedagogical relationship between teacher and student or student and peers as they are separated in space and also (sometimes) time. We need to ask:

- How presence is communicated and felt in online (sometimes only textual) communication?

- How space is created between teachers and learners and the nature of these spaces, the intersection between virtual and real worlds, the development of a number of individual learners to a virtual community in an online space?

- How interactions are facilitated and experienced across a variety of modes of communication?

Moreover, we might inquire into the role of social media, rules and routines for interaction, management of alternatives to face-to-face interaction in online pedagogy, and teachers' and students' roles, and issues of marginalization.

Social spaces created within, for example, Facebook, Twitter and Second Life merge personal, professional and public identities and lives, and present new fora for pedagogy research. These new spaces also bring new ethical and methodological questions for researchers of pedagogy. The distinction between public and private space is not always clear in online environments. Questions arise around the privacy of participants, the written intentions of participants and how these may vary across different media and settings, for example blogging, archived emails, bulletin boards, social networking sites, instant messaging and chats. Taking, for example, a message left on a Facebook wall of a friend, while textual information may be available online, does not mean that the writer intended it for a public audience.

Similarly, researchers have to be careful when deciding to use direct quotes (as in qualitative research) from online participants, as these can be tracked and anonymity for participants cannot be guaranteed (Halfpenny and Proctor 2015). Gaining informed consent can be difficult, as it is likely that the researcher may never actually meet the participants of the study. This links to further issues for the researcher in online spaces around access to participation, securing trust and developing the relationship with participants necessary for some research methods, and leads to the question of under what circumstances can or should researchers contact participants in the so-called real world. We need to be mindful that participants may (mis)represent themselves in an online space in a way that could challenge the validity of the data collected. Most importantly, when researching in online spaces we have to be mindful of the ethical challenges (Wishart and Thomas 2015) and understand that the digital data collected (textual, audio, visual, etc.) come from individuals and have repercussions for their online and offline lives. Case Example 9.5 explores methodological choices made by researchers of a series of online spaces and it provides evidence of the many ethical decisions inherent around the spaces for research in virtual worlds. The authors use netnography (Kozinets 2010), which is a particular development of **virtual ethnography** (Hines 2000).

Case example 9.5: Reconceptualizing fieldwork in a netnography of a global online community of English language teachers (Kulavuz-Onal and Vásquez 2013)

Context: A multisite study of an online community of practice of professionals (teachers, teacher educators, teacher candidates,

Case example 9.5

etc.) from around the world of English as a Second/Foreign Language (ESL/EFL). Participants communicate and chat, but also follow a weekly syllabus (where they read blogs and complete tasks including sharing, exchanging and exploring the pedagogical uses of web-based communication tools in language teaching). On completion, they 'graduate' as Webheads. Online spaces include Yahoo groups and email, Messenger, Tapped In, Facebook, Twitter, Second Life and a biannual online all day conference.

Goals: To explore new types of culture-building and culture-sharing groups in an online multisite netnography (Kozinets 2010) and to understand the nature of one exclusively online, global, multisited and practice-oriented community of practice through a focus on its main activities, practices and perspectives.

Outcomes: The focus was specifically a methodological one, and outcomes discussed are around the researcher experiences of methodological issues, specifically defining the field, the nature of researcher participation, data, impact of medium and survival skills for online fieldwork.

Research methods: Fieldwork over twelve months through online participant observation, prior to which a website detailing research aims, procedures and information on the researchers was put online and shared with participants. Data collection undertaken using netnography (Kozinets 2010) through researcher participation in main online events, analysis of archived email communication, online interviews with site moderators, community founder and five members, reflective observational field notes and screenshots.

Kulavuz-Onal and Vásquez (2013) show how ethnographic fieldwork changes when carried out in online spaces. They explain how the first task for the researcher in online spaces must be the development of an understanding of this space, so as to define the field where the research is to be undertaken. In their study, the researchers traced activities of the virtual rather than geographical community of practice to a variety of online sites and spaces, and the first task became how the researcher could develop boundaries for the research. Trying to understand the spaces involved, the researchers conclude that in redefining the field in online research, 'the field may no longer be a website/site, but rather a set of practices and activities carried out over multiple online platforms' (Kulavuz-Onal and Vásquez 2013: 288).

With the field defined, the next step for Kulavuz-Onal and Vásquez was to decide the nature of their own participation while researching the online community of practice. The researcher may be an observer or a fully active participant in the practice, or live in spaces in between, observing in some contexts and participating in others. Presence and visibility are key issues. As an observer, if the researcher logs on or connects to the online practice of the community under study, her presence may not necessarily be visible to the research participants. This carries ethical and methodological concerns and links to researcher decisions around synchronous or asynchronous access of data in online spaces and how their choices in design influence the data collected and their experience of the research.

Data collected in netnographic (or any virtual ethnographic) observation may vary from that of traditional ethnographic research, as data collection involves 'watching text and images on a computer screen' (Garcia et al. 2009: 58). Observing or participating in online activities and analysing archived data requires researchers to read extensive text and reconstruct meanings within fragments of dialogue or interactions. In the study by Kulavuz-Onal and Vásquez (2013), field notes recorded what was seen on screen, and reflections and interpretations based on experiences in the community of practice. An interesting facet of researching in online spaces in this regard is the opportunity for synchronous and asynchronous engagement with group activities such as group chats. In this example, there was engagement with the biannual one-day conference and online workshops, where researchers could later come back and analyse their own engagement and their interaction with others in archived video or text files.

Kulavuz-Onal and Vásquez (2013) also had to consider carefully the impact of the technology necessitated in online research on more traditional methods such as interviews, questionnaires, focus groups and so on. In this study researchers experienced difficulties when it came to the interview element of their research design, as not all participants wished to use webcams for this part of the study. This led to difficulties for researchers in picking up and making clear social cues such as active listening. Even when participants opted to use a webcam for their interviews, researchers found the social elements of interviewing problematic, for example timing of question and responses and making eye contact with the interviewee (as looking the interviewee in the eye, from their point of view, necessitated that the interviewer look directly at their webcam instead of the interviewee). Engaging with participants across a range of sites also necessitated technological expertise among the researchers as they had to hold and use accounts on several websites and media platforms.

Conclusion

This chapter has explored methods for space and, in particular, its physical, social, temporal, experiential and virtual dimensions in pedagogy research. You might find it useful to map these out in your own research arena. Pushing methodological (and spatial) boundaries, as the title of this chapter suggests, we see space as both shaped by and shaping pedagogical interaction and experience. Understanding space in this way as dynamic and unbounded, this chapter suggests a variety of methods and methodological approaches to make visible and unchain hidden and entangled spatial pedagogical practices. As we move between the chains within pedagogical space, what is most evident is how one space leads into and through the next as they all become part of the moment in pedagogical practice.

Further reading

The special 2004 issue of *Forum*, 46(1) provides a variety of theory and research focused on understandings of place and space in teaching, learning and research. Teachers, architects, academics, educationalists and policy advisers with a common interest in space and schools share articles that put forward the idea that space makes a difference.

Higgs, J., A. Titchen, D. Horsfall and D. Bridges (eds) (2011), *Creative Spaces for Qualitative Researching: Living Research*, Netherlands: Sense. This book explores a variety of qualitative research studies that investigate the living worlds of participants.

2015 Special Issue, *International Journal of Research and Method in Education*, 28(3), *E-research in Educational Contexts: The Roles of Technologies, Ethics and Social Media*, provides useful papers exploring methods for studying education in digital spaces.

Conclusion

To conclude the book, we revisit what we set out to do with it. In the most basic sense, we sought to explain pedagogy and to explore issues that need to be considered when researching it. We knew from the outset that one of our challenges was that, while aspects of pedagogy are often researched, the concept itself is poorly understood. We would need, therefore, to explicate our stance on pedagogy, and discuss research methods and methodologies in relation to this. Thus, our goal was to exemplify the relationships between theoretical stance, pedagogical context and research approach using a range of studies across sectors and cultures. We wanted to make more transparent the decision-making processes that researchers of pedagogy go through, thereby aiding readers to reflect on their own processes. We also wanted to widen and deepen readers' thinking about the available options by discussing not just the expected research approaches – of action research, ethnography, discourse analysis and so on – but also less obvious approaches such as sensory ethnography and lesson study. Some of questions we set out to explore included: What do we, as pedagogy researchers, look at? Where do we look? How do we look? And what is visible and invisible from different points of view? Thus, we would be discussing what constitutes pedagogical texts, data or evidence, and how these might be differently generated and understood.

Reflecting back on what we have done with our intentions for the book, we conclude that we have achieved a number of core things. We have discussed pedagogy as a concept that encompasses teaching and learning plus matters of curriculum, assessment, relationships and values. We have shown it to be about what people perceive to be meaningful, important and relevant. Moreover, we have shown that neither pedagogy nor research methodology is ever 'innocent' as Bruner put it; they are imbued with values. We have provided a sociocultural framework to guide methodological thinking pertaining to researching pedagogy in a range of settings, broadening the focus away from just schools and formal learning contexts.

Our discussion of research methods for pedagogy has taken us back to the fundamentals of what counts as research and what constitutes data in pedagogy research. We have explored methods suited to conceptualizations of pedagogy as specified, pedagogy as enacted and pedagogy as experienced, focusing more on the latter two. We have explored methods, too, in terms of which are suited to conceptualizations of pedagogy as an art, craft or science, focusing more on the first two. Our discussions have led into identifying research methods that put different elements of pedagogy at the centre of the research process, for example, dialogue (Chapter 2), classroom interaction (Chapter 4) and classroom talk (Chapter 5), pedagogic relationships (Chapter 6), teachers' decision-making (Chapter 7), bodies (Chapter 8) and use of pedagogic space (Chapter 9). The discussions have raised questions about the ethical sensitivities and dilemmas associated with different research methods and their application to pedagogy. We have examined the way in which methods may be advanced by technology, particularly digital video technology, but, more importantly, we have examined how pedagogic and research values translate into practice. Our tools in our task have been our reflections on our own methodological decision-making and, where transparent, those of other pedagogy researchers. In addition, by using the case examples, we have been able to illustrate methods in action in pedagogy research and to illuminate the debates, dilemmas and concerns for the researcher.

Throughout the book, we have argued that our theoretical stance on pedagogy is fundamentally important to how we research it; that theories, practices and research approaches and methods messily and inevitably intertwine. Methods of teaching and learning and methods of researching them, we maintain, may be overlapping and blurred. It has been our contention that teachers and pedagogy researchers may be one and the same, or they may share common ground, common approaches to generating data, or work with the same data, in related ways. There is, as we have painstakingly shown, more to researching pedagogy than seeking to understand 'what works' in teaching in learning. Identities, power relations, interests, purposes, agendas, resources, organizational and institutional practices, lived realities, past experiences, conventions and perspectives all matter for pedagogy and for researching pedagogy. These affect our ways of knowing. Researching pedagogy requires attention to its enmeshed, constitutive, situational nature and to its 'attendant discourses' (Alexander 2004: 11). As we have shown, these vary across sectors and contexts with particular methods suited to researching the early years or to pedagogy in the absence of a formal curriculum or teacher, for example.

Readers may not have been surprised to find in the book an exploration of how different kinds of pedagogy take us to different methodological places and different methods. You may have been less prepared for an exploration of the methodological implications of recognizing that pedagogy is embodied and of seeing the pedagogical body in relation to pedagogical structures, other bodies and physical, social, temporal, experiential and virtual space. In culminating with this approach to research methods for pedagogy, we have worked to push at the boundaries of what methods the texts in education ordinarily cover. Our ultimate purpose in this regard has been about pursuing what is inescapable from our perspective – that pedagogy is hard to know. If, as a pedagogy researcher, adopting a sociocultural stance perhaps, you want to get at the complexities of pedagogy beneath and inside what is more readily knowable, then the methodological journey may take you into new territory.

REFERENCES

Aberg, M., A. Makitalo and R. Saljo (2010), 'Knowing and Arguing
in a Panel Debate: Speaker Roles and Responsivity to Others', in
K. Littleton and C. Howe (eds), *Educational Dialogues: Understanding
and Promoting Productive Interaction*, 13–30, London: Routledge.

Adams, P. (2011), '(Dis)continuity and the Coalition: Primary Pedagogy
as Craft and Primary Pedagogy as Performance', *Educational Review*,
63 (4): 467–83.

Agnew, J. (2005), 'Space: Place', in P. J. Cloke (ed.), *Space of Geographical
Thought: Deconstructing Human Geography*, 81–96, London: Sage.

Ainscow, M., T. Booth and A. Dyson (2004), 'Understanding and
Developing Inclusive Practices in Schools: A Collaborative Action
Research Network', *International Journal of Inclusive Education*,
8 (2): 125–39.

Ainscow, M., A. Dyson and S. Weiner (2013), *From Exclusion to
Inclusion: Ways of Responding in Schools to Students with Special
Educational Needs*, Reading: Cfbt Education Trust.

Alexander, R. (2000), *Culture and Pedagogy: International Comparisons
in Primary Education*, Oxford: Blackwell.

Alexander, R. (2001), *Culture and Pedagogy: International Comparisons
in Primary Education*, Oxford: Blackwell.

Alexander, R. (2004), 'Still No Pedagogy? Principle, Pragmatism and
Compliance in Primary Education', *Cambridge Journal of Education*,
34 (1): 7–33.

Alexander, R. (2005), *Towards Dialogic Teaching: Rethinking Classroom
Talk*, Cambridge: Dialogos.

Alexander, R. (2008), 'Pedagogy, Curriculum and Culture', in K. Hall,
P. Murphy and J. Soler (eds), *Pedagogy and Practice: Culture and
Identities*, 3–27, London: Sage.

Alexander, R. (2009), 'Pedagogy, Culture and the Power of Comparison',
in H. Daniels, H. Lauder and J. Porter (eds), *Educational Theories,
Cultures and Learning: A Critical Perspective*, 10–26, Abingdon:
Routledge.

Alexandersson, M. (1994), *Metod och Medvetande* (Method and
Consciousness). PhD Thesis, University of Gothenburg.

Alvesson, M. (2009), 'At Home Ethnography: Struggling with Closeness and Closure', in S. Ybema, D. Yanow, H. Wels and F. Kamsteeg (eds), *Organizational Ethnography: Studying the Complexities of Everyday Life*, 156–73, London: Sage.

Amidon, E. and N. Flanders (1967), 'Interaction Analysis as a Feedback System', in E. Amidon and J. Hough (eds), *Interaction Analysis: Theory, Research and Application*, Reading, MA: Addison-Wesley.

Arnot, M. and D. Reay (2007), 'A Sociology of Pedagogic Voice: Power, inequality and Pupil Consultation', *Discourse: Studies in the Cultural Politics of Education*, 28 (3): 311–25. doi: 10.1080/01596300701458814

Auer, P. (2014), 'There's No Harm in Glossing But a Need for a Better Understanding of the Status of Transcripts', *Research On Language and Social Interaction*, 47 (1): 1–5.

Banbury, M. M. and C. R. Hebert (1992), 'Do You See What I Mean?' *Teaching Exceptional Children*, 24: 34–8.

Bates, C. (2014), *Video Methods: Social Science Research in Motion*, London: Routledge.

Benjamin, S., M. Nind, J. Collins, K. Hall and K. Sheehy (2003), 'Moments of Inclusion and Exclusion: Children Negotiating Classroom Contexts', *British Journal of Sociology of Education*, 24 (5): 547–58.

Bereiter, C. (1986), 'The Reading Comprehension Lesson: A Commentary on Heap's Ethnomethodological Analysis', *Curriculum Inquiry*, 16: 65–72.

Bernstein, B. (1977), 'Class and Pedagogies: Visible and Invisible', in J. Karabel and A. H. Halsey (eds), *Power and Ideology in Education*, 511–34, New York: Oxford University Press.

Bernstein, B. (1990), *Class Codes and Control: Vol. 4. The Structuring of Pedagogic Discourse,* London: Routledge and Kegan Paul.

Berry, T. R. (2010), 'Engaged Pedagogy and Critical Race Feminism', *Educational Foundations*, Summer-Fall, 24: 19–26.

Bertram, T. and C. Pascal (2002), *Early Years Education: An International Perspective*, London: QCA.

Bertram, T. and C. Pascal (2006), *Baby Effective Early Learning (BEEL): A Handbook for Evaluating, Assuring and Improving Quality in Setting for Birth to Three-Year-Olds*, Birmingham: Amber.

Bertram, T. and C. Pascal (2007), 'Children Crossing Borders: Enhancing the Inclusion of Children in Pre-School Settings', *Childcare in Europe*, May, http://www.childrenineurope.org/english.php (accessed 14 April 2015).

Bertram, T. and C. Pascal (2008), *Opening Windows: A Handbook for Enhancing Equity and Diversity in Early Childhood Settings*, Birmingham: Amber.

Bertram, T., C. Pascal and M. Saunders (2010), *The Accounting for Early Life Long Learning Programme*, Birmingham: Amber.

Bezemer, J. and G. Kress (2014), 'Touch: A Resource for Making Meaning', *Australian Journal of Language and Literacy*, 37 (2): 77–85.

Bezemer, J. and Mavers, D. (2011), 'Multimodal Transcription as Academic Practice: A Social Semiotic Perspective', *International Journal of Social Research Methodology*, 14 (3): 191–206.

Biesta, G. (2007), 'Why "What Works Won't Work": Evidence-based Practice and the Democratic Deficit in Educational Research', *Educational Theory*, 57 (1): 1–22.

Black, P. and D. Wiliam(1998), 'Assessment and Classroom Learning', *Assessment in Education*, 5 (1): 7–71.

Black-Hawkins, K., L. Florian and M. Rouse (2007), *Achievement and Inclusion in Schools*, London: RoutledgeFalmer.

Blackmore, J., G. Aranda, D. Bateman, A. Cloonan, M. Dixon, M.Loughlin, J. O'Mara and K. Senior (2013), 'The Embodied Pedagogic Voice: Exploring Methodological Approaches to investigating Spatialised Pedagogical Practices', in Innovative Learning Environments, Report. Available at http://www.learningspaces.edu.au/docs/learningspaces-visual-methodologies-report.pdf (accessed 29 April 2015).

Blackmore, J., D. Bateman, J. O'Mara and J. Loughlin (2010), 'The Connections between Learning Spaces and Learning Outcomes: People and Learning Places?'. Available at http://www.deakin.edu.au/research/src/crefi/documents/built-learning-spaces.pdf (accessed 29 April 2015).

Bloom, B. S. (1953), 'Thought-Processes in Lectures and Discussions', *Journal of General Education*, 7: 160–9.

Bloome, D., M. Beierle, M. Grigorenko and S. Goldman (2009), 'Learning Over Time: Uses of Intertextuality, Collective Memories, and Classroom Chronotopes in the Construction of Learning Opportunities in a Ninth-Grade Language Arts Classroom', *Language and Education*, 23 (4): 313–34.

Booth, T., M. Ainscow and D. Kingston (2006), *Index for Inclusion: Developing Play, Learning and Participation in Early Years and Childcare*, Bristol: Centre for Studies in Inclusive Education.

Bourne, J. (2004), 'Framing Talk: Towards a "Radical Visible Pedagogy"', in J. Mullar, B. Davies and A. Morais (eds), *Reading Bernstein, Researching Bernstein*, 61–74, London: RoutledgeFalmer.

Bourne, J. and C. Jewitt (2003), 'Orchestrating Debate: A Multimodal Analysis of Classroom Interaction', *Literacy*, 37 (2): 64–72.

Bragg, S. (2011), '"Now It's Up to Us to Interpret It": Youth Voice and Visual Methods in Creative Learning and Research', in P. Thomson and J. Sefton-Green (eds), *Researching Creative Learning: Methods and Issues*, 88–103, London: Routledge.

Broadhead, P. (2001), 'Investigating Sociability and Co-Operation in 4 and 5-year-olds in Reception Class Settings', *International Journal of Early Years Education*, 9 (1): 23–35.

Broadhead, P. (2006), 'Developing an Understanding of Young Children's Play: The Place of Observation, Interaction and Reflection', *British Educational Research Journal*, 32 (2): 191–207.

Broadhead, P. (2009), 'Conflict Resolution and Children's Behaviour: Observing and Understanding Social and Cooperative Play in Early Years Educational Settings', *Early Years*, 29 (2): 105–18.

Broderick, A. A., G. Hawkins, S. Henze, C. Mirasol-Spath, R. Pollack-Berkovits, P. Prozzo Clune, E. Skovera and C. Steel (2012), 'Teacher Counter Narratives: Transgressing and "Restorying" Disability in Education', *International Journal of inclusive Education*, 16 (8): 825–42.

Brooks-Gunn, J., W. J. Han and J. Waldfogel (2002), 'Maternal Employment and Child Cognitive Outcomes in the First Three Years of Life: The NICHD Study of Early Childhood Care', *Child Development*, 73: 1052–72.

Brown, J. S. and P. Duguid (1996), 'Stolen Knowledge', in H. Mclellan (ed.), *Situated Learning Perspectives*, 47–56, Englewood Cliffs, NJ: Educational Technology.

Brown, S. A. and D. Mcintyre (1993), *Making Sense of Teaching*, Buckingham: Open University Press.

Bruner, J. (1996), *The Culture of Education*, Cambridge, MA: Harvard University Press.

Bryman, A. (2013), *Triangulation: Encyclopedia of Social Science Research Methods,* 1142–3, Thousand Oaks, CA: Sage.

Buchanan, I. (1992), 'Extraordinary Spaces in Ordinary Places: De Certeau and the Space of Postcolonialism'. Available at http://www.mcc.murdoch.edu.au/readingroom/litserv/span/36/jabba.html (accessed 29 April 2015).

Buchanan, T. K., D. C. Burts, J. Bidner, V. Faye White and R. Charlesworth (1998), 'Predictors of the Developmental Appropriateness of the Beliefs and Practices of First, Second, and Third Grade Teachers', *Early Childhood Research Quarterly*, 13 (3): 459–83.

Bucholtz, M. (2000), 'The Politics of Transcription', *Journal of Pragmatics*, 32: 1439–65.

Bucknall, S. (2014), 'Doing Qualitative Research with Children and Young People', in A. Clark, R. Flewitt, M. Hammersley and M. Robb (eds), *Understanding Research with Children and Young People*, 69–84, London: Sage.

Burke, C. (2008), '"Play in focus": Children's visual voice in participative research', in P. Thomson (ed.), *Doing Visual Research with Children and Young People*, 23–36, London: Routledge.

Calderhead, J. (1981), 'Stimulated Recall: A Method for Research on Teaching', *British Journal of Educational Psychology*, 51: 211–17.

Carr, M. (2001), *Assessment in Early Childhood Settings*, London: PCP.

Carr, M. and W. Lee (2012), *Learning Stories: Constructing Learner Identities in Early Education*, London: Sage.

Carson, R. L., H. M. Weiss and T. J. Templin (2010), 'Ecological Momentary Assessment: A Research Method for Studying the Daily Lives of Teachers', *International Journal of Research and Method in Education*, 33 (2): 165–82. doi: 10.1080/1743727X.2010.484548

Carter, K. (1993), 'The Place of Story in the Study of Teaching and Teacher Education', *Educational Researcher*, 22 (1): 5–12.

Cazden, C. (1988, 2001), *Classroom Discourse: The Language of Teaching and Learning*, Portsmouth, NH: Heinemann.

Cerbin, W. and B. Kopp (2006), 'Lesson Study as a Model for Building Pedagogical Knowledge and Improving Teaching', *International Journal of Teaching and Learning in Higher Education*, 18 (3): 250–7.

Challen, D. (2013), 'A Pedagogical Exploration of Guided Reading in Three Primary Classrooms', PhD thesis, University of Southampton, Available online http://eprints.soton.ac.uk/358500/ (accessed 11 May 2015).

Charlesworth, R., C. H. Hart, D. C. Burts and S. Hernandez (1990), *Kindergarten Teachers' Beliefs and Practices* (Report No. PS018 757), Boston, MA: American Educational Research Association.

Charlesworth, R., C. H. Hart, D. C. Burts, R. H. Thomasson, J. Mosley and P. O. Fleege (1993), 'Measuring the Developmental Appropriateness of Kindergarten Teachers' Beliefs and Practices', *Early Childhood Research Quarterly*, 8: 255–76.

Chavaudra, N., N. Moore, J. Marriott and M. Jakhara (2014), 'Creating an Evidence Base to Support the Development of a Holistic Approach to Working with Children and Young People in Derbyshire: A Local Authority Case Study On the integration of Social Pedagogy in Children and Young People's Services', *International Journal of Social Pedagogy*, 3 (1): 54–61.

Child, S. (2014), 'Social Experiences and Belonging: An Ethnography of Children in Two Primary Schools Supporting Children with Social, Emotional and Behavioural Difficulties', PhD thesis, University of Southampton. Available online http://eprints.soton.ac.uk/374160/ (accessed 7 January 2015).

Chuang, H-H. and C. J. Ho (2011), 'An investigation of Early Childhood Teachers' Technological Pedagogical Content Knowledge (TPACK) in Taiwan', *Ahi Evran Üniversitesi Kırşehir Eğitim Fakültesi Dergisi*, 12 (2): 99–117.

Chung, S. and D. J. Walsh (2000), 'Unpacking Child-Centredness: A History of Meanings', *Journal of Curriculum Studies*, 32 (2): 215–34.

Clandinin, D. J. (1992), 'Narrative and Story in Teacher Education', in T. Russell and H. Munby (eds), *Teachers and Teaching: From Classroom to Reflection*, 124–37, London: Falmer Press.

Clark, A. (2001), 'How to Listen to Very Young Children: The
    Mosaic Approach', *Child Care in Practice*, 7 (4): 333–41. doi:
    org/10.1080/13575270108415344
Clark, A. (2011), 'Breaking Methodological Boundaries? Exploring Visual,
    Participatory Methods with Adults and Young Children', *European
    Early Childhood Education Research Journal*, 19 (3): 321–30.
Clark, A. and P. Moss (2001), *Listening to Young Children: The Mosaic
    Approach*, London: National Children's Bureau for the Joseph
    Rowntree Foundation.
Clark, A. and P. Moss (2005), *Spaces to Play: More Listening to Young
    Children Using the Mosaic Approach*, London: National Children's
    Bureau.
Clark, C. M. and P. L. Peterson (1981), 'Stimulated Recall', in B. R. Joyce,
    C. C. Brown and L. Peck (eds), *Flexibility in Teaching: An Excursion
    into the Nature of Teaching and Training*, 256–61, New York:
    Longman.
Clark, M. A., H. S. Chiang, T. Silva, S. Mcconnell, K. Sonnenfeld, A.
    Erbe and M. Puma (2013), *The Effectiveness of Secondary Math
    Teachers From Teach for America and the Teaching Fellows Programs
    (NCEE 2013-4015)*, Washington, DC: National Center for Education
    Evaluation and Regional Assistance, Institute of Education Sciences,
    US Department of Education.
Cochran-Smith, M. and S. Lytle (1993), *Inside Outside: Teacher Research
    and Knowledge*, New York: Teachers College Press.
Cole, M. (1996), *Cultural Psychology: A Once and Future Discipline*,
    Cambridge, MA: Harvard University Press.
Comber, B. (2001), 'Critical Literacies and Local Action: Teacher
    Knowledge and a "New" Research Agenda', in B. Comber and A.
    Simpson (eds), *Negotiating Critical Literacies in Classrooms*, 301–13,
    Mahwah, NJ: Lawrence Erlbaum.
Comber, B. and B. Kamler (2004), 'Getting Out of Deficit: Pedagogies of
    Reconnection', *Teaching Education*, 15 (3): 303–20.
Cook, T. D. and D. T. Campbell (1979), *Quasi-Experimentation: Design
    and Analysis Issues for Field Settings*, Boston, MA: Houghton Mifflin.
Cook-Sather, M. (2006), 'Change based on what students say: preparing
    teachers for a paradoxical model of leadership', *International Journal
    of Leadership in Education*, 9 (4): 345–35.
Corbett, J. (1999), 'Special Needs, Inclusion and Exclusion', in A. Hayton
    (ed.), *Tackling Disaffection and Social Exclusion*, 178–90, London:
    Kogan Page.
Corbett, J. (2001), *Supporting Inclusive Education: A Connective
    Pedagogy*, London: RoutledgeFalmer.
Corbett, J. and B. Norwich (2005), 'Common or Specialized Pedagogy',
    in M. Nind, J. Rix, K. Sheehy and K. Simmons (eds), *Curriculum and*

Pedagogy in Inclusive Education: Values into Practice, 34–47, London: Routledge/Falmer.

Cowan, K. (2014), 'Multimodal Transcription of Video: Examining Interaction in Early Years Classrooms', *Classroom Discourse*, 5 (1): 6–21. doi: 0.1080/19463014.2013.859846

Craft, A. (2000), *Creativity across the Primary Curriculum: Framing and Developing Practice*, London: RoutledgeFalmer.

Craft, A. (2001), 'Analysis of Research and Literature on Creativity in Education' (pdf), a Report Prepared for QCA by Anna Craft, March. Available at http://www.ncaction.org.uk/creativity/resources.htm (accessed 7 January 2015).

Cremin, T., P. Burnard and A. Craft (2006), 'Pedagogy and Possibility Thinking in the Early Years', *Thinking Skills and Creativity*, 1 (2): 108–19.

Cremin, T., M. Mottram, F. Collins, S. Powell and R. Drury (2015), *Researching Literacy Lives: Building Communities between Home and School*, Oxford: Routledge.

Curtin, A. (2011), 'From Exceptions to Exceptional: Choreographing Adolescent Literacy and Identity in the Everyday', Doctoral thesis, Department of Education, UCC.

Dadds, M. (1993), 'The Feeling of Thinking in Professional Self-Study', *Educational Action Research*, 1 (2): 287–303.

Dahlberg, G., P. Moss and A. Pence (2007), *Beyond Quality in Early Childhood Education and Care: Languages of Evaluation*, 2nd edn, London: RoutledgeFalmer.

David, T., B. Raban, C. Ure, K. Goouch, M. Jago, I. Barriere and A. Lambirth (2000), *Making Sense of Early Literacy*, London: Trentham.

Davies, J. (2005), 'We Know What We're Talking About, Don't We? An Examination of Girls' Classroom-Based Learning Allegiances', *Linguistics and Education*, 15: 199–216.

Dede, C., J. Clark, D. Ketelhut, B. Nelson and C. Bowman (2005), *Fostering Motivation, Learning, and Transfer in Multi-User Virtual Environments*. Harvard Graduate School of Education [online] Available at http://muve.gse.harvard.edu/muvees2003/documents/dede_games_symposium_aera_2005.pdf (accessed 27 May 2015).

Degerbøl, S. and C. Svendler Nielsen (2015), 'Researching Embodied Learning by Using Videographic Participation for Data Collection and Audiovisual Narratives for Dissemination – Illustrated by the Encounter between Two Acrobats', *Ethnography and Education*, 10 (1): 60–75. doi: 10.1080/17457823.2014.929018

Dempsey, N. P. (2010), 'Stimulated Recall Interviews in Ethnography', *Qualitative Sociology*, 33: 349–67.

Denzin, N. K. and Y. S. Lincoln (eds) (2011), *The Sage Handbook of Qualitative Research*, 3rd edn, Thousand Oaks, CA: Sage.

Department for Education and Skills (DfES) (2006), *Primary National Strategy: Primary Framework for Literacy and Mathematics*, London: Crown Copyright. Available at http://www.educationengland.org.uk/documents/pdfs/2006-primary-national-strategy.pdf (accessed 7 July 2015).

Derry, S. (2007), 'The Guidelines for Video Research in Education: Recommendations from an Expert Panel'. Available at http://drdc.uchicago.edu/what/video-research-guidelines.pdf (accessed 27 May 2015).

Dicks, B., R. Flewitt, L. Lancaster and K. Pahl (2011), 'Multimodality and Ethnography: Working at the Intersection', Special Issue: *Qualitative Research*, 11 (3): 227–346.

Dixon, K. (2011), *Literacy, Power and the Schooled Body: Learning in Time and Space*, London: Routledge.

Dixon, M. and K. Senior (2011), 'Appearing Pedagogy: From Embodied Learning and Teaching to Embodied Pedagogy', *Pedagogy, Culture and Society*, 19 (3): 473–84. doi: 10.1080/14681366.2011.632514

Dochy, F., I. Berghmans, E. Kyndt and M. Baeten (2011), 'Contributions to innovative Learning and Teaching? Effective Research-Based Pedagogy – a Response to TLRP's Principles from a European Perspective', *Research Papers in Education*, 26 (3): 345–56.

Dodd, M. (2014), 'Making Connections: Problems, Progress and Priorities – a Practitioner's Viewpoint', University of Southampton Doctoral thesis. Available at http://eprints.soton.ac.uk/366262/ (accessed 30 April 2015).

Duck, C. and K. Hutchison (2005), 'Animating Disenchanted Writers', in B. Comber and B. Kamler (eds), *Turn Around Pedagogies: Literacy Interventions for At-Risk Students*, 15–30, Newtown, NSW: Primary English Teachers Association.

Dyson, A., A. Howes and B. Roberts (2002), 'A Systematic Review of the Effectiveness of School-Level Actions for Promoting Participation by All Students' (EPPI-Centre Review, Version 1.1*), in *Research Evidence in Education Library*, London: EPPI-Centre, Social Science Research Unit, Institute of Education.

Edwards, A. (2007), 'Researching Pedagogy: A Sociocultural Agenda', *Pedagogy, Culture and Society*, 9 (2): 161–86.

Eisner, E. W. (1979), *The Educational Imagination: On the Design and Evaluation of School Programs*, New York: Macmillan.

Elbaz, F. L. (1983), *Teacher Thinking: A Study of Practical Knowledge*, London: Croom Helm.

Elliot, A. (2006), *Early Childhood Education: Pathways to Quality and Equity for All Children*, Camberwell, Victoria: Australian Council for Education Research.

Erickson, F. (2011), 'Uses of Video in Social Research: A Brief History', *International Journal of Social Research Methodology*, 14 (3): 179–89.

Estola, E. and F. Elbaz-Luwisch (2003), 'Teaching Bodies at Work', *Journal of Curriculum Studies*, 35: 697–719.

EURYDICE (2013), 'NFER Compulsory Age of Starting School in European Countries', *Evening Standard*, 9 November 2006, Discipline Fears as Female Teachers Outnumber Male Peers by 12 to 1.

Farrell, T. S. C. (2006), 'The Teacher is an Octopus: Uncovering Preservice English Language Teachers' Prior Beliefs through Metaphor Analysis', *Regional Language Centre Journal*, 37 (2): 236–48.

Fenstermacher, G. D. (1994), 'The Knower and the Known: The Nature of Knowledge in Research On Teaching', *Review of Research in Education*, 20 (1): 3–56. doi:10.3102/0091732X020001003

Fielding, S. (2000), 'Walk On the Left! Children's Geographies and the Primary School', in S. Holloway and G. Valentine (eds), *Children's Geographies: Playing, Learning, Learning*, 199–211, London: Routledge.

Fisher, K. (2004), 'Revoicing Classrooms: A Spatial Manifesto', *Forum*, 46 (1): 36–8.

Fleet, A., T. Honig, J. Robertson, A. Semann and W. Shepherd (2011), *What's Pedagogy Anyway? Using Pedagogical Documentation to Engage with the Early Years Framework*, New South Wales, Australia: Children's Services Central.

Fleet, A., C. Patterson, M. Hammersley, L. Schillert and E. Stanke (2006), 'Five Voices: Interrupting the Dominant Discourse', in A. Fleet, C. Patterson and J. Robertson (eds), *Insights: Behind Early Childhood Pedagogical Documentation*, 311–30, Sydney: Pademelon.

Flewitt, R. (2006), 'Using Video to investigate Preschool Classroom Interaction: Education Research Assumptions and Methodological Practices', *Visual Communication*, 5 (1): 25–50.

Flewitt, R., N. Kucirkova and D. Messer (2014), 'Touching the Virtual, Touching the Real: iPads and Enabling Literacy for Students Experiencing Disability', *Australian Journal of Language and Literacy*, 37 (2): 107–16.

Flewitt, R. S., M. Nind and J. Payler (2009), 'If She's Left with Books She'll Just Eat Them': Considering Inclusive Multimodal Literacy Practices', *Journal of Early Childhood Literacy*, 9: 211–33.

Florian, L. (2009), 'Towards Inclusive Pedagogy', in P. Hick, R. Kershner and P. Farrell (eds), *Psychology for inclusive Education: New Directions in Theory and Practice*, 38–51, London: RoutledgeFalmer.

Florian, L. and K. Black-Hawkins (2011), 'Exploring inclusive Pedagogy', *British Educational Research Journal*, 37 (5): 813–28.

Foucault, M. (1980), '"Body/Power" and "Truth and Power"', in C. Gordon (ed.), *Michel Foucault: Power/Knowledge*, 55–62, Brighton, UK: Harvester.

Fox-Turnbull, W. (2009), 'Stimulated Recall Using Autophotography – A Method for investigating Technology Education', in Proc.PATT-2 Conference, 204–17. Delft, The Netherlands, Available at http://www.

iteaconnect.org/conference/patt/patt22/foxturnbull.pdf (accessed 27 May 2015).

Freire, P. (1970), *Pedagogy of the Oppressed*, New York: Continuum.

Gage, N. (1985), *Hard Gains in the Soft Sciences: The Case of Pedagogy*, Bloomington, IN: Phi Delta KappA.

Gallacher, L. and M. Gallagher (2008), 'Methodological Immaturity in Childhood Research? Thinking through "Participatory Methods"', *Childhood*, 15 (4): 499–516.

Galton, M., L. Hargreaves, C. Comber, D. Wall, and T. Pell (1999), 'Changes in Patterns of Teacher Interaction in Primary Classrooms: 1976-96', *British Educational Research Journal*, 25 (1): 23–37.

Gamble, J. (2001), 'Modelling the invisible: The Pedagogy of Craft Apprenticeship', *Studies in Continuing Education*, 23 (2): 181–96.

Gamble, J. (2002), 'Teaching Without Words: Tacit Knowledge in Apprenticeship', *Journal of Education*, 28: 63–82.

Gamble, J. (2004), 'Tacit Knowledge in Craft Pedagogy: A Sociological Analysis', Unpublished PhD Dissertation, University of Cape Town.

Gamble, J. (2009), 'The Relation between Knowledge and Practice in Curriculum and Assessment', a concept paper commissioned by Umalusi, October.

Garcia, A. C., A. I. Standlee, J. Bechkoff and Y. Cui (2009), 'Ethnographic Approaches to the Internet and Computer-Mediated Communication', *Journal of Contemporary Ethnography*, 38 (1): 52–84. doi:10.1177/0891241607310839

Garfinkel, H. (1967), *Studies in Ethnomethodology*, New York: Prentice-Hall.

Gass, S. M. and A. Mackey (2000), *Stimulated Recall Methodology in Second Language Research*, Mahway, NJ: Erlbaum.

Gee, J. P. (1999), *An Introduction to Discourse Analysis: Theory and Method*, London: Routledge.

Gee, J. P. (2003), *What Video Games Have to Teach Us About Learning and Literacy*, New York: Palgrave-Macmillan.

Gee, J. P. and J. L. Green (1997), 'Discourse Analysis, Learning, and Social Practice: A Methodological Study', *Review of Research in Education*, 23: 119–69.

Goldstein, Samantha H. (1996), '"A Position Only a Mother Could Love": The Female Teacher as Text in the College Writing Classroom', *Composition Forum*, 7: 40–9.

Gómez, A., L. Puigvert and R. Flecha (2011), 'Critical Communicative Methodology: Informing Real Social Transformation through Research', *Qualitative Inquiry*, 17: 235–45.

Goodey, C. (1999), 'Learning disabilities: the researcher's voyage to planet Earth', in S. Hood, B. Mayall and S. Oliver (eds), *Critical Issues in Social Research*, 40–53, Buckingham: Open University Press.

Granger, D. A. (2010), 'Somaesthetics and Racism: toward an Embodied Pedagogy of Difference', *Journal of Aesthetic Education*, 44 (3): 69–81.

Gray, M. and A. Sanson (2005), 'Growing Up in Australia: The Longitudinal Study of Australian Children', *Family Matters*, 72 (Summer): 4–9.

Greeno, J. G. (2006), 'Theoretical and Practical Advances through Research on Learning', in J. Green, G. Camilli and P. B. Elmore (eds), *Handbook of Complementary Methods in Education Research*, 795–821, New York: Routledge.

Gubrium, J. and J. Holstein (2000), 'Analyzing Interpretative Practice', in N. K. Denzin and Y. S. Lincoln (eds) (2003), *Strategies of Qualitative inquiry*, 487–508, London: Sage.

Guzmán, V. C. (2009), 'Developing Craft Knowledge in Teaching at University: How Do Beginning Teachers Learn to Teach?', *European Educational Research Journal*, 8 (2): 326–35.

Habermas, J. (1987), *The Theory of Communicative Action: Vol. 1. Reason and the Rationalization of Society*, Boston: Beacon Press.

Halfpenny, P. and R. Proctor (2015), *Innovations in Digital Research Methods*, London: Sage.

Hall, K. (2002), 'Negotiating Subjectivities and Knowledge in a Multi-Ethnic Literacy Class: An Ethnographic-Sociocultural Perspective', *Language and Education*, 16 (3): 178–94.

Hall, K. and Chambers, F. (2012), 'Discourse Analysis and the Beginner Researcher', in K. Armour and D. Macdonald (eds), *Research Methods in Physical Education and Youth Sport*, 295–305, London: Routledge.

Hall, K. and A. Curtin (2015), 'The Rise of Neuroscientific Discourse in Early Childhood', in T. David, K. Goouch and S. Powell (eds), *The Routledge International Handbook of Philosophies and Theories of Early Childhood Care and Education*, 200–8, London: Routledge.

Hall, K., A. Curtin and V. Rutherford (eds) (2014), *Networks of Mind: Learning, Culture, Neuroscience*, Routledge: London.

Hall, K., P. Murphy and J. Soler (eds) (2008), *Pedagogy and Practice: Culture and Identities*, London: Sage.

Hammersley, M. (2001), 'On "Systematic" Reviews of Research Literatures: A "Narrative" Response to Evans and Benefield', *British Educational Research Journal*, 27 (5): 543–54.

Hargreaves, A. (2001), 'Emotional Geographies of Teaching', *Teachers College Record*, 103 (6): 1056–80.

Harms, T., R. M. Clifford and D. Cryer (2005), *Early Childhood Environment Rating Scale*, rev. edn, New York: Teachers College Press.

Harper, D. (2002), 'Talking About Pictures: A Case for Photo Elicitation', *Visual Studies*, 17 (1): 13–26.

Harris, M. (2007), 'Introduction: Ways of Knowing', in M. Harris (ed.), *Ways of Knowing: New Approaches in the Anthropology of Experience and Learning*, 1–24, Oxford: Berghahn.

Harris, M. and O. Johnson (2000), *Cultural Anthropology*, 5th edn, Needham Heights, MA: Allyn and Bacon.

Hart, S., A. Dixon, M. Drummond and D. McIntyre (2004), *Learning Without Limits*, Maidenhead: Open University Press.

Hattam, R., M. Brennan, L. Zipin and B. Comber (2009), 'Researching for Social Justice: Contextual, Conceptual and Methodological Challenges', *Discourse: Studies in the Cultural Politics of Education*, 30 (3): 303–16.

Heap, J. L. (1986), 'Cultural Logic and Schema Theory: A Reply to Bereiter', *Curriculum Inquiry*, 16: 73–86.

Hedges, H. (2012), 'Teachers' Funds of Knowledge: A Challenge to Evidence-Based Practice', *Teachers and Teaching: Theory and Practice*, 18 (1): 7–24.

Hemmeter, S. and M. M. Ostrosky (2008), 'Preparing Early Childhood Educators to Address Young Children's Social-Emotional Development and Challenging Behavior: A Survey of Higher Education Programs in Nine States', *Journal of Early Intervention*, 30 (4): 321–40.

Hewett, D. (2007), 'Do Touch: Physical Contact and People Who Have Severe, Profound and Multiple Learning Difficulties', *Support for Learning*, 22 (3): 116–23.

Higgins, S., E. Hall, K. Wall, P. Woolner and C. Mccaughey (2005), 'The Impact of School Environments: A Literature Review', 47, Centre for Learning and Teaching, School of Education, Communication and Language Science, University of Newcastle: Design Council. Available online http://128.240.233.197/cflat/news/dcreport.pdf (accessed 27 May 2015).

Higgs, J., A. Titchen, D. Horsfall and D. Bridges (eds) (2011), *Creative Spaces for Qualitative Researching: Living Research*, Netherlands: Sense.

Hines, C. M. (2000), *Virtual Ethnography*, London: Sage.

Hogan, D. (2011), 'Yes Brian, At Long Last There is Pedagogy in England- and in Singapore too. A Response to TLRP's "Ten Principles for Effective Pedagogy"', Research Papers in Education, 26 (3): 367–79.

Holland, J., T. Gordon and E. Lahelma (2007), 'Temporal, Spatial and Embodied Relations in the Teacher's Day at School', *Ethnography and Education*, 2 (2): 221–37. doi: 10.1080/17457820701350673

Hollway, W. (2001), 'The Psycho-social Subject in "Evidence-based practice"', *Journal of Social Work Practice*, 15 (1): 9–22.

Hooks, B. (1994), *Teaching to Transgress: Education as the Practice of Freedom*, New York: Routledge.

Howe, C. (2010), 'Peer Dialogue and Cognitive Development: A Two-Way Relationship?', in K. Littleton and C. Howe (eds), *Educational Dialogues: Understanding and Promoting Productive Interaction*, 32–47, London: Routledge.

Hughes, M. and A. Pollard (2006), 'Home–School Knowledge Exchange in Context', *Educational Review*, 58 (4): 385–95.

Hunt, C. (2006), 'Travels with a Turtle: Metaphors and the Making of a Professional Identity', *Reflective Practice*, 7 (3): 315–32.

Hyson, M. C., K. Hirsh-Pasek and L. Rescorla (1990), 'The Classroom Practices Inventory: An Observation Instrument Based on NAEYC's Guidelines for Developmentally Appropriate Practices for 4 and 5 year-old Children', *Early Childhood Research Quarterly*, 5: 475–94.

James, M. and A. Pollard (2011), 'TLRP's Ten Principles for Effective Pedagogy: Rationale, Development, Evidence, Argument and Impact', *Research Papers in Education*, 26 (3): 275–328.

Jeffery, B. (2001), 'Challenging Prescription in Ideology and Practice: The Case of Sunny First School', in J. Collins, K. Insley and J. Soler (eds), *Developing Pedagogy: Researching Practice*, 143–60, London: Paul Chapman.

Jewitt, C. (2002), 'The Move From Page to Screen: The Multimodal Reshaping of School English', *Visual Communication*, 1 (2): 171–95.

Johnson, R. T. (2000), *Hands Off! The Disappearance of touch in the Care of Children*, New York: Peter Lang.

Johnston, R. and J. Warson (2005), 'The Effects of Synthetic Phonics Teaching on Reading and Spelling Attainment', Scottish Executive Education Department Full Report, available online www.Scotland.Gov.Uk.

Jones, P., T. Whitehurst and K. Hawley (2012), 'Reclaiming Research: Connecting Research to Practitioners', in P. Jones, T. Whitehurst and J. Egerton (eds), *Creating Meaningful Inquiry in Inclusive Classrooms: Practitioners' Stories of Research*, 1–16, Abingdon: Routledge.

Jordon, S. (2001), 'Embodied Pedagogy: The Body and Teaching Theology', *Teaching Theology and Religion*, 4 (2): 98–101.

Kamler, B. and B. Comber (2005), 'Turn Around Pedagogies: Improving the Education of At Risk Students', *Improving Schools*, 8 (21): 121–31. doi: 10.1177/1365480205057702

Kamler, B. and B. Comber (2008), 'Making a Difference: Early Career English Teachers Research their Practice', *Changing English: Studies in Culture and Education*, 15 (1): 67–76.

Kazan, T. S. (2005), 'Dancing Bodies in the Classroom: Moving towards and Embodied Pedagogy', *Pedagogy*, 5 (3): 379–408.

Keesing-Styles, L. (2003), 'The Relationship between Critical Pedagogy and Assessment in Teacher Education', *Radical Pedagogy*, 5 (1): 1–19.

Kehily, M. J. (2002), *Sexuality, Gender and Schooling: Shifting Agendas in Social Learning*, London: Routledge/Falmer.

Kellett, M. and M. Nind (2003), *Implementing Intensive Interaction in Schools: Guidance for Practitioners, Managers and Coordinators*, London, David Fulton.

Kemmis, S. (2009), 'Action research as a practice-based practice', *Educational Action Research*, 17 (3): 463–74.

Kennedy, H. and M. Landor (2015), 'Introduction', in H. Kennedy, M. Landor and L. Todd (eds), *Video Enhanced Reflective Practice: Professional Development through Attuned Interactions*, 18–34, London: Jessica Kingsley.

Kennedy, H., M. Landor and L. Todd (eds) (2015), *Video Enhanced Reflective Practice: Professional Development through Attuned Interactions*, London: Jessica Kingsley.

Kerkham, L. and K. Hutchison (2005), 'Principles, Practices and Possibilities', in B. Comber and B. Kamler (eds), *Turn Around Pedagogies: Literacy Interventions for At-Risk Students*, 109–23, Newtown, NSW: Primary English Teachers Association.

Kiilakoski, T. and A. Kivijärvi (2015), 'Youth Clubs as Spaces of Non-Formal Learning: Professional Idealism Meets the Spatiality Experienced by Young People in Finland', *Studies in Continuing Education*, 37 (1): 47–61.

Kilburn, D. (2014), 'Methods for Recording Video in the Classroom: Producing Single and Multi-Camera Videos for Research into Teaching and Learning', NCRM Working Paper. NCRM. Available online http://eprints.ncrm.ac.uk/3599/ (accessed 7 January 2015).

Kim, M. and W.-M. Roth (2014), 'Argumentation as/in/for Dialogical Relation: A Case Study from Elementary School Science', *Pedagogies: An International Journal*, 9 (4): 300–21.

Kind, V. (2009), 'Pedagogical Content Knowledge in Science Education: Perspectives and Potential for Progress', *Studies in Science Education*, 45 (2): 169–204. doi: 10.1080/03057260903142285

Koole, T. (2010), 'Displays of Epistemic Access: Student Responses to Teacher Explanations', *Research on Language and Social Interaction*, 43 (2): 183–209.

Kornbeck, J. and N. Jensen (2009), *The Diversity of Social Pedagogy in Europe*, Bremen: Europäischer Hochschulverlag.

Koshik, I. (2002), 'Designedly Incomplete Utterances: A Pedagogical Practice for Eliciting Knowledge Displays in Error Correction Sequences', *Research on Language and Social Interaction*, 35: 277–309.

Kovalainen, M., K. Kumpulainen and S. Vasama (2002), 'Orchestrating Classroom Interaction in a Community of Inquiry: Modes of Teacher Participation', *Journal of Classroom Interaction*, 37 (1): 17–28.

Kozinets, R. V. (2010), *Netnography: Doing Ethnographic Research Online*, Thousand Oaks, CA: Sage.

Kresh, E. (1998), 'The Effects of Head Start: What Do We Know?', *National Head Start Association Research Quarterly*, 1 (4): 112–23.

Kress, G. and T. Van Leeuwen (2001), *Multimodal Discourse: The Modes and Media of Contemporary Communication*, London: Hodder Arnold.

Kulavuz-Onal, D. and C. Vásquez (2013), 'Reconceptualising Fieldwork in a Netnography of an Online Community of English Language Teachers', *Ethnography and Education*, 8 (22): 224–38.

Kyriacou, C., I. T. Ellingsen, P. Stephens and V. Sundaram (2009), 'Social Pedagogy and the Teacher: England and Norway Compared', *Pedagogy, Culture and Society*, 17 (1): 75–87.

Lancaster, L. (2001), 'Staring at the Page: The Functions of Gaze in a Young Child's Interpretation of Symbolic Forms', *Journal of Early Childhood Literacy*, 1 (2): 131–52.

Larson, R. and M. Csikszentmihalyi (1983), 'The Experience Sampling Method', in H. T. Reis (ed.), *Naturalistic Approaches to Studying Social Interaction: New Directions for Methodology of Social and Behavioral Science*, 41–56, San Francisco, CA: Jossey-Bass.

Lather, P. (1992), 'Post-Critical Pedagogies: A Feminist Reading', in C. Luke and J. Gore (eds), *Feminisms and Critical Pedagogy*, 120–37, New York: Routledge.

Lave, J. (1996), 'Teaching as Learning in Practice', *Mind, Culture and Activity*, 3 (3): 149–64.

Leach, J. and B. Moon (2008), *The Power of Pedagogy*, London: Sage.

Learning and Teaching Scotland (2005), 'Let's Talk About Pedagogy: Towards a Shared Understanding for Early Years Education in Scotland', Perspectives: A Series of Occasional Papers on Early Years Education. Scottish Executive.

Lewis, C., P. Enciso and E. B. Moje (2007), *Reframing Sociocultural Research on Literacy: Identity, Agency and Power*, New York: Routledge.

Lin, A. M. Y. (2007), 'What's the Use of "Triadic Dialogue"? Activity Theory, Conversation Analysis, and Analysis of Pedagogical Practices', *Pedagogies: An International Journal*, 2 (2): 77–94.

Lincoln, Y. S., S. A. Lynham and E. G. Guba (2011), 'Paradigmatic Controversies, Contradictions, and Emerging Confluences, Revisited', in Y. S. Lincoln and N. K. Denzin (eds), *The Sage Handbook of Qualitative Research* (4th edn), 97–128, Thousand Oaks, CA: Sage.

Littleton, K. and C. Howe (2010), 'Introduction', in K. Littleton and C. Howe (eds), *Educational Dialogues: Understanding and Promoting Productive Interaction*, 1–7, London: Routledge.

Littleton, K. and N. Mercer (2010), 'The Significance of Educational Dialogues between Primary School Children', in K. Littleton and C. Howe (eds), *Educational Dialogues: Understanding and Promoting Productive Interaction*, 271–88, London: Routledge.

Luke, A. (2006), 'Editorial introduction: Why Pedagogies?', *Pedagogies: An International Journal*, 1 (1): 1–6.

Luke, C. and J. Gore (1992), 'Introduction', in C. Luke and J. Gore (eds), *Feminisms and Critical Pedagogy*, 1–14, New York: Routledge.

Lusted, D. (1986), 'Why Pedagogy?', *Screen*, 27 (5): 2–14.

Lyle, J. (2003), 'Stimulated Recall: A Report on Its Use in Naturalistic Research', *British Educational Research Journal*, 29 (6): 861–78.

Lynch, R. G. (2005), 'Early Childhood investment Yields Big Payoff. *Policy Perspectives*', San Francisco, CA: Wested.

Lytle, S. (2008), 'At Last: Practitioner Inquiry and the Practice of Teaching: Some Thoughts on Better', *Journal of Research in Teaching*, 42(3): 373–79.

Mackey, A. and S. M. Glass (2005), *Second Language Research: Methodology and Design*, Mahwah, NJ: Lawrence Erlbaum.

Macnaughton, G., S. A. Rolfe and I. Siraj-Blatchford (2001), *Doing Early Childhood Research: International Perspectives on Theory and Practice*, Maidenhead: Open University Press.

Mahlios, M., D. Massengill-Shaw and A. Barry (2010), 'Making Sense of Teaching through Metaphors: A Review across Three Studies', *Teachers and Teaching: Theory and Practice*, 16 (1): 49–71.

Mahruf, M., C. Shohel and A. J. Howes (2007), 'Transition from Nonformal Schools: Learning through Photo Elicitation in Educational Fieldwork in Bangladesh', *Visual Studies*, 22 (1): 53–61. doi: 10.1080/14725860601167200

Makoelle, T. M. (2014), 'Pedagogy of inclusion: A Quest for inclusive Teaching and Learning', *Mediterranean Journal of Social Sciences*, 5 (20): 1259–67.

Marchand, H. J. (2008), 'Muscles, Morals and Mind: Craft Apprenticeship and the Formation of Person', *British Journal of Educational Studies*, 56 (3): 245–71.

Marcon, R. A. (1988), 'Cluster Analysis: Creating independent Variables in Evaluation Research', Paper presented at the Meeting of the American Psychological Association, August, Atlanta, GA.

Margutti, P. (2010), 'On Designedly Incomplete Utterances: What Counts as Learning for Teachers and Students in Primary Classroom Interaction', *Research on Language and Social Interaction*, 43 (4): 315–45.

Marland, P. (1984), 'Stimulated Recall from Video: Its Use in Research on the Thought Processes of Classroom Participants', in O. Zuber-Skerritt (ed.), *Video in Higher Education*, 156–65, London: Kogan Page.

Marland, P. and B. Osborne (1990), 'Classroom Theory, Thinking, and Action', *Teaching and Teacher Education*, 6: 93–109.

Massumi, B. (2002), *Parables for the Virtual: Movement, Affect, Sensation*, Durham, NC: Duke University Press.

McDaniel, E. and P. A. Andersen (1998), 'The International Patterns of Interpersonal Tactile Communication: A Field Study', *Journal of Nonverbal Behavior*, 22: 59–75.

McDermott, R. (1993), 'The Acquisition of a Child by a Learning
    Disability', in S. Chaiklin and J. Lave (eds), *Understanding Practice*,
    269–305, New York: Cambridge University Press.
McGregor, J. (2004a), 'Space, Power and the Classroom', *Forum*, 46 (1):
    13–18.
McGregor, J. (2004b), 'Spatiality and the Place of the Material in Schools',
    Pedagogy, Culture and Society, 12 (3): 347–72.
McGuinness, C., L. Sproule, K. Trew and G. Walsh (2009a), 'The Early
    Years Enriched Curriculum Evaluation Project (EYECEP), End of
    Phase 2, Report 1: Overview: Evaluation Strategy and Curriculum
    Implementation', Belfast, N. Ireland: Report for Northern Ireland
    Council for Curriculum Assessment and Examinations (CCEA).
McLaren, P. (2000), 'Paulo Freire's Pedagogy of Possibility', in S. Steiner, H.
    Krank, P. McClaren and R. Bahruth (eds), *Freirean Pedagogy, Praxis and
    Possibilities: Projects for the New Millennium*, 1–22, New York: Falmer.
McLaughlin, M. (2008), 'Beyond Misery Research – New Opportunities
    for Implementation Research, Policy and Practice', in C. Sugrue (ed.),
    The Future of Educational Change: International Perspectives, 175–90,
    Abingdon: Routledge.
McWilliams, E. (1996), 'Touchy Subjects: A Risky Inquiry into Pedagogical
    Pleasures', *British Educational Research Journal*, 22: 305–19.
McWilliams, E. (1999), *Pedagogical Pleasures*, New York: Peter Lang.
Mehan, H. (1979), 'What Time is it Denise? Asking Known Informational
    Questions in Classroom Discourse', *Theory into Practice*, 18 (4): 285–94.
Mercer, N. (2000), *Words & Minds: How We Use Language to Think
    Together*, London: Routledge.
Mercer, N. (2008), 'The Seeds of Time: Why Classroom Dialogue Needs a
    Temporal Analysis', *Journal of the Learning Sciences*, 17 (1): 33–59.
Mercer, N. (2010), *'The Analysis of Classroom Talk: Methods and
    Methodologies'*, British Journal of Educational Psychology, 80: 1–14.
Mercer, N. and K. Littleton (2007), *Dialogue and the Development of
    Children's Thinking: A Sociocultural Approach*, London: Routledge.
Messiou, K. (2013), 'Embedding Students' Voices in the Lesson Study
    Approach as a Strategy for Teacher Development', SAALED
    Professional Development Conference, July, Johannesburg, South Africa.
Miles, M. and M. Huberman (1984), 'Drawing Valid Meaning from
    Qualitative Data: Toward a Shared Craft', *Educational Researcher*,
    13 (5): 20–30.
Mitchell, C., S. Weber and K. O'Reilly-Scanlon (eds) (2005), *Just Who Do
    We Think We Are: Methodologies for Autobiography and Self-Study in
    Teaching*, New York: Routledge.
Mitchell, L. and P. Cubey (2003), 'Characteristics of Professional
    Development Linked to Enhanced Pedagogy and Children's Learning

in Early Childhood Settings: Best Evidence Synthesis', Report Prepared for the New Zealand Ministry of Education, Wellington, NZ: Ministry of Education.

Mitchell, W. J. (2005), *What Do Pictures Want? The Lives and Loves of Images*, Chicago: University of Chicago Press.

Moje, E. (2000a), 'Changing Our Minds, Changing Our Bodies: Power as Embodied in Research Relations', *Qualitative Studies in Education*, 13 (1): 25–42.

Moje, E. (2000b), '"To Be a Part of the Story": The Literacy Practices of Gangsta Adolescents', *Teachers College Record*, 102 (3): 651–90.

Morgan, A. (2007), 'Using Video-Stimulated Recall to Understand Young Children's Perceptions of Learning in Classroom Setting', *European Early Childhood Education Research Journal*, 15 (2): 213–26. doi: 10.1080/13502930701320933

Moustakas, C. (1994), *Phenomenological Research Methods*, Thousand Oaks, California: Sage.

Moyles, J., S. Adams and A. Musgrove (2002), 'Using Reflective Dialogues as a Tool for Engaging with Challenges of Defining Effective Pedagogy', *Early Child Development and Care*, 172 (5): 463–78. doi: 10.1080/03004430214551

Moyles, J., L. Hargreaves, R. Merry, F. Paterson and V. Estarte-Sarries (2003), *Interactive Teaching in the Primary School: Digging Deeper into Meanings*, Maidenhead: Open University Press.

Muijs, D. and D. Reynolds (2005), *Effective Teaching: Evidence and Practice*, 2nd edn, London: Sage.

Neelands, J. (2000), 'Drama Sets You Free, or Does It?', in J. Davison and J. Moss (eds), *Issues in English Teaching*, 73–89, London: Routledge.

Newspaper articles http://www.thisislondon.co.uk/news/article-23373976-details/discipline+fears+as+female+teachers+outnumber+male+peers+by+12+to+1/article.do; http://archive.oxfordmail.net/2006/11/9; http://www.thisislondon.co.uk/standard/article-23416963-details/damning+ofsted+report+accuses+'failing'+secondaries/article.do (accessed 11 May 2015).

Nind, M. (1996), 'Efficacy of Intensive Interaction: Developing Sociability and Communication in People with Severe Learning Difficulties Using an Approach Based On Caregiver–Infant Interaction', *European Journal of Special Needs Education*, 11 (1): 48–66.

Nind, M. (2003), 'Enhancing the Communication Learning Environment of an Early Years Unit through Action Research', *Educational Action Research*, 11 (3): 347–64.

Nind, M. (2014a), 'Inclusive Research and Inclusive Education: Why Connecting Them Makes Sense for Teachers' and Learners' Democratic Development of Education', *Cambridge Journal of Education*, 44 (4): 525–40. doi: 10.1080/0305764X.2014.936825

Nind, M. (2014b), *What is Inclusive Research?* London: Bloomsbury.

Nind, M. and S. Cochrane (2002), 'Inclusive Curricula? Pupils on the Margins of Special Schools', *International Journal of inclusive Education*, 6 (2): 185–98.

Nind, M. and D. Hewett (1994), *Access to Communication: Developing the Basics of Communication with People with Severe Learning Difficulties through Intensive Interaction*, London: David Fulton.

Nind, M. and D. Hewett (2001), *A Practical Guide to Intensive Interaction*, Kidderminster: British Institute of Learning Disabilities.

Nind, M., S. Benjamin, J. Collins, K. Sheehy and K. Hall (2004), 'Methodological Challenges in Researching Inclusive Education', *Educational Review*, 56 (3): 259–70.

Nind, M., R. Flewitt and J. Payler (2010), 'The Social Experience of Early Childhood for Children with Learning Disabilities: Inclusion, Competence and Agency', *British Journal of Sociology of Education*, 31 (6): 653–70.

Nind, M., R. S. Flewitt and J. Payler (2011), 'Social Constructions of Young Children in "Special", "Inclusive" and Home Environments', *Children and Society*, 25 (5): 359–70.

Nind, M., D. Kilburn and R. Wiles (2015), 'Using Video and Dialogue to Generate Pedagogic Knowledge: Teachers, Learners and Researchers Reflecting together On the Pedagogy of Social Research Methods', *International Journal of Social Research Methodology*, July. doi: 10.1080/13645579.2015.1062628

Nishizaka, A. (2015), 'Facts and Normative Connections: Two Different Worldviews', *Research on Language and Social Interaction*, 48 (1): 26–31.

Norris, S. (2002), 'The Implication of Visual Research for Discourse Analysis: Transcription Beyond Language', *Visual Communication*, 1 (1): 97–121.

Nutbrown, C. (1994), *Threads of Thinking: Young Children Learning and the Role of Early Education*, 1st edn, London: Paul Chapman.

Nystrand, M. (1997), 'Dialogic Instruction: When Recitation Becomes Conversation', in M. Nystrand with A. Gamoran, R. Kachur and C. Prendergast (eds), *Opening Dialogue: Understanding the Dynamics of Language and Learning in the English Classroom*, 1–29, New York: Teachers College Press.

Nystrand, M., L. Wu, S. Zeiser and D. Long (2003), 'Questions in Time: Investigating the Structure and Dynamics of Unfolding Classroom Discourse', *Discourses Processes*, 35: 135–98.

O'Brien, J. (1993), 'Action Research through Stimulated Recall', *Research in Science Education*, 23: 214–21.

Oakley, A. (2002), 'Social Science and Evidence-Based Everything: The Case of Education', *Educational Review*, 54 (3): 277–86.

Olsson, L. M. (2009), *Movement and Experimentation in Young Children's Learning: Deleuze and Guattari in Early Childhood Education*, Abingdon: Routledge.

Özmanter, M. F. (2011), 'Rethinking About the Pedagogy for Pedagogical Content Knowledge in the Context of Mathematics Teaching', *Eurasia Journal of Mathematics, Science and Technology Education*, 7 (1): 15–27.

Parks, A. N. (2011), 'Diversity of Practice within One Mathematics Classroom', *Pedagogies: An International Journal*, 6 (3): 216–33.

Pascal, C. and T. Bertram (2014), 'Transformative Dialogues: The Impact of Participatory Research on Practice', in A. Clark, R. Flewitt, M. Hammersley and M. Robb (eds), *Understanding Research with Children and Young People*, 269–84, London: Sage.

Pascal, C., T. Bertram, M. Gasper, C. Mould, F. Ramsden and M. Saunders (1999), 'Research to Inform the Evaluation of the Early Excellence Centres Pilot Programme', Centre for Research in Early Childhood, University College, Worcester.

Patton, M. (2002), *Qualitative Research and Evaluation Methods*, Thousand Oaks, CA: Sage.

Perry, M. and C. L. Medina (eds) (2015), *Methodologies of Embodiment: Inscribing Bodies in Qualitative Research*, Abingdon/New York: Routledge.

Petrie, P., J. Boddy, C. Cameron, C., Heptinstall, S. McQuail, A. Simon and V. Wigfall (2005), 'Pedagogy – a Holistic, Personal Approach to Work with Children and Young People, Across Services: European Models for Practice, Training, Education and Qualification', Thomas Coram Research Unit Briefing Paper, June.

Pickering, C. and J. Painter (2005), 'Using Shrek and Bart Simpson to Build Respectful Learning Communities', in B. Comber and B. Kamler (eds), *Turn Around Pedagogies: Literacy Interventions for At-Risk Students*, 109–23, Newtown, NSW: Primary English Teachers Association.

Pinar, W. and R. Irwin (eds) (2005), *Curriculum in a New Key – The Collected Works of Ted T. Aoki*, Mahwah, NJ: Lawrence Erlbaum.

Pink, S. (2007), 'Walking with Video', *Visual Studies*, 22 (3): 240–52. doi: 10.1080/14725860701657142

Pink, S. (2008), 'Mobilising Visual Ethnography: Making Routes, Making Place and Making Images', *Forum*, 9: 3.

Pink, S. (2009), *Doing Sensory Ethnography*, London: Sage.

Pink, S. (2010), 'What is Sensory Ethnography', in NCRM Research Methods Festival 2010, July, St Catherine's College, Oxford (unpublished) Available online http://eprints.ncrm.ac.uk/1354/ (accessed 7 January 2015).

Piper, H. and H. Smith (2003), '"Touch" in Educational and Child Care Settings: Dilemmas and Responses', *British Educational Research Journal*, 29 (6): 879–94.

Powell, E. (2005), 'Conceptualising and Facilitating Active Learning: Teachers' Video-Stimulated Reflective Dialogues', *Reflective Practice*, 6 (3): 407–18. doi: 10.1080/14623940500220202

Pramling Samuelsson, I. and M. Asplund Carlsson (2008), 'The Playing Learning Child: towards a Pedagogy of Early Childhood', *Scandinavian Journal of Educational Research*, 52 (6): 623–41. doi: 10.1080/00313830802497265

Pratte, R. and J. Rury (1991), 'Teachers, Professionalism, and Craft', *Teachers College Record*, 93 (1): 59–72.

Prosser, S. (ed) (1998), *Image–based Research: Source book for qualitative researchers*, London: Falmer Press.

Puigvert, L., M. Christou and J. Holford (2012), 'Critical Communicative Methodology: including Vulnerable Voices in Research through Dialogue', Cambridge Journal of Education, 42: 513–26.

Quinn Patton, M. (ed.) (2002), *Qualitative Research and Evaluation Methods*, 3rd edn, Thousand Oaks, CA: Sage.

Raudenbush, S. W. and A. S. Bryk (2002), *Hierarchical Linear Models: Applications and Data Analysis Methods*, 2nd edn, Thousand Oaks, CA: Sage.

Reis, H. T. and S. L. Gable (2000), 'Event-sampling and other methods for studying everyday experience', in H. T. Reis and C. M. Judd (eds), *Handbook of Research Methods in Social and Personality Psychology*, 190–222, New York: Cambridge University Press.

Rex, L. A., S. C. Steadman and M. K. Graciano (2006), 'Researching the Complexity of Classroom Interaction', in J. Green, G. Camilli and P. B. Elmore (eds), *Handbook of Complementary Methods in Education Research*, 727–71, New York: Routledge.

Richardson, L. (1994), 'Writing: A Method of Inquiry', in N. K. Denzin and Y. S. Lincoln (eds), *Handbook of Qualitative Research*, 516–29, Thousand Oaks, CA: Sage.

Richardson, L. (2000), *Qualitative Research and Evaluation Methods*, Ed. M. Quinn Patton (2002), 3rd edn, California: Sage.

Richardson, L. and E. St. Pierre (2002), *Qualitative Research and Evaluation Methods*, Ed. M. Quinn Patton, 3rd Edn, Thousand Oaks, CA: Sage.

Robinson, K. (2008), 'In the Name of "Childhood Innocence": A Discursive Exploration of the Moral Panic Associated with Childhood and Sexuality', *Cultural Studies Review*, 14 (2): 113–29.

Rogers, R. (ed.) (2011), *An Introduction to Critical Discourse Analysis in Education*, 2nd edn, New York: Routledge.

Rogers, R., E. Malancharuvil-Berkes, M. Mosley, D. Hui, and J. Glynis (2005), 'Critical Discourse Analysis in Education: A Review of the Literature', *Review of Educational Research*, 75 (3): 365–416.

Rogers, S. and J. Evans (2007), 'Rethinking Role Play in the Reception Class', *Educational Research*, 49 (2): 153–67.

Rogoff, B. (1995), 'Observing sociocultural Activity on Three Planes: Participatory Appropriation, Guided Participation, and Apprenticeship', in J. V. Wertsch, P. del Rio and A. Alvarez (eds), 139–64, *Sociocultural Studies of Mind*, Cambridge: Cambridge University Press.

Rogoff, B. (2003), *The Cultural Nature of Human Development*, Oxford: Oxford University Press.

Rogoff, B. (2008), 'Observing Sociocultural Activity on Three Planes: Participatory Appropriation, Guided Participation, and Apprenticeship', in K. Hall, P. Murphy and J. Soler (eds), *Pedagogy and Practice: Culture and Identities*, 58–74, London: Sage.

Roth, W. and Y. Lee (2006), 'Contradictions in Theorizing and Implementing Communities in Education', *Educational Research Review*, 1: 27–40.

Rowe, V. C. (2009), 'Using Video-stimulated Recall as a Basis for Interviews: Some Experiences from the Field', *Music Education Research*, 11(4): 425–37.

Rudduck, J. and J. Flutter (2004), *How to Improve your School: Giving Pupils a Voice*, London: Continuum Press.

Ruthven, K. and S. Goodchild (2008), 'Linking Researching with Teaching: Towards Synergy of Scholarly and Craft Knowledge (rev. edn)', in L. English (ed.), *Handbook of International Research in Mathematics Education*, 2nd edn, 561–88, New York: Routledge.

Saban, A. (2010), 'Prospective Teachers' "Metaphorical Conceptualizations" of Learner', *Teaching and Teacher Education*, 26: 290–305.

Sachs, H. (1992), *Lectures On Conversation*, Oxford: Blackwell.

Sammons, P., K. Sylva, E. C. Melhuish, I. Siraj-Blatchford, B. Taggart and K. Elliot (2002), 'Measuring the Impact of Pre-School on Children's Cognitive Progress Over the Preschool Period', Technical Paper 8a, London: Institute of Education, University of London.

Sanoff, H. (2001), 'School Buildings Assessment Methods', North Carolina State University and National Clearinghouse for Educational Facilities, Washington, DC.

Schegloff, E. A. (1993), 'Reflections on Quantification in the Study of Conversation', *Research On Language and Social Interaction*, 26 (1): 99–128.

Schmidt, D., E. Baran, A. Thompson, P. Mishra, M. J. Koehler and T. Shin (2009), 'Technological Pedagogical Content Knowledge (TPACK): The Development and Validation of an Assessment instrument for Preservice Teachers', *Journal of Research On Technology in Education*, 42 (2): 123–49.

Schön, D. (1983), *The Reflective Practitioner*, New York: Basic Books.

Schultz Colby, R. and R. Colby (2008), 'A Pedagogy of Play: Integrating Computer Games into the Writing Classroom', *Science Direct: Computers and Composition*, 25: 300–12.

Schweinhart, H. V. Barnes and D. P. Weikart (1993), *Significant Benefits: The High/Scope Perry Preschool Study through Age 27*. Yipsilanti, MI: High Scope Press, ED 366 433.

Sebba, J. (2004), 'Developing Evidence-informed Policy and Practice in Education', in G. Thomas and R. Pring (eds), *Evidence Based Practice in Education*, 34–44, Buckingham: Open University Press.

Sellar, S. (2009), 'The Responsible Uncertainty of Pedagogy', *Discourse: Studies in the Cultural Politics of Education*, 30 (3): 347–60. doi: 10.1080/01596300903037077

Shavelson, R. J., N. M. Webb and L. Burstein (1986), 'Measurement of Teaching', in M. Wittrock (ed.), *Handbook of Research on Teaching*, 3rd edn, 50–91, New York: Macmillan.

Shor, I. (1992), *Empowering Education: Critical Teaching for Social Change*, Chicago: University of Chicago Press.

Shor, I. (1996), *When Students Have Power*, Chicago: University of Chicago Press.

Shulman, L. (1986), 'Those Who Understand: Knowledge Growth in Teaching', *Educational Researcher*, 15 (2): 4–14. doi: 10.3102/0013189X015002004

Shulman, L. (1987), 'Knowledge and Teaching: Foundations of the New Reform', *Harvard Educational Review*, 57 (1): 1–23.

Sinclair, J. M. and R. M. Coulthard (1975), *Towards an Analysis of Discourse: The English Used by Teachers and Pupils*, Oxford: Oxford University Press.

Siraj-Blatchford, I. and K. Sylva (2004), 'Researching Pedagogy in English Pre-Schools', *British Educational Research Journal*, 30 (5): 713–30.

Siraj-Blatchford, I., K. Sylva, S. Muttock, R. Gilden and D. Bell (2002), 'Researching Effective Pedagogy in the Early Years', Research Report No. 356, London: Dfes/Queens PrInter.

Slavin, R. E. (2002), 'Evidence-Based Education Policies: Transforming Educational Practice and Research', *Educational Researcher*, 31 (7): 15–21.

Slavin, R. E. (2004), 'Education Research Can and Must Address "What Works" Questions, *Educational Researcher,* 33 (1): 27–8.

Slee, R., G. Weiner and S. Tomlinson (eds) (1998), *School Effectiveness for Whom? Challenges to the School Effectiveness and School Improvement Movements*, London: Falmer.

Sproule, L., C. McGuinness, K. Trew and G. Walsh (2009), 'The Early Years Enriched Curriculum Evaluation Project (EYECEP). End of Phase 2, Report 4: Outcomes for Pupils over Time', Belfast, N. Ireland: Report Produced for Northern Ireland Council for Curriculum Assessment and Examinations (CCEA).

Stake, R. E. (1995), *The Art of Case Study Research*, Thousand Oaks, California: Sage.

Stake, R. E. and D. Kerr (1994), 'Rene Magritte, Constructivism and the Researcher as Interpreter', paper presented to the American Educational Research Association (AERA), Annual Conference, New Orleans, April.

Steensig, J. and T. Heinemann (2015), 'Opening Up Codings?', *Research on Language and Social Interaction*, 48 (1): 20–5.

Stivers, T. (2015), 'Coding Social Interaction: A Heretical Approach to Conversation Analysis', *Research on Language and Social Interaction*, 48 (1): 1–19.

Stone, A. A. and S. Shiffman (1994), 'Ecological Momentary Assessment (EMA), in Behavioural Medicine', *Annals of Behavioral Medicine*, 16 (3): 199–202.

Strozzi, P. (2001), 'Daily Life At School: Seeing the Extraordinary in the Ordinary', in C. Giudici, C. Rinaldi and P. Barchi (eds), Harvard University, Graduate School of Education, Harvard Project Zero, and Reggio Children, *Making Learning Visible: Children as individual and Group Learners*, Cambridge, MA: Harvard Graduate School of Education.

Tannen, D. (1984), *Conversational Style: Analyzing Talk Among Friends*, Westport, CT: Albex.

ten Have, P. (2007), *Doing Conversation Analysis*, 2nd edn, London: Sage.

Thackray, D. (2013), 'An Investigation into the Clinical Reasoning of Cardiorespiratory Physiotherapists Using a Simulated Patient and Simulated High Dependency Unit', University of Southampton Doctoral Thesis, http://eprints.soton.ac.uk/366487/

Thomson, P. (2011), 'When Only the Visual Will Do', in P. Thomson and J. Sefton-Green (eds), *Researching Creative Learning: Methods and Issues*, 104–12, London: Routledge.

Tilley, L. and K. Woodthorpe (2011), 'Is This the End for Anonymity as We Know It? A Critical Examination of the Ethical Principle of Anonymity in the Context of 21st Century Demands on the Qualitative Researcher', *Qualitative Research*, 11(2): 197–212.

Tobin, J. J., D. Y. H. Wu and D. H. Davidson (1989), *Preschool in Three Cultures, Japan, China and the United States*, New Haven, CT: Yale University Press.

Traianou, A. (2006), 'Understanding Teacher Expertise in Primary Science: A Sociocultural Approach', *Research Papers in Education*, 21 (1): 63–78. doi: 10.1080/02671520500445466

Ulmer, G. (1985), *Applied grammatology: Post(e)-pedagogy from Jacques Derrida to Joseph Beuys*, Baltimore: Johns Hopkins University Press.

Valuti, S. (1999), 'How Early Childhood Teacher Beliefs Vary Across Grade Level', *Early Childhood Research Quarterly*, 14 (4): 489–514.

Van Drie, J. and R. Dekker (2013), 'Theoretical Triangulation as an Approach for Revealing the Complexity of a Classroom Discussion', *British Educational Research Journal*, 39 (2): 338–60.

Van Horn, L. M. and S. L. Ramsey(2003), 'The Effects of Developmentally Appropriate Practices on Academic Outcomes among Former Head Start Students and Classmates, Grades 1–3', *American Educational Research Journal*, 40 (4): 961–90.

Van Horn, L. M., E. O. Karlin, S. L. Ramey, J. Aldridge and S. W. Snyder (2005), 'Effects of Developmentally Appropriate Practices on Children's Development: A Review of Research and Discussion of Methodological and Analytic Issues', *The Elementary School Journal*, 105: 4325–51.

Van Maanen, J. (1995), 'An End to Innocence: The Ethnography of Ethnography', in J. Van Maanen (ed.), *Representation in Ethnography*, 1–35, Thousand Oaks, CA: Sage.

Van Maanen, M. (1990), *Researching Lived Experience*, New York: State University of New York Press.

Vesterinen, O., A. Toom and S. Patrikainen (2010), 'The Stimulated Recall Method and ICTs in Research on the Reasoning of Teachers, *International Journal of Research and Method in Education*, 33 (2): 183–97.

Wadsworth, Y. (2001), 'The Mirror, the Magnifying Glass, the Compass and the Map: Facilitating Participatory Action Research', in P. Reason and H. Bradbury (eds), *Handbook of Action Research: Participative inquiry and Practice*, 420–32, London: Sage.

Waller, T. and A. Bitou (2011), 'Research with Children: Three Challenges for Participatory Research in Early Childhood', *European Early Childhood Education Research Journal*, 19 (1): 5–20. http://dx.doi.org /10.1080/1350293x.2011.548964

Walmsley, J. and K. Johnson (2003), *Inclusive Research with People with Learning Disabilities: Past, Present and Futures*, London: Jessica Kingsley.

Watson, S., P. Schafer and B. Squires (2000), *Think Global, Document Local: Using Data and information Technologies to Move the Early Childhood Agenda*. The Finance Project. Retrieved From http://www. financeproject.org/think_global.pdf (accessed 30 April 2015).

Wells, G. (1999), *Dialogic inquiry: Towards a Sociocultural Practice and Theory of Education*, New York: Cambridge University Press.

Wenger, E. (1998), *Communities of Practice: Learning, Meaning and Identity*, Cambridge: Cambridge University Press.

Wikeley, F., K. Bullock, Y. Muschamp and T. Ridge (2007), *Educational Relationships Outside School: Why Access Is Important*, Bath: Joseph Rowntree Foundation.

Wiles, R., A. Coffey, J. Robison and J. Prosser (2012), 'Ethical Regulation and Visual Methods: Making Visual Research Impossible or Developing Good Practice', *Sociological Research Online*, 17 (1): 1–17.

Wiles, R., J. Prosser, A. Bagnoli, A. Clark, K. Davies, S. Holland and E. Renold (2008), 'Visual Ethics: Ethical Issues in Visual Research', NCRM Working Paper. Available online http://eprints.ncrm.ac.uk/421/ (accessed 30 April 2015).

Williams, J. S. (2009), 'The Learner, the Learning Process and Pedagogy in Social Context', in H. Daniels, H. Lauder and J. Porter (eds), *Educational Theories, Cultures and Learning*, 81–91, London: Routledge.

Wishart, J. and M. Thomas (2015), 'Introducing e-Research in Educational Contexts, Digital Methods and Issues Arising', *International Journal of Research and Method in Education*, 38 (3): 223–29. doi: 10.1080/1743727X.2015.1036852

Woodgate-Jones, A. (2014), 'Primary Teachers in Times of Change: Engaging with the Primary Modern Foreign Language initiative in England', PhD thesis, University of Southampton.

Woods, P. (1995), *Creative Teachers in Primary Schools*, Buckingham: Open University Press.

World Bank (2000), School Start Dates. Available online http://data.worldbank.org/indicator/se.prm.ages (accessed 29 April 2015).

Wurm, J. (2005), *Working in the Reggio Way: A Beginner's Guide for American Teachers*, St Paul, MN: Redleaf Press.

Wylie, C., J. Thompson and C. Lythe (2001), *Competent Children at 10. Families, Early Education and Schools*. Wellington: NZCER.

Zembylas, M. 2007. 'The Specters of Bodies and Affects in the Classroom: A Rhizo-Ethological Approach', *Pedagogy, Culture and Society*, 15: 19–35.

Zill, N., G. Resnick and K. O'Donnell (2001), *Growth in Children's Literacy Skills in Head Start and Early Elementary School. Implications for Preschool Curricula*. Washington, DC: US Department of Health and Human Services.

Zuengler, J., C. Ford and C. Fassnacht (1998), 'Analyst Eyes and Camera Eyes: Theoretical and Technological Considerations in "Seeing" the Details of Classroom Interaction', National Centre on English Learning and Achievement, University of Albany, New York. Report Series 2.40 http://cela.albany.edu/analysteyes/index.html (accessed 30 April 2015).

INDEX